A Population of Selves

Erving Polster

· · · · · · · · · · · · ·

A Population of Selves

• •

A Therapeutic Exploration
of Personal Diversity

Jossey-Bass Publishers
San Francisco

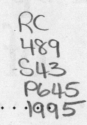

Copyright © 1995 by Jossey-Bass Inc., Publishers, 350 Sansome Street, San Francisco, California 94104. Copyright under International, Pan American, and Universal Copyright Conventions. All rights reserved. No part of this book may be reproduced in any form—except for brief quotation (not to exceed 1,000 words) in a review or professional work—without permission in writing from the publishers.

The Poem "Death of a Psychiatrist (for Volta Hall)" in Chapter Seven is reprinted from *A Private Mythology* by May Sarton with the permission of W. W. Norton & Company, Inc. Copyright © 1966 by May Sarton. In the United Kingdom reprinted with the permission of A. M. Heath.

Substantial discounts on bulk quantities of Jossey-Bass books are available to corporations, professional associations, and other organizations. For details and discount information, contact the special sales department at Jossey-Bass Inc., Publishers. (415) 433–1740; Fax (800) 605–2665.

For sales outside the United States, please contact your local Paramount Publishing International office.

 Manufactured in the United States of America on Lyons Falls Pathfinder Tradebook. This paper is acid-free and 100 percent totally chlorine-free.

Library of Congress Cataloging-in-Publication Data

Polster, Erving.
    A population of selves: a therapeutic exploration of personal diversity/Erving Polster.—1st. ed.
        p. cm.—(The Jossey-Bass social and behavioral science series)
    Includes bibliographical references (p. 239) and index.
    ISBN 0-7879-0076-1 (acid-free paper)
    1. Self psychology. 2. Gestalt therapy. I. Title. II. Series: Jossey-Bass social and behavioral science series.
RC489.S43P645   1995
616.89—dc20   94-42595

HB Printing   10 9 8 7 6 5 4 3 2 1   FIRST EDITION

Contents

• •

Preface

In forty-five years of practice, I have seen how often the search for a sense of self has been one of the primary factors that motivates people to seek therapy. Underneath the symptoms that trouble them, patients have a widespread concern with the simple question of who they are. In searching out the answer, rather than discovering one fundamental, unified, unchanging self, we uncover a number of different aspects—selves—that are often so much at odds with one another that they may seem to belong to several different people.

A single, basically healthy individual may, at various moments and under changing moods and circumstances, seem almost to *be* different people: by turns infantile, cunning, rebellious, tender, and silly. This multiplicity within the person, with all its contradictions, poses a challenge to embrace the unruly population of selves that exists within every human being. The wish for a greater, overarching sense of self, a comprehensive representation of who we are, is thwarted by the diversity of the many less comprehensive selves that are often in conflict.

When I refer to selves, I mean the personal summations that transform characteristics into characters in a life-defining drama. Although these inner characters are part of a personal dynamic understood by professional psychologists, they also make sense to nonprofessionals. For example, when a person recognizes that she has been aggressive, she understands the difference between the aggressive behavior and the recognition of an enduring aggressive self within. By focusing on particular selves—naming them, address-ing them, influencing them, creating dialogue among them—ther-apist and patient can see how each plays a role in the complex life of the person, how each contributes to a dependable integration of selves. Some of these representations of self—for example, the gen-erous self, the hardworking self, or the paternal self—may form the nucleus of a patient's chosen identity. Others—the greedy self, the shirking self, the subversive self—are perhaps suppressed and silenced, feared, rejected, and misunderstood. All of them are important, however. Creating a lively understanding of these vari-ous members of the self is the essential step toward forming a pow-erful and enduring sense of a greater self.

The main purpose of this book is to show therapists how they can work with dissonant selves: first to recognize characteristics that can be transformed into selves and then to help the patient develop a live-and-let-live attitude, neither excluding necessary selves nor allowing domination by unwanted selves.

My approach has two main elements. First, it expands beyond theories that propose a real or true self, or only a few universal selves, in which the multifaceted makeup of a person is overshad-owed by a single, higher self. Second, it provides a new slant on syn-thesis, one that maintains the uniqueness of each element of the person while encouraging integration into one whole.

A common view of synthesis is that it *fuses* elements; that is, in the parlance of self, two alienated parts of the person may influence each other, forming a third entity. For example, a person may have dichotomous aspects: a driving business executive, let us say, and a relaxed music listener. In fusing, the two may join to form an exec-utive who listens. That may be a desirable fusion, but I am propos-ing an additional form of synthesis. This person may well continue to alternate between being a driving business executive and a relaxed music listener, much as the bark of a tree and the leaves remain separate while nevertheless being integrated as parts of a whole tree. Dissonant or not, many selves continue to make them-selves individually heard within the diversity each person houses.

On the subject of diversity and synthesis, I have been challenged as a gestalt therapist, as therapists of any theoretical orientation are, to recover the disregarded principles within my method. Much as people seek to restore the discarded aspects of themselves, in this book I have tried to navigate the dissonant currents of thought in gestalt methodology.

When I first came to gestalt therapy in 1953, I was attracted by its breadth, its ability to touch and even embrace a wide variety of concepts, ranging from those of the psychoanalytic dissidents like Jung, Rank, Reich, and Moreno to existentialism to behaviorism to the quest for social change. But breadth was not enough for me. I also wanted clear techniques and concrete therapeutic tools to present to my patients.

One of my teachers was Fritz Perls. One of the secrets of his therapeutic brilliance was the power of simple directives and simple principles. But he went too far in the direction of simplification, undermining the breadth he introduced. For example, he once insisted that to eliminate depersonalization, I should avoid using the word *it*, replacing it instead with *I*. When I impudently asked him whether it would be right to say, "I am raining," he admitted that I had a point, but the exchange stayed with me as an example of the deadening effect that oversimplification can have in therapeutic circles.

My own vulnerability to the narrowing of principles was brought home to me at a seminar a few years ago. I heard my audience— some of whom, but not all, were gestalt therapists—express the belief that gestalt therapy had neglected the concept of the self. I was surprised to hear this, and argued that, on the contrary, the self was heavily represented in gestalt therapy by its concept of self splitting and its view of the synthesizing properties of the mind, basic to the formation of self. I believed that my fellow therapists were oversimplifying gestalt therapy by tuning in only to its most highly emphasized aspect: its focus on the raw experience of what people say and do and feel.

They were, indeed, oversimplifying gestalt therapy, but they were also expressing another truth: that gestalt therapy theorists had themselves deemphasized the contrapuntal principles for showing what people fundamentally *are*. The seminar group felt that the gestalt notions of the self were necessarily at odds with its experiential concerns. As I found myself arguing that they were not at odds, that in fact explorations of the self had already been widely applied in gestalt practice, I came to realize the point that had to be made. Whether gestalt therapy actually postulated a concept of the self or merely applied it, the concept had taken a back seat to the emphasis on direct experience.

Gestalt therapy had indeed swept itself into the primacy of raw experience rather than focusing on the question of who people are. These priorities resulted from the way the basic theory had been skewed, not only by others but also by myself. I determined to explore the self freshly, to emphasize what is basic to gestalt therapy: a compatibility between experiences themselves and the classification of experiences represented in the self. This exploration grew close to my heart, and it is the basis for this book.

To make A *Population of Selves* useful for practitioners as well as students, I have used many case examples from my own practice—with names, occupations, and other identifying traits changed, of course, to protect the privacy of my patients. In these, I have given considerable detail about the interaction between myself and my patients. Each chapter highlights one or another of the primary therapeutic pathways to the person's selves and shows how therapists can use these principles to identify and restructure the patient's sense of self.

Among my aims in this book are the broadening of theoretical principles and an expansion of procedural diversity. As a result, I have filled it with the thinking of therapists from a wide range of theoretical persuasions, including those with an eclectic background. The material is also relevant for professionals in the mental health field who are not therapists but are interested in how people may discover who they are. The book also addresses the concerns of a great many ordinary people who are interested in psychological exploration.

Organization

A *Population of Selves* is divided into two parts, one exploring how the self is formed and the other delineating the procedural principles that guide the actual therapy. In Chapter One, I address the universal need for a sense of self. In Chapter Two, I lay the groundwork for self, showing the factors that influence the formation of selves. Chapter Three elaborates on the concept of a population of selves, demonstrating how they can be identified and applied in therapy.

Part Two begins with Chapter Four, whose subject is attention and its impact on all human experience. I try to harness attention in the service of a therapy of selves. Chapter Five shows therapists how to use the hypnomeditative influence of finely tuned therapeutic sequences to open the patient to new levels of potential change. The stories that emerge naturally from sensitive sequencing are described in Chapter Six, and their role in evoking and recognizing both new and old selves is developed. Chapter Seven focuses on techniques for improving contact between various selves and, on a different level, between therapist and patient. Chapter Eight celebrates the power of empathy and its indivisible connection to contact. To find ways to be empathic with one's own selves, as well as just recognizing them, is a key factor in creating personal wholeness.

Chapter Nine addresses the importance of merger as a fundamental human need, joined inextricably with contact and empathy. Two roles of merger are elaborated: one as a source of synthesis among selves, the other as a source of the enlarged influence that therapy may exercise in expanding communal options for belonging. Chapter Ten shows how therapists can evoke a patient's awareness, injecting liveliness as well as clearer identity into a patient's sense of self. Chapter Eleven closes the book by pointing the way to action, the outward creator of a strong sense of self in relation to the external world.

Not surprisingly, this book has itself turned out to contain multiple aspects, and here is a final one: through the models and ideas on these pages, I would like to encourage versatility in therapists and the development of individual repertoires and styles.

I see it as part of the therapist's task to recognize and honor the multiplicity of selves that make all people the various, complex beings they are. In doing so, the many selves of *therapists* will be registered in their work, so that they can take advantage of their own wide variety of human traits. Wisecracking, sympathetic, impatient, workmanlike, analytical, inspirational—within the technical requirements of therapy, there is room for the therapists to be regular people, professionally tuned in to their patients and yet engaged with them on a human level. I hope to show that through theoretical, emotional, and procedural versatility, every therapist can bring more timeliness and inspiration to every session, and so help patients in their search for self.

Acknowledgments

A writer is a funnel through which the ideas of many people flow. I want to thank Tom Pace for pressing me to expand and clarify my views of the self. I also want to thank my editors at Jossey-Bass for the valuable help they gave. Becky McGovern remained enthusiastic about the book's merits while still finely tuned to the flaws that had to be addressed—just the combination I needed. Marta Maretich's organizational clarity and tough-minded sensitivity for both the pruning and expansion of the original manuscript got me to work hard on specific troublesome areas. My friend Michael Miller once gave me a basic rule for authors: kill all your darlings. In revisions of this manuscript, Marta encouraged me to these murderous acts. Grim though I first felt about the process, I felt all the more grateful to her for enabling me to express what I wanted to get across.

I also want to thank Gordon Wheeler for his careful and illuminating examination of an early draft. Suggestions from Elaine Breshgold, Herman Gadon, Rich Hycner, Lynne Jacobs, Natasha Josephowitz, Milton Richlin, Jeanne Weissman, Gary Yontef, and Stephen Zahm were helpful. To Kathryn Conklin, my secretary, I want to express my thankfulness for all she has meant to me and in particular all the many ways she helped me get this manuscript off, including the times she rescued me from becoming a victim of my own computer. She is sunny, competent, and a breath of fresh air.

Finally, I always have my major support in my wife, Miriam. Her judgments about language, thematic validity, and sense of proportion, as well as her editorial acumen, are always factors in practically everything I do, so much so that it would be easy to take them for granted. Fortunately, I don't.

My writing of this book began with the presentation of three papers (1987, 1990, 1992), each of which was later published in an anthology. The material in these papers has been greatly expanded and considerably revised, but occasional passages from the papers are reproduced here unaltered.

The impersonal pronoun will be male or female in alternate chapters.

La Jolla, California   Erving Polster
February 1995

To Miriam

The Author

. . . .

ERVING POLSTER is director of the Gestalt Training Center in San Diego, California, and clinical professor in the Department of Psychiatry at the School of Medicine, University of California, San Diego. He provides training, workshops, and lectures throughout the United States and abroad and is on the editorial board of *The Gestalt Journal*. His previous books include the best-selling *Gestalt Therapy Integrated* (1973), cowritten with his wife, Miriam Polster, and *Every Person's Life Is Worth a Novel* (1987). Among his contributions to various anthologies are "Escape from the Present: Transition and Storyline" (1987) and "The Self in Action: A Gestalt Outlook" (1992) in *The Evolution of Psychotherapy* volumes edited by Jeffrey Zeig.

He received his doctorate in clinical psychology from Case Western Reserve University in 1950, was a founder of the Gestalt Institute of Cleveland in 1953, and served as its faculty chair until 1973, when he began to work in California.

A Population of Selves

Part I

. . . .

How the Self Is Formed

Why the Self?

Fifty years ago, Popeye, the one-eyed, pipe-smoking cartoon-strip sailor, used to sing, "I am what I am, I'm Popeye the sailor man." The simple self-respect of this peculiar man who always knew who he was charmed generations of moviegoers and comics fans.

What is notable about the popularity of Popeye's theme song is that it only mirrors what everybody is already guaranteed: to be what they are. Being what you are is one of the great tautologies, as assured as daytime at noon. There is, after all, nothing else to be.

Yet being yourself remains an elusive goal. People commonly yearn wistfully to be themselves. So compelling has this wish become that the concept of the self may well be the successor to its venerable predecessors, the soul and the unconscious, in the search for our true natures.

The soul served as a guide for centuries and the unconscious became its successor in the twentieth century. But both soul and unconscious have major shortcomings; each concept is nebulous in its own way, directing the person to what goes on beneath the actual experiences of daily living.

The soul goes underground more mystically than the unconscious, intoning a personal essence, offering many people a reassuring belief about what they *really* are, a warm core that is disembodied and eternal, yet compassionate and deep. As an example of the indeterminacy of the soul, take the words of Thomas Moore, who says it is impossible to define the soul; that definition is an "intellectual enterprise," whereas "the soul prefers to imagine" (Moore, 1992, p. 1). People who are oriented to their souls try to live as the soul would direct them, but the soul does not speak clearly, and the interpretations of its directions are very diffuse. Furthermore, since this life is a temporary interlude in the soul's eternal life, the mundane challenges take a back seat to the soul's invincible purity, a purity few people experience.

Most people nowadays do not talk about their souls. Almost none of my patients does, nor do I bring it up. Still the soul has a sense of the human spirit, undefinable but dear. Historically, it has been a great force in people's attempts to understand their deepest natures. It is a lyrical and benevolent representation of what people are really like.

In this century, the unconscious has largely replaced the soul as a conceptual orientation to what we really are. It does not have the soul's value implications. Instead it has been a no-holds-barred dynamic where the id, ego, and superego wrestle for dominion. The unconscious has been far more fruitful in explaining otherwise incomprehensible experience, and it has been incontrovertible as a source of impelling energy. But it has also been a source of separation between that which the person knows about herself and what the unconscious represents. Though more experience rooted than the soul, the unconscious nevertheless maintains only a ghostly link to surface experience, which is directed by cryptic motives buried in unreachable filing systems. The unconscious so often contradicts the surface of existence that it has become easier than ever to be confused about who you *really* are. Popeye would have no part of such complexity.

Dynamics of the Self

Now, after a century of extensive writings, the self has recently received a new level of acceptance and may well serve as the contemporary conceptual heir to the soul and the unconscious. The concept of the self that I am proposing and that I will elaborate in this book has four key processes that deepen an understanding of the person, on both the surface level and the deeper levels normally attributed to both the soul and the unconscious:

1. Point/counterpoint relatedness
2. Configuration
3. Animation
4. Dialogue

Point/Counterpoint

The concept of self addresses the interplay among whatever aspects of the person come into focus, crossing the line between surface experience and depth. This interplay takes surface experience at face value, not as simply a substitute for what is obscured. In the language of the self, this means that there is no "real" self, hidden by surface experience, but rather a community of selves that vie for ascendancy. For example, an intellectual man, feeling unhappily caught into a studious way of life, gets fed up and says his "real" self is a surfer. Not so. In terms of the interplay among his options, he is talking about two of his selves—the intellectual self and the surfer self—each with its own character.

Therapists considering the population of selves that I propose can learn a lesson from music, where point/counterpoint interaction is a familiar compositional factor. In point/counterpoint, independent musical voices are set against one another. Some are complementary, others dissonant, but all contribute to the integrity and richness of the entire piece of music. In a culture where harmony in music, as in other things, is frequently considered the ideal, anything short of a smooth blending of voices can seem like a blemish that distracts attention. Yet, as the musicologist Arthur Bullivant says, "There is no fundamental reason why contrapuntal music should be more difficult to appreciate than harmonic, and the listener who is prepared to forget past prejudices will find the experience infinitely rewarding" (Bullivant, 1983, p. 501).

In contrapuntal music, neither the primary melody nor its counterpoint loses its individuality, yet both contribute to the character of the total work. So it is with the self and its many contrapuntal voices. The disparate voices are not there merely to be smoothed over and made harmonious but rather to invite the listeners—therapists and patients—to encompass variety and appreciate the unity that arises from the complexity of the point and counterpoint patterns.

That some of a person's selves are obscured from attention does not mean that they are more real than the manifested self. It means that these selves need to be coordinated with each other. Though these obscured selves may seem very close in concept to the unconscious, they are not the same. Each self has an identity of its own, rather than a substitutive role in the person's makeup. For example, it has been easy for therapists guided by the concept of the unconscious to say that a person who indicates love for his mother "really" hates her in his unconscious mind. In contrast, what I am proposing is that the selves in the background are counterpoint voices, perhaps unheard, to the ascendant selves; the aim of wholeness is to hear these voices simultaneously.

Classes of self, like the intellectual self and the surfer self, are usually recognized by directly observable experiences; they are more easily fleshed out than the misty characterizations of the soul and unconscious. These classes of self may be formed by the most intense experiences, like being screamed at or worshipped by mother, or by defining statements, like "Whenever the chips are down, you leave."

This focus on observable behavior and feeling is hospitable to ordinary experiences. When the therapist responds compassionately to these experiences, she helps register the human quality the soul is associated with. The social value that the concept of soul fosters, including especially the goal of being a good person, contrasts with the scientism of the unconscious, which lets the chips fall where they may.

Building on the ancestry of humanity and experiential accountability, the self I will describe offers greater detail of everyday personal experience than the soul and greater empathy with internal dynamisms than the unconscious. The interplay between surface and depth goes on always as self formation goes easily in and out of awareness. This fluctuation between surface and depth makes the self a bridge between unconscious and conscious experience. Yet, as I shall show, the self is more enduring than the continual fluctuations of ephemeral experiences.

Configuration

Selves are formed by a configurational reflex, which takes the disparate details of personal experience and forms them into a unified pattern. Such organizational reflexes result in shorthand identifications of clusters of experiences. Through these clusters of experiences, a person may be identified in innumerable forms: an iconoclast, a robber, a singer, a coward, or a noble person. At some point, as the significance of these characteristics evolves, these clusters may merit designation as selves.

Let's look at how many different ways we can organize these experiences into selves with which we may identify. At its highest sweep, the self integrates the events of a lifetime. An epitaph is one example. "Here lies Eric, friend to all; all ways and always." For those who knew Eric, this self designation may be a fitting summary and it may even be evocative of many stories in Eric's life. But this epitaph does not encompass the breadth of his life. Eric survived a fall into one of Venice's slippery and polluted canals, he played practical jokes on whomever he thought would sit still for them, he daydreamed whenever he could.

Yet, even though everyone's life has comparable breadth, many people search for a unified summary of their existence. Joaquim

Machado de Assis, a nineteenth-century novelist, recognized this minimalist yearning for one self, *the* self, when he wrote: "Among civilized people [epitaphs] are an expression of a secret . . . egoism that leads men . . . to rescue from death at least a shred of the soul that has passed on" (Machado de Assis, 1990, p. 202).

The urge to rescue a shred of their souls, a fragment that will register their existence, makes many of our patients feel compelled to spend their lives reaching for hints of their true proportions within what they fear is a shapeless existence. Because shapelessness is often seen as fractured identity, they may give their sense of self premature shape, falling for flawed summations and getting stuck with them. Often they have no idea what is wrong because they don't realize how they have summed themselves up or how misrepresentative the troublesome summations may be. The concept of the self not only helps recognize this trouble but also gives new guidance for reconstructing the person's summary conclusions.

Still, in contrast to the multiform nature of the self, the notion of a single image of who we are remains a strong attraction. A 1994 article in the *New York Times* reports on the results of a poll in which 1,136 people were asked to say who they were, in one word. For some it was a befuddling task; others quickly found the word. Jesse Jackson said he was "somebody." Martina Navratilova said she was "kind." Mario Cuomo called himself a "participant." Margaret Atwood said she was "indescribable." Michael Kinsley said it was a stupid question. Although the *Times* writer recognized the scientific limits of the poll, he believed it "provides a compelling sociological snapshot" (Barron, 1994, p. B1). For some people this search for an easy sense of identity is nothing more than the wistful despair of people grieving over an ancient fragment of themselves. Other people seriously try to harmonize their behavior with their most desired qualities.

We see this quest all the time in therapy. Here are two stanzas of a poem written by one of my patients:

She looked through the veil she had woven,
From threads of her everyday life,
Forming scaffolds she willingly clung to,
In the attempt to reach paradise.

But too close was the weave and the pattern,
It allowed not a breath to escape,
So it caused her to spin in confusion
And she landed . . . somewhere . . . out there in space.

At what threshold do elemental experiences, the "threads of everyday life," qualify as ingredients in the formation of self? A sly remark, a dog growling menacingly, a toy broken, the smile on a teacher's face for a perfect answer to her question, witnessing an auto accident? These experiences are often so transitory or their meanings so blurred or neutralized that they are below the registration level needed for self formation. But there are many stronger experiences also, more likely to be registered: early brutalization by bullies, marvelous storytelling by an uncle, annual trips to a vacationland, being often told you are lazy, brilliant, mischievous, or rebellious.

In any person, these experiences combine into certain configurations. First the raw data of the person's life are registered, then they evolve into a recognition of personal characteristics, then to formation of self. The therapeutic challenge is to get a fresh view of these incremental influences, which could coalesce into a new sense of self. But lowering the threshold for new and therapeutic self formations is difficult when the patient's mind is already made up about what counts.

For example, a patient comes in depressed. His wife left him and the divorce settlement leaves him feeling financially destitute. Because of economic downturns, his professional practice is slowly going bankrupt. In his mind, he *is* his marriage, his practice, his

financial predicament. Since his favorite ingredients of self definition are gone, he no longer knows who he is, perhaps doesn't even
care. The fact that he is brilliant, affable, enduring, kind, recedes
far into the background. His addiction to the existing self criteria
must be dissolved. Therapy must then reengage and reconfigure
both his sorrows and his multiple self possibilities.

Animation

The self is more than a simple accounting of experiences. It is composed by the human inclination to create fiction, forming characters out of characteristics. It is a named entity, representing clusters
of experienced events. Thus a person who is highly tuned to giving
gifts may be said to have a gift-giving self; a person who loves sailing, a sailor self. When the therapist personifies characteristics, giving them humanlike identity, she animates these characteristics.

In this transformation from a characteristic to a self is selective.
If, for example, I were to tell a person he was being gullible, this
would simply be my reference to one of his characteristics, a familiar form of communication. However, when I want to emphasize
the enduring nature of his gullibility and the experiences that cluster around his gullibility, I may take the designation to a new level
by telling him that his gullible self was speaking.

In a sense, this person is composed of a population of selves that
represent him, one of which is his gullible self. We dramatize his
gullibility by translating this directly describable characteristic into
the more tangibly accentuated language of internal characters. My
patient's depression was reduced when we transformed his characteristics of affability, competence, and dedication into selves that
he experienced as true members of his total, complex being. These
internal characters give a heightened realization of what, in his
depressed state, he may have only dimly registered.

A vital factor in this personal registration process, and crucial in
the use of the word *self*, is the anthropomorphic reflex. This reflex
inspires people to see the human state everywhere—in nature, in

inanimate objects, and even inside themselves. The wind sighs, a bridge groans, thunder roars, clouds race, trees dance, the ocean is wondrously peaceful or tormented or angry. Isn't it logical that people would also populate themselves with these humanlike entities? The anthropomorphic adds drama, understanding, and empathy to raw experience, in much the same way that absorption in the drama of fictional characters derives from an identification with them. The anthropomorphic self, and the deep caring that is inherent in it, give lucidity and psychological life to otherwise transitory experience.

We need look no further than the realization of God for the strength of anthropomorphic identification. The personification of God and the ease thereby gained in the experience of knowing him are monumental entries into the psyche of multitudes of people. Some people try to transcend such anthropomorphism by saying God is only a reference to qualities, such as spirit or goodness or everlastingness. But even these people are caught up in anthropomorphism when they speak of God as "he" rather than the more grammatically correct "it."

Another example of anthropomorphism, taken from psychological theory, is Buber's I–Thou relationship. He applied the term *thou* to deeply experienced "others," by which he meant inanimate objects as well as people. For Buber, immersion in the other is what makes him or her or it into a "thou." If the relationship is more casual, the person or object is an "it." Thus a sunset, deeply experienced, can be a "thou."

Individuals also coalesce their personal reality. The human split between the observer and the observed, the doer and the done-to, makes two people out of one person. It is an internal relationship, neither party ever alone. As a result of this internal interactive phenomenon, a person's raw experiences—be they the seeds of altruism, dependency, enterprise, endurance—may become recognized, united, and named as altruistic self, dependent self, enterprising self, enduring self. By the act of coloring experiences by transforming them into an identification, the person comes to care more than he would about simple descriptive designations. Through this process of special recognition and accentuation, the person anthropomorphically empathizes with his self, much as he might with a character in a novel.

This empathy with self is required indefinitely. The therapist must tap into this self empathy in order to smooth the way into new appreciations of the individual's personhood. Until this quality of empathy—not pity or despair or resignation—is restored, we face the same neutered reaction the reader of a novel may face when, no matter how good the writing may be, he does not care about the characters. It is this empathy with the self that mobilizes the person to continue and persevere in self acceptance, even in the face of disappointment and confusion.

The restoration of caring has often been recognized as a key factor in therapy. Caring for the self, empathy for the self, leads to more than an impersonal talking about one's self. It replaces token communication with an appreciation of self, even the love that serves as prime human motivation.

Dialogue

Selves vie with each other for a place in the life of the host person, creating internal friction. When that person comes to therapy he is, often unknowingly, trying to reduce that friction by updating the proportion of influence of the various selves. In the process some selves, long relegated to the background, are accentuated and others may diminish in influence.

To reestablish a mutuality of influence among selves, as I am calling them, Fritz Perls in his early writings and workshops featured personlike identities as a centerpiece of both his theory and his method (Perls, 1947; Perls, Hefferline, and Goodman, 1951). These identities, such as top dog and underdog, were animated, personlike inner characteristics, tantamount to selves. Perls gave sharp attention to neurotic splitting, not only between top dog and underdog but between any paired characteristics that are alienated from each other, such as indomitability and resignation. These splits were transformed from mere conceptual orientations about the person into working dialogues between the two members of the split pair.

By means of the dialogue among these internal characters, not yet called selves, gestalt therapy introduced a graphic depiction of the person's internal struggles. Conflict could be seen as the dramatic interplay between internal beings inimical to each other. Therapy sought to name these mutually alienated beings and, through guided dialogue, to restore harmony among them. The aim was to merge the disharmonious aspects of the person so that they could become joint contributors to the person's wholeness. Live engagement through dialogue would evoke the empathy of the host person for his characters within.

By this means, the point/counterpoint interrelationship in the internal struggle for personal breadth was addressed. If diversity and dissonance add spice and depth to music, why not to the concept of self? One reason is that in music, the counterpoint voices are heard simultaneously and are very difficult to disregard. When a person hears two melodies at the same time, it would be a prodigious act to exclude one or the other; both melodies enter the ear at once. Where selves are concerned, it is easier to uncouple them and select which one will be attended to. Taking the easy way out, where counterpoint is distracting, any particular self is more readily set aside. However, as is true of musical counterpoint, people may relish the dissonances among the variety of selves that any person must coordinate to live a full life.

When I address the point/counterpoint dimension, I find myself in what I call the *radical middle*—radical because is it fundamental to be at the center of all personal experience and because it represents free reactivity, moving in whatever direction my choices go. The radical middle is not a point of neutralization but rather the place where the therapist encompasses everything from what T. S. Eliot (1943) called the "still point of the turning world" where "the dance is" (p. 11). Eliot's image summons us to the uncanny core of a swirling eventfulness, magnet to all experience, a locus of concentration and inclusion.

Perls (1947) referred to this point as "creative indifference" (p. 15), but that term falls short of communicating either the excitement or the rootedness that exists at the center. From this position I discover an abundance of options and, better yet, the special alertness that the dynamism of integrating these options creates. When I welcome dissonance, not only do I face a choice between focusing on the patient's enduring self and focusing on her transitory experience, but I also broaden the scope of my theoretical guides. I may focus on such point/counterpoint dissonances as content *and* process, introspection *and* action, here and now *and* there and then, commonality *and* the idiosyncratic, neediness *and* self-sufficiency, individuality *and* merger, hatred *and* love, chicanery *and* altruism, and all the varieties of experience that call out from the maelstrom of human divergence.

Within such multiplicity, the natural reflex to synthesis is our ally. Where the person is overburdened with the requirements for synthesis, gestalt therapy has taken a simplified and active approach to the problem by directly identifying and energizing alienated aspects of the person. Perls (1947) said, "By remaining alert in the centre, we can acquire a creative ability of seeing both sides of an occurrence and completing an incomplete half. By avoiding a one-sided look we gain a much deeper insight into the structure and function of the organism" (p. 15).

From this perspective, the dynamic middle came alive with the concept of the top dog/underdog polarity, each personified part alienated from the other and each called into a therapeutically guided dialogue with the other. From the perspective of the Hegelian thesis–antithesis–synthesis sequence, two alienated selves in good-quality dialogue would fuse into a third entity representing both. This union would be no victory for either top dog or underdog but rather a composition of both. Gestalt therapy seeks synthesis not only among such highly generalized selves as top dog and underdog but also for the more specific selves representing complexes of characteristics, such as ambition and passivity. A person suffering from this split in her self structure might identify these selves, for example, as a driving business executive or a wimp. In dialogue, these selves become synthesized as a new fusion of selves—perhaps an executive who listens.

However, important though this form of synthesis is, I want to propose the point/counterpoint interrelationship as a new slant on synthesis, different from the fusion that Perls advocated and, I believe, more suited to the treatment of selves. Whereas the synthesis of selves is commonly thought by gestalt therapists to be the creation of a third quality, a fusion of previously alienated aspects of the person, point/counterpoint is characterized not by fusion but by the retention of dissonant selves, each one continuing to play out its own original quality within the diversity of the person's voices.

As I recognize the voices of these selves, I help my patient register them as part of her total self, each with its own character, and thereby create a synthesis within diversity. In musical terms, the melody and its counterpoint are both heard as individual voices, neither of which loses its individuality. The dissonant voices are simultaneously encompassed by the listener, who is able to synthesize them while continuing to hear both as independent voices. An example is an anecdote about the composer Charles Ives when he was a student of composition. He liked dissonance a little too much for his teacher, who forced him to resolve his chords. Ives's father, a musician who liked his son's musical eccentricities, was indignant and said, "Tell [him] that every dissonance doesn't need to resolve, if it doesn't happen to feel like it, any more than every horse should have its tail bobbed just because it's the prevailing fashion" (Kirkpatrick, 1972, p. 116).

Nor do psychological dissonances all have to be resolved into a fusion. The driving business executive I described earlier can, in full function, be flexibly ambitious or passive, according to the circumstances and her reactions. Her pressured ambition may not be experienced as contradictory to her passivity, and her ambition is no contradiction to her becoming appropriately passive. The synthesis of multiple voices *without changing them* is illustrated by the synthesis of furniture pieces, art objects, and flowers that become a well-appointed room, though they always remain furniture pieces, art objects, and flowers.

Dangers of the Classified Self

The four conditions of self formation—the point/counterpoint union of surface and depth, configuration, animation, and dialogue—are all part of an enlivening process that could counteract the stagnancy of classifications. Nevertheless, when we speak, for example, of a gullible self as opposed to a person being gullible, we edge close to the famous existentialist controversy between essence and existence.

Essence represents what people characteristically are, be it parent or carpenter, compassionate or exploratory. Existence refers to actual experience—individualized, unlimited, released from defining classifications. As Rollo May pointed out, existentialism derived its name and its character through its reaction against the Western concern with the essences of people, who were often cavalierly classified and catalogued (May, Angel, and Ellenberger, 1958). To be defined by one's nationality, family membership, sexual or racial identity, chosen organizations, IQ, career skills, and the like is alien to the boundary-expanding options our culture has come to insist on. The self, therefore, as an enduring classification of one's characteristics, might threaten this need for freedom.

But our patients are already suffering from exactly such a threat. They are already stuck with narrow classifications of their natures. It is a primary aim of psychotherapy to release them from what they already experience as the givens of their lives, to recognize flux in their environment and versatility of their own powers. The release from these destructive classifications is not necessarily a release from classification itself, but rather a rebirth through new, fruitful classifications.

In the early days of existentialism, the restrictive forces of classification were especially evident. Jean-Paul Sartre inspired a revolt against assigning essence status to behavior as the defining factor in forming people's character. Proclaiming "man is nothing else but that which he makes of himself" (Sartre, 1948, p. 28), he assigned to people the full and continuing responsibility as agents of their existence. His words were full of bravado and helped stamp personal freedom into the minds of many people. But his aphorisms, catchy slogans taken out of context, came back to haunt him. He was misunderstood by people who were eager for philosophical release from constraint.

Sartre never meant his views to be taken as a dismissal of the enduring nature of identity. After the misunderstandings accumulated, he explained that existence preceded essence but did not replace it; that is, we are as we carve ourselves out to be. Essence exists, but as a counterpoint to existence. Yet, since his genie was already out of the bottle, his corrections didn't help much. Given the postwar reformulations of human possibilities and the widespread urge to jettison many major behavioral and attitudinal fixities, the increased fluidity of values challenged previous customs. The emphasis on existence rather than essence encouraged people to think they could do or be anything and that social concerns were not so pointedly the concerns of the individual.

Fritz Perls, in spite of his innovative designations of such enduring internal characters as top dog and underdog, retained a strong anticlassification mindset. As part of this theoretical atmosphere, gestalt therapy emphasized the action properties of the self. The view, in a nutshell, was that the self was a system of ever-fluid contacts, a process rather than a structure, a result of a continuum of engagement and awareness. As Perls and his colleagues said: "The self is not . . . a fixed institution; it exists wherever and whenever there is . . . interaction. To paraphrase Aristotle, when the thumb is pinched, the self exists in the painful thumb" (Perls, Hefferline, and Goodman, 1951, p. 373).

This was a key perspective honoring versatility of mind, but at the same time it ignored the self as an enduring composition of characteristics. Even though Perls and colleagues said that the self exists in the painful thumb, the infinite succession of all of our experiences was still of greater interest than the abstract self. Misgivings about abstractions and a yearning for greater appreciation of the uniqueness of each experience permeated nonpsychology circles as well.

One of the many voices warning against the petrification that occurs in classifying experience was the novelist Joyce Cary (1961), who observed that if you tell a child the name of a bird, he loses the bird. The fear was warranted, but it is also apparent that there is an equal but opposite truth: if you know the name of the bird, its history, and its habits, you may know the bird better.

Given these opposite prospects—losing the bird and enhancing the bird—it is evident that the principles which win out in any method, the ones that come to be a method's major theme, relegate counterpoints to the background. So the classification of experience lost out temporarily. Though this configurational counterpoint could enrich the person's sense of self much like harmonic undercurrents deepen primary musical themes, many people could not hear it. In music, as I have said, disparate voices can resonate simultaneously in the listener's ear, but the verbal mind easily narrows in on the main theme, avoiding contrapuntal intricacy.

Trying to live with the existential credo of personal freedom caused many therapists to give only background importance to the enduring and identifying characteristics in a person's life. My wife Miriam and I took a step toward the classificatory experience through our concept of the I–boundaries (Polster and Polster, 1974). Through this concept we proposed that the quality of continuing experience was best when the individual's range of acceptable self was not threatened by the prospective new experience. For example, if my sense of acceptable self does not include crying or anger or assertiveness or submission, I will be careful not to engage with others in a way that might call forth these behaviors; or if I do engage it will probably be awkward and have reduced benefit.

We named and described some large classes—essences—of these I–boundaries: value boundaries, expressive boundaries, body boundaries, familiarity boundaries, and exposure boundaries. Each boundary delineated parameters of the self, of that sense of what it is to be "me." Within these boundaries this feeling of being "me" was so compelling that to rend the boundaries would be disturbing. Thus these boundaries were the range of experiences wherein each person's self was recognizable and acceptable.

These classes of experience were actually the raw material for the forming of selves, and these raw materials were extensively elaborated. The rest of our book described the contacts, awarenesses, and experiments in the marketplace of experience. The existence factors were given greater attention than the essence factors of the self, itself. Now, in revising this proportion and accentuating the self as an enduring formation of raw experiences and characteristics, it is important not to turn things around and neglect these experiential facets of living.

Yet, dangers notwithstanding, classifications must be given greater attention even though they collide with the individuality so highly prized in psychotherapeutic circles. Over the years of being oriented to individuality, psychotherapists have increased their skills in fostering stronger, more personalized behavior in their patients and they have guided them to new levels of individual personal awareness. They often did this instead of seeing the enduring community of people and institutions as a key support for an enduring sense of self. Now, when the isolations in our society are of greater concern, it has become important to recognize that therapy's emphasis on personal accomplishments has overshadowed the durable qualities of belonging. These qualities must be accommodated to maintain context, continuity, dependability, and coherent change.

Shared identities are brought into unforgettable relief by an infinite range of simple experiences, such as "a candle lit at a ritual, the flap of a flag, or the odor of onions and thyme sauteeing in olive oil"

(Moerman, 1993, p. 96). More than a sentimental crutch or a nostalgic rush, these kindlings of our self realizations enable us to drink in the special assurances that group identification provides.

These assurances may be empty when the individual fails to participate with the depth that is called for. Those most absorbed in the group to which they belong will most readily recognize the self that is reflected in the membership: as a member of a group of friends or a worker proud of his company's productions or a member of a beloved family or a participant in a square dancing group or a bowling club or a stamp collectors' society. These associations are self clarifying only to the extent that one's current life experiences fit the membership. In full identity with the group, membership may create a brightened self, recognizable and refreshing. This brightness must be continually maintained by the special fluctuations and experiences of the individual's actual behavior.

The enduring membership in an enduring community offers a major reference point, a guide to a sense of self through the great flux in personal accomplishment. One is continually challenged to create, as Rogers might have said, congruence between self and community as well as between self and continuing personal experience. The self that is defined by belonging must form side by side with the self that is defined by advances in such functions as assertiveness, goal directedness, confidence, ability to be affectionate, and receptivity—all of which are important for friendships, business success, entertainment opportunities, good sex, or happy marriage.

All these personal functions, the improvement of which has been the core purpose of therapy, have been also crucial to the formation of self, constituting the substance from which it evolves. We must ask, however, whether it is sufficient for a person to reach experiential goals if he has not also increased his sense of who it is who has done it. To paraphrase the New Testament, what will it profit this person if through all his advances, he fails to get a resonant sense of his own self.

2

The Creation of Self

I now come to a key discrimination about the self, without which the concept of the self will always remain elusive to therapists and patients alike. This source of elusiveness is the failure to differentiate clearly enough between the concept of the self and the person. Often the reference to "self" is just another way of referring to the person himself, using the term as though it were a pronoun, standing in place of the person.

The word *self* is especially vulnerable to that confusion since people refer to themselves all the time. They will say, "I did that myself" or "I am proud of myself" when referring to their own actual acts and feelings, like painting the house or feeling exhilarated. Or they may ask, "What is true about me, the person I am? Am I intelligent? peculiar? reliable?" They are simply looking inward to their own characteristics; there is no implication of the self as a new psychological entity.

Differentiating the Person and the Self

The purpose of a theory of the self must be to recognize a new entity serving to enhance understanding of the person, not just to serve as a linguistic convenience for referring to the person. In describing the self earlier, I conceptualized an entity within the person, much as we see it in the establishment of id, ego, and superego, metaphorical compositions of intrapsychic functions. But the differentiation of the self from the person is more difficult.

The self in its largest amplitude is so supraordinate a configuration, as for example in thinking of the "real me," that it is almost coextensive with the person. Yet in its smaller arcs—the rational self or the dominating self, for example—it is more clearly a constituent of the person rather than the person himself. It is necessary therefore to understand the fact that, pronoun function notwithstanding, the self is always a summation of large or small clusters of characteristics within the person, a metaphorical dynamism that guides the person's behavior and feelings. This is sometimes so fine a differentiation from the person himself that almost all theorists go in and out of using the self as a special composition created by the person, often using it when they are actually talking about the person.

To understand this problem more fully, we can look at how it is manifested in those who theorize about the self. One of the most important of these theorists is James Masterson, who, in specifying the distinction between person and self, gets caught up in blurring it. On the one hand, he is clear about the self as an intrapsychic entity, distinct from the person, when he objects to those who "define the self as a whole person" (Masterson, 1985, p. 19). Yet in naming the nine capacities of the self, he could just as well be naming the capacities of the person.

To illustrate the blurring, let us look at just the first of his designated capacities: the "spontaneity and aliveness of affect." This represents "the capacity to experience affect deeply with liveliness, joy, vigor, excitement and spontaneity" (Masterson, 1985, p. 26). These capacities of the self may just as well be understood to be capacities of the person, possibly heavily influenced by his self, which is organized around these capacities. Nevertheless, though these capacities are pivotal in the formation of his sense of self, the self must be distinguished as the person's configurational creation, not merely his behavioral capacities.

The same is true of another important theorist, Heinz Kohut, who speaks of the self in a similarly ambiguous way. He refers to the self as "a psychological sector"—intrapsychic—yet having "ambitions, skills and ideals" which permit "joyful creative activity," language we usually associate with the person's achievement (Kohut, 1977, p. 63). How do we distinguish between a joyfully creative self, a fictional dynamism driving the person, and the person who experiences joyful creative activity?

This confusion is all the more disconcerting coming from Masterson and Kohut, leading figures in recognizing the intrapsychic quality of self, for it only reflects the unruly nature of the problem. There will always be some confusion because of the overlapping language of self and person and because the self has a dynamism of its own. But the self is always the configurational entity within the person. It will never wear a pair of shoes.

There is nothing new about this dilemma. Philosophers have had similar difficulty in making the distinction between self and person, and this difficulty has often led to a depreciation of the concept of the self. Michael J. Mahoney (1991) tells us about David Hume's search for his own self, a search that showed Hume what many people, perhaps most people, experience. Hume found nothing that was different from simple experience and concluded that the concept of self would add nothing to his already recognized ordinary human qualities. Mahoney observes that what Hume disregarded was the search itself, which in its "life-ordering" function could lead to insightful abstractions that united behavioral qualities otherwise observed in isolation from each other. In other words, for Mahoney, the internal search is a condition required for the recognition of the existence of the self.

What I am trying to describe, however, goes beyond this internal search, though the search may be important in the conscious recognition of one's selves. Those selves may be formed independently of this active inward search just as naturally as the perceptions and other experiences on which the reflexive formation of self is grounded. The nature of self is elusive because it cannot be identified by simple registration of experience. It is identified, instead, by the functions of summation or representation of experience. This summation process in its many forms is as compelling as is the registration of simple experience. The summation process, within awareness or not, is the vehicle directing the person's search for the self.

The self has often been said to be illusory. The process of configuration—or summation, which is one of the attributes of configuration—is no more illusory than any other psychological agency for making sense of the world. The Buddhists, more mystical than Hume, are among those who believed the self to be an illusion—with our thoughts we make the world. So are constructivist thinkers who believe we create our own reality and take the Buddhists' illusionary perspective to the edge of reality by discounting the reality of anything but the mind's own creative compositions.

These views of illusion as unreal perception should be differentiated from my view of the self. As the inherent artistry of the human mind operates, the self—a representational portrayal of aspects of the person—is not an unreal perception. Far from being merely a perceptual shadow, the self elaborates experience so as to reveal what is otherwise unrealized by raw experience alone. A person who thrives on discovering a new book or examining a broken piece of pottery or taking a bus wherever it may be going is more than any of these isolated experiences portrays. Together, organized and personified, the experiences are alive inside this person as, perhaps, an exploratory self.

This process resembles art forms that provide symbolic integration for otherwise isolated experiences. The fractured faces in a surrealistic painting, for example, although not literal organizations of reality as is the exploratory self, may nevertheless be said to organize many complex phenomena: the broken nature of people or relativity of perception or vulnerability. Often the specialized perceptions of art form will enhance understanding where ordinary description fails. In the same way, the self, through extrapolating and animating this or that hint of the patient's experiences, helps focus a sense of enduring reality, where such experiences deserve more than transitory attention.

This creation that I am proposing as the self is an example of natural gestalt formation and greatly reduces the confusion between person and self. First, the self is a psychological event intending to illuminate and animate reality, not to replace it. Second, this configurative process is fluid and is the creator of many selves. It is easier to distinguish between the self and the person when there are many selves (a phenomenon I will elaborate in the next chapter) because it is very clear about any person that there is only one of him.

Further heightening the distinction between person and self is that selves may exist outside awareness and receive only wispy recognition. So tempting is this vague realization that people commonly feel within reach of it when they say they want to "find themselves." They often treat this intuitive sense of the self's existence as though this self were an identifiable singleness which, once admitted, will enhance the reality of an otherwise indistinct existence.

The Real Self

Before we get to the description of the variety of selves and how vital they are in psychotherapy (Chapter Three), we must take account of the immense appeal of a comprehensive self. People seek clear, global, and dependable answers to the question of who they are. We see a similar phenomenon in theoretical circles as well. The search for a comprehensive self has been widespread. Winnicott looks at true and false selves (Ogden, 1986); Horney (1942) at real self, actualized self, and idealized self; Miller at true and false selves (1986); and Masterson at real self (1985). All of these theorists assume a self based on the early loss of one's basic nature; it apparently starts out pure but becomes sullied, then abandoned, in the course of socialization. They observe that what begins as an original and simple reality of self is distorted through the inevitable influence of acculturation.

The loss of this original purity becomes at least a subtle abrasive for everybody, and for many people it is a disaster. For all, the recovery of this early unadulterated self becomes urgent, driven by a longing to close the gap between early ephemeral bliss and current personal complexity.

The drug culture beginning in the 1960s has been devoted to the restoration of primordial, therefore presumably real, experience. LSD evoked phantasmagoric imagery, unbounded by culturally familiar perceptions; marijuana created peace and unhurried time; cocaine created excitement, endurance, and joy. Nowadays, drugs are becoming neurologically more sophisticated and controversially promise to be nonaddictive, noninvasive, and specific, directed not just to the removal of symptoms but to changes in how people see themselves.

Kramer (1993) writes—with futuristic implications for the pharmacological creation of self—about many patients whose characteristic behaviors have been dramatically altered by Prozac. He believes the drug has a fundamental impact in restoring basic self functions, similar to the "real" self people often seek: free of intimidation, functioning with zest and clarity, unhampered by threats of rejection, self-sufficient but communally active. In effect, he sees Prozac as promising nothing less than a return to a utopian security and harmony. His buoyant observations of pharmacological successes are not shared by all, but he does report a researcher's dream— an incidental discovery of self reformation, surpassing the original intention to provide more specific relief from depression and other psychiatric diseases.

Theories about a real self have validly pointed to internal conflict between what, on the one hand, seems rooted in the person— even normal, as Masterson puts it—and what, on the other hand, is a sacrificial effect of living in the world. However, these root experiences often remain key points of reference as criteria for a desirable sense of self. Later self formations are unfortunately seen to be only distortions of this early self. To me they are more than distortions. They are the creative enterprise of self formation, each new configuration building on what is continually happening. When the struggle begins between the "real" and the acculturated formations, it is a struggle of contradictions among the diverse conclusions about the self drawn by complex people. (See observations on composition in Polster and Polster, 1973, chap. 3.)

The selves that are in disharmony with the felt preference for an early idyllic experience may be desirable or not, "normal" or not, conflicting or not, overlooked or not. All of them represent developmental reality. All have their own potential for freshness, direction, and zest, often overshadowed by the nostalgia for the original freshness. For all of us, how good it is to taste ice cream again as we did as a child, or to remember being soothed, or to reexperience the wonderment of an early puppet show or magic act. How, then, in the face of such precedents can a jaded adult return to the experience of novelty when, for example, he is listening to an abstract and repetitive lecture or tackling confusing responsibility or being distracted by too many options?

Alas, in the search for the simple realization of self, the so-called real self remains a compelling goal, and many people can feel satisfied only when reaching it. The damage created by excessive focus on such selves is that these criteria for selfness make all else shrivel in comparison. Even though achieving this realization of a "real me" is rightly cherished, it is also a large source of disappointment when many experiences that could be rewarding and self-sustaining on their own merits don't measure up to the inflated standard. Instead of regarding formative experiences as forces destructive to some pure, original self, I prefer to view these experiences, positive and negative, as the base for the coherent self that they are now seeking to identify. It is better to examine the point/counterpoint implications of self formation, which calls for including the melodies that all these selves play as they make their contributions to the forming person.

In the following example I try to show the value of restoring the multiplicity of selves, which had been abandoned because of a fear of their coexistence. This patient returned to a blessed moment, briefly recaptured, that served as his reference point for acceptable self identification.

Shelly was chronically angry. One day he realized, as though hit between the eyes, how hard his life had been. In great self empathy, instead of getting angry this time, Shelly yielded to his softer inclinations and in long-absent sadness cried convulsively. After he finished crying, released from his anger and tension, he said, "This is the real me, peaceful and soft." He loved this self, the self who was free to cry when overwhelmed and free to enjoy the breath of fresh air inside and the temporary end of conflict. For the moment, he rediscovered how to yield. The release felt much better than the anger, which made him feel strong but isolated.

Real? Yes. But it is also important to keep in mind that Shelly's anger was the instrument of an important self within. Although in this case it was prodded by a bloated righteousness, this angry self should also be real to him. His so-called real self, peaceful and soft, could now appear and give a necessary new dimension to his angry self. His angry self now had some lessons to learn from his "real" self. But he needed to know that it was his angry self that helped him to survive.

In spite of the attractions of a "real" self, it is clearly an oversimplification of a person's existence. Though the real self is often a useful reference for what people would like to be or what they believe they once were, there is always a wider scope of personal options and developments. Unfortunately, the use of generic entities like a real self makes individual personal development seem a compromise rather than a fresh creation. It is better to know that the prospect of multiple selves, each with its own place in the individual, offers the patient a recognition that all internal dynamics are the raw material from which one's sense of self is always being created and recreated.

Nevertheless, the realization of the "real me" is a noteworthy achievement, as it was for Shelly—not only for the moment of pleasure but even more as a reference point for subsequent experience and as a reminder of possibilities forgotten. In this discovery of desirable selfness we see a steadying point for the elusive personal standard of self, one with which an individual can totally and happily identify. However, in order not to get stuck with unreachable standards, the person must become reoriented, not only by primal origins but by current experiences that give his behavior an individualized place in the community of possible behaviors.

To have such standards as the real self may give dimension to experience but only if the new experiences retain a validity of their own. In a sense, one is already inescapably what one has become, not merely a negation of what one originally was. The task of therapy is to restore regard for what one is so poignantly as to be at the starting point for what one would like to be.

Underneath this multiplicity of selves we have a vast range of raw materials of experience that may or may not fit any particularly coveted sense of self. The raw materials of many contacts, many awarenesses, and many actions are the ingredients of what the person is. The recognition and the naming of each self contend with the infinity of events and personal characteristics, which have unruly organizational possibilities. Thus the therapist enters into this burbling population of experience, grounded in billions of neurons, offering to create new organizations of these experiences so that the patient will know his own nature more clearly than the jumbled understandings and fixed beliefs with which he entered therapy.

Introjection: A Therapeutic Resource

One vital tool in the creation of these flawed versions of what the patient is like is the introjection process. Through the overloaded requirements the patient is faced with in imbibing the world of experience, he develops skewed visions of his self. However, introjection, a source for mistaken self formation, may also serve as an ally in the therapeutic process. As introjection opens the patient to a flawed organization of messages about himself, so also may it in therapy open him to new messages and a reorganization of the old ones.

Introjection is the reflexive ingestion of experience. Through it the individual is merged with society. The offerings of society are imbedded into his psyche from the beginning, largely without choice. This phenomenon, ominous in its possibilities for poisoning the mind, is also the most wondrous source of learning. Language, customs, purposes, and information become transmitted, and each person becomes oriented to how he will take his place in the generational transitions on which every society depends.

There is in each of us a clear and compelling introjective hunger for absorbing the world around us. That is how we gather the experiences that form the self. Nevertheless, though the achievements of introjection can be a fundamental source of societal unity and self creation, they have largely been seen by psychotherapists as the source of personal handicap, a cross people must bear in payment for getting along.

Perls (1947), for example, considered introjections the basis for maintaining structures that the person needed to destroy and "in every case contrary to the requirements of the personality" (p. 29). In the face of this dark view of introjection, Perls emphasizes the healthy antidote of chewing, actual and metaphorical. Actual chewing transforms the infant from someone who receives food in the form offered into a person who can and must change food's structure before taking it in. A baby can't swallow a cracker, but as he grows, he breaks it down to size by chewing it.

The metaphor of chewing—modifying—extends to other experiences: unwelcome instruction, cold weather, troublesome opinion, personal rejection, and so on. Rather than ingesting these experiences as given, people alter them to make them fit their individual needs. The success of this process (which I will discuss later in this chapter as tailoring) will be crucial in creating a harmonious sense of existence. As Perls (1947) says, "Any introjection must go through the mill of the molars if it is not to become . . . a foreign body—a disturbing isolated factor in our existence" (p. 132).

From this position, Perls provides a vehicle for processing what is introjected so that it may fit harmoniously. However, for Perls the introjection is of value only if it passes through metaphorical chewing, which includes weighing another's opinion, looking beyond rote instructions to do things individualistically, and so forth. The implication is that introjection is an invasive factor in the life of the passively introjecting person, creating a mindless copy of other people's opinions. If parents don't listen when a child talks, he assumes he is not worth listening to; if people laugh derisively at him, he believes he is a shameful person; if people play with him happily, he infers he has a right to whatever he wants.

According to this narrow and erroneous understanding, introjection is often seen exclusively as a major source of mistaken beliefs about one's self. It is true that many distorted self images are created through introjection. One patient, for example, characterized by a helpless self formed when he was repeatedly beaten up by his father, was so invaded by the introjective powers of his helplessness that he was fused into it. For him to identify with being helpless was more compelling than to recognize it as a case of mistaken identity. One of his helpless memories concerned a boy who had pinned him to the ground. So irresistibly was the image fixed into his mind that only with considerable encouragement could he even visualize pressing forcefully against this boy. To fight back, even in fantasy, was a disconfirmation of his investment in his helpless self.

But pathological results of introjection are only half the story. To incorporate the other half of the story, the healthy component, I would like to redefine introjection as spontaneous receptivity, unimpeded by the deliberative faculties of the mind. Introjection, in this sense, is to receptivity what Freudian free association is to verbal expression. From this perspective we may better appreciate two of introjection's major contributions to the powers of therapy.

The first attribute of introjection is that it is a wondrous source of learning, hospitable to the abundance of the world's offerings, including what the therapy has to offer. Though introjection is receptivity, it can be appetitive rather than passive. The restoration of both appetite and receptivity is a major goal of therapy. If we look to ordinary events, we see the effects of introjective vibrancy all the way from the infant who spontaneously picks up his native language to the concertgoer blissfully soaking in the music. This same appetite and receptivity are available in psychotherapy, where the patient may be fascinated with the new messages.

The second attribute of introjection, crucial to the healthy learning process, is that it does not stand alone. By itself, introjection has no implications for psychological well-being—no more so than blood circulation does for blood pressure levels. The key to well-being is not whether we introject but how well the introjected experiences are integrated into the person.

The Introjection Triad

Integration is facilitated by three operations that together compose the process of introjection, an introjection triad of contact, configuration, and tailoring.

Contact

Though the gestalt principles of contact are extensive, perhaps it is enough to say here that contact is the instrument of connection between the individual and the world. (This is described more fully in Chapters Seven, Eight, and Nine.) Only through contact does the individual meet the world and find anything to introject. Even in infancy, where introjection is primary, the baby doesn't just drink the milk. He feels the touch of mother, tastes and smells the milk, and senses its fluidity and texture. He hears mother's cooing or scolding voice. He sees a smile or a scowl. He is touched gently or harshly. Such contacts, multiplied in power and complexity, are the raw material for introjection.

Although it is often mistakenly believed that a person in good contact does not introject, contact and introjection are actually interwoven. So close in touch is the contacting person, as a matter of fact, that he merges momentarily with the other person while paradoxically maintaining his individual identity. This closeness to the contacted person is, in a sense, a lubricant for the introjective process because it opens the person to receptivity.

Take, for example, a person who comes to therapy because he has always felt isolated and continues to live his life according to introjected expectations of isolation. If, in good contact with his therapist or others, he begins to feel understood and valued, this new feeling will open him to relax his isolated self while safely introjecting a sense of belonging. That is, he doesn't just figure out he is understood and valued. He drinks it in, sometimes hardly realizing it has happened. This is not necessarily a function of the therapist's dominating influence but just as easily a measure of mutual respect and trust that opens the person to self-benefiting beliefs.

Configuration

The second phase of the introjection process is configuration, a process designed to create internal unity. This ideal of unity is so compelling, yet so easily thwarted by the complexities of experience, that it can comprise a life's work. Given the early circumstance of great fluidity in registering these introjected experiences and weak organizational development, it is questionable whether self exists yet at all. The experiences that register are only loosely organized in the beginning but are subject to a more stable organization at a later time.

At first, the child seems largely to be a yes/no organism, accepting whatever comes in or rejecting it, with little sense of the relationship among experiences. These early experiences, weakly organized, will become the ingredients of a later self formation. The individual seeks to fit new experiences into his total picture of himself, thus giving relevance and coherence to as much experience as possible. The success of this configurational reflex in fitting things together is a crucial determinant of the future of the introjection, particularly as to whether it turns out to be "healthy" or not.

In the earliest days of a person's life the configurational process is relatively simple. The child with only scant experience has very little to which he must connect any new experience. Furthermore, his skill in determining what fits is minimal. Certain early difficulties, such as awful milk and brutal treatment, would be manifestly alien to the already formed biological needs. Also, sleep patterns and eating cycles would be difficult to organize if the parental pressures didn't fit the individual needs of the child. But even with a number of such exceptions, most of what comes in, comes in on the ground floor of the organism, and the child has great freedom to introject because it is easy to fit his experiences into a relatively meager context.

When much of what happens just fits, it is only natural to feel life is just as it uncomplicatedly is. Thus the child learning to speak has very little context, either of speech movements or meanings, into which the speech must be fitted. Parents' behaviors, including laughter or depression, kindness or severity, inventiveness or fixity, are taken simply as though that's what the world is like.

The fewer the contradictions between what already exists in the child and what he is newly receiving, the easier the configurational process is. But, as his world of connections achieves greater definition—as in having already learned a particular language, having already developed individual bodily posture, living already by certain moral rules, already recognizing dangers—the requirements for acceptable fit become more challenging.

For example, at seven months of age it makes a bigger difference who is tending the baby than at two months. It is more difficult for the seven-month-old baby to accept a substitute for the strongly formed connection with mother. Other examples of contradictory experiences that would be hard to integrate are feeling hunger while food is delayed, aggressive impulses when parents have suppressed such behavior, expressions of sensuality when there is a requirement for distance. Another example: a generous child may have to reconcile his own actual generosity with his father scolding him for being stingy to his sibling. Or a child trained to crave success may be thrown by being told he is stupid. Clearly, it is no small matter to navigate through the sea of contradictions we all face, especially as the formation of self is always on the line.

The work of configuration must be differentiated from assimilation. Assimilation refers to the process "through which the 'unlike' is made 'like.' . . . Learning, when it is digested and not swallowed whole, is said to be assimilated" (Perls, Hefferline, and Goodman, 1951, pp. 190, 421) Thus the assimilated is said to become an undifferentiated part of the assimilating whole. What is to be said for assimilation is that where the person is all of a piece, melded into unity, where internal distinctions are no longer to be made, assimilation is an apt word.

Such melding of experience is especially evident in physiological experience, where the nourishing ingredients of food, for example, become dissolved into a relatively undifferentiated composition. It is also true of many psychological experiences, those that are just part of the total experience. The feeling of being strong, for example, may be based on many personal experiences that, though they have fed this feeling, no longer have any individual identifiability. They are a melded part of feeling strong—just assimilated.

However, this melding is not true for many experiences that may be harmonized but are diverse and retain individuality. A walk in Central Park, a telephone call from a friend, getting a new job: all part of one's life, but each retaining individual identity in memory or planning, much as nose, eyes, and ears have individual identity while also being a face. That is how it is with self formation also, each self with its own identity, configured rather than assimilated.

In consistency with the concept of gestalt formation, it is therefore important to think of configuration as well as assimilation, since configuration is more congenial to the recognition that individual aspects join into a pattern without losing individual identity. Where assimilation is concerned, there would be no point in speaking of selves, which are grounded in configurations among identifiable aspects of the person, each existing with its own identity, interrelated in harmony or dissonance.

Tailoring

The third phase in introjection is tailoring, a process similar to the Perlsian concept of the mill of the grinding molars: destructuring food in order to be able to take it in and make it digestible. You can't eat an apple without taking a bite out of it. Though the primal destructuring process of chewing is developmentally crucial in its literal meaning, figuratively it is vastly more significant.

For more general and lifelong purposes, the term *chewing* is too narrow and the term *destructuring* too one-sided. Tailoring, on the other hand, expands the concept of chewing to include all forms of remodeling, reshaping as well as destructuring. With this meaning in mind, it is easier to examine tailoring in its pervasive role in living.

This larger view of tailoring encompasses the fact that we create newness everyday out of seemingly old situations, ranging from simply bringing a smile to a clerk's face by thanking him warmly to the most inventive strategies for getting a job assignment we want. Knowing cognitively how things are formed and how they may be reshaped is included in the tailoring process. To build a bridge, for example, requires knowing about the nature of steel, formulas for safe support, finances, hiring workers, the needs of the community, setting up infrastructures for maintenance, and so on. In the same way, it is important for the patient to understand the role of his cognitive powers in tailoring his world. If he knows his wife will be more accessible to him if he tells her about his day's experience, he may do it. If he knows he is good at designing houses, he gets the education to do it.

The tailoring factor is so pervasive a function that to think of it as an antidote to introjection would be a trivialization of its key role in people's lives. Through its shaping of external reality, it is a partner to introjection. To the extent it is in good working order, it provides confidence that with skill in tailoring, we will be glad about what we have ingested.

This tailoring process is not much available in the beginning of life. As the child grows, this function also develops. The tailoring process helps maximize the success of the configurational reflex in connecting all that is taken in. What is not suitably tailored, yet ingested, may create configurational problems as the new learning, untailored, does not fit what the person is already oriented by. Failures in the configuration of ingested experiences accumulate, causing psychological discomfort.

Through tailoring the individual improves the prospects for successful configuration. He does this by rejecting those experiences that wouldn't fit and remodeling those experiences that would fit only if altered. Common means of remodeling are criticizing, selecting, objecting, revising, educating, digesting, suggesting, commanding, and all the range of other things people do to try to make the world of ideas, things, and people harmonious with themselves.

Reforming the Introjected Self

What all of this indicates is that introjection, so long seen as the enemy of the self, can work to the advantage of self formation as well. The introjected self, born of the triad of contact, configuration, and tailoring, must be reborn into a new self by the same triad, newly operative in the therapy experience, where the patient's receptivity to new views of self is increased.

Many people are, of course, unable to let the therapy in because of their fixed positions, imposed by other people's beliefs, admonitions, and pressures. The task of therapy is to restore the introjection triad when it has atrophied or when it is inappropriately directed. Here is an example of a case where lack of choice followed poor contact, poor tailoring, and a fragmented self configuration.

Allan, forty years old, had been repeatedly and sadistically scorned by his father as though he were a freak. Geared by this introjection to be cast out—the role of his freak self—he tended to break off contacts with people, so much so that he occasionally experienced extreme dissociation. He had so strongly introjected the shame his father imbued in him that only after two years of therapy was he able to tell me about an experience that symbolized his shame. By this time he was sufficiently confident that whatever he would absorb from me would be promising rather than poisonous. It took two years for him to feel this trust, through introjecting my appreciation of him, and to place his father's degradation of him into the background.

When he was nineteen years old, Allan got a job supervising a group of young athletes, thirteen to fifteen years old. The job gave him a new level of personal success. The kids loved his coaching and he began to appreciate himself. Then a challenge to this new self-image came through a brutal playground game called poling. The boys, including Allan's kids, would randomly select another boy from the playground—in a sense, capture him. These terrorists would then forcefully spread-eagle his legs and fling him, scrotum first, against a pole.

Allan had heard of these personal raids but had never encountered one until one day, one of his athletes, a 230-pound brute, suggested poling a boy who was innocently eating a meal nearby. The boys asked Allan whether they should do it. At the time Allan felt he was fading out of his contact with the boys, about to be cast off once again. He found himself saying, "Do it"—abandoning his own tailoring function, which would have led him to a quite different judgment. They poled the screaming kid, and Allan had suffered the pain silently for all these years. In a sense he had his fling at being the perpetrator of terror, allying himself uncritically with the sadism whereby he had often been victimized.

Since the reformation of selves must include new experiences of contact, I asked Allan to revisit the ringleader boy and imagine himself speaking to him as though he were there. He started by humanely sharing guilt. But then, as a new track for his tailoring function, he began what was also necessary: to differentiate himself from this kid. By the time he warmed to the differences, he began to rage at the boy for his cruelty. This represented both the contact and the tailoring ingredients of the introjection triad, and it obliterated his original mindless harmony with the gang. Through the new contact and tailoring, his rage and discrimination let him know firsthand the difference between his own moral and compassionate sensibilities and those of the ringleader boy.

Almost needless to say, this new differentiation did not excuse him from abandoning his responsibility. What it did, though, was to restore his internal connectedness. No longer did he need to keep this moment of his sadistic self dissociated, lurking always in the background and interfering with his own sense of wholeness. Once the right contact and tailoring were restored, the configurational task of including this experience as part of his life was made easier because it involved less contradiction; as a result he felt more whole.

Clearly, there is heartache embodied within the coordination of contact, configuration, and tailoring. We are all more or less in trouble because, to get a coherent sense of self, we often have to isolate those parts of our experiences that don't fit. Such a sacrifice of certain selves in the service of coherence is a major source of personal distortion. Certain parts of the person come to count more than the whole person. Thus it is not the introjection, itself—I am a freak, I am a sadist—that causes trouble but the fact that these are alienated introjections with a dissociated influence. My patient was primarily a kind man and a competent man, and for him to suffer the shame of being either a sadist or a freak was a distortion of the rightful configuration of his self.

My task as a therapist is not just to find a pure, original self or to promote an exclusively positive vision of self but to bring to light the variety of selves and to bring them together in whatever point/counterpoint synthesis is achievable. These selves are forced into the background by the surpassingly dominant impressions that have been introjected, that have been force fed, like Allan's ingestion of his freak self. These impressions either stand out prominently, blotting out large elements of the patient's self formation, such as Allan's basic kindness, or they are denied, feared, protected secrets, eroding confidence and creating wariness and distraction, all of which, acknowledged or not, contribute to a person's sense of wholeness and harmony.

3

The Diversity of Selves

In this chapter, we shall explore the individual person as host to a *population* of selves and the therapeutic applications of this phenomenon. Drawing elemental experiences together with the fluidity of metal filings being attracted to moving magnets, the person creates and recreates multiple selves. These selves may be either highly generalized or narrow, like a radiant self and a gardening self. They may be biologically or culturally universal, like a mothering self, or they may be altogether idiosyncratic, like a coin-collecting self. They may be parallel, like a doctor self and a musical self, or interactive, as in a struggle for ascendancy between an energetic self and a lazy self. They may be temporary or permanent. They may coordinate well with each other or be alienated, even dissociated, from each other.

I propose two primary classes of these selves: essential selves and member selves. Essential selves are extremely enduring; the individual experiences a compelling identity with them. Member selves are in greater flux, more responsive to immediate experience, and often overshadowed in awareness by the larger goal of consummate self designation. Though these two classes of selves have some overlap, there is enough distinction to be therapeutically meaningful. The distinctions are especially relevant in assessing the patient's amenability to change and also in orienting the therapist for the transformation of selves from essential to member or vice versa, as the therapeutic need determines.

Essential Selves

The enduring nature of essential selves makes them seem like the sine qua non of people's existence. Some of these selves are highly beneficial because they are positive and fit the experiences that the person has actually lived through. For example, a person who grows up feeling secure may live a life in which her secure self is a guiding force, keeping her steady in a risky world. The essential quality of this self makes it feel an inextricable part of her, not easily altered by occasional contradictory feelings of insecurity. When the essential selves are harmful, they also become fixed firmly in position and resist change. These selves, because they cause psychological pain, become the object of therapeutic focus, calling for remodeling through new experiences. Adding to the problem created by actual harmful experiences, people often jump to erroneous conclusions about the events that create essential selves, distorting any clear sense of who they are.

The traumatic experience of injuring a sibling in anger, for example, may take on such great importance that it skews one's version of one's self, perhaps into that of a bad-tempered self. Rightly or wrongly, this self, particularly when bolstered by other experiences, may dominate the mind, leading to irritability with one's children or stubbornness with friends. But this bad-tempered self may be a false guide, overshadowing compensatory qualities—clarity, humor, generosity, dedication, and so on. Valid achievements, lacking sufficient perceived weight to compete with the bad-tempered self, may seem insubstantial against the defining experience of injuring the sibling. Where essential selves are concerned, the difficulty of changing is aggravated by the fact that people would generally rather continue to suffer great psychic pain than give up the selves with which they most deeply identify.

Furthermore, the criteria for dissolving the bad-tempered self may be impossible to meet if they include such requirements as never having created the injury in the first place or forgiveness specifically by a now-dead parent or living a perfectly virtuous life. Defining such fixed criteria for a desirable self realization is a common barrier to successful therapy because it sets up unrealizable conditions.

Under such rigid conditions, even when changes in the essential self may seem successfully accomplished, the person may still feel vulnerable as though living in a psychological haunted house. The deeply familiar essential self, though inactive, casts a shadow obscuring a more current self formation. Registration of current living, leading to new configurations of self, may need to be so strong and so frequently repeated that the old essential self will disappear into the background.

The person with the essential bad-tempered self would have to have many experiences of joking with his special friends before his joking self would seriously register in his own self composition. Bringing member selves such as his joking self into ascendancy may help redirect the patient's areas of concern. The essential bad-tempered self may not be erased, but it occupies a new proportion of the person's psychic space. The following case is an example of this kind of transformation.

Harry, forty-five, came to therapy because he felt unintelligent. He had felt that way as far back as he could remember. Harry grew up in a family where the only prized accomplishment was to be a doctor; it was considered the criterion of intelligence. Harry's brilliant older brother became one, but not Harry. We will never know what might have happened had Harry not had a childhood learning disability. That disability would have been enough reason for him to feel unintelligent but the family code created a more indelible imprint. Being a doctor, his secret longing, had always been altogether out of reach, but it also turned into an immutable reference point for his intelligence. That cluster of experiences created an unintelligent self;

it animated his fixed belief and gave it stronger personal registration than his mechanical appraisal of his intelligence.

What was so remarkable about Harry, and so characteristic of essential selves, was his imperviousness to actual experience. Unintelligent self or not, Harry was no dolt. He had developed a business from nothing and later sold it for a hundred million dollars! He was beloved to many people who benefited from both his generosity and his ebullience. He had created excellent friends.

Building on the facts of his adult life, it was not difficult for Harry to recognize a beloved self inside him, beloved by his associates, and a successful businessman self. Harry was not blind to being either beloved or successful. He recognized and valued these selves, but he did not see them as the real thing. To him they were merely evolutions from his experiences in life—member selves; they were not something built into his nature, as he felt intelligence would be. The actual achievements were fortuitous, and they were no commentary on his intelligence—his mind was made up about that. Essential selves often evoke that kind of certainty.

To show how invincible Harry's essential self was, we may look at Harry's interpretations of his business success. Where most other people would have taken this as a confirmation of his intelligence, he believed that he was merely in the right place at the right time, merely foresaw the future for his product, merely developed a good distribution system, merely hired the right people, merely hit it lucky, and so on. In spite of the depressivelike self-depreciation, he spoke in a style just short of manic, peppy and without enough pause for things to sink in. Much of what I said slid right past him.

To get past his stale beliefs and to accentuate his successful businessman self, I asked him detailed questions about each of his business operations. How did he get into the right place, how did others in the same place manage, was there any risk involved, how did he evaluate the risk, did things ever go wrong, what had he done about them, who were the people he hired, what were their characteristics and contributions, how did he relate to them and contribute to their work, how much time did he spend working? Through these explorations, some new experience of his intelligence seeped into him but not in the revelatory dimension he deserved. Not being a doctor, he couldn't call himself intelligent but his concern with his intelligence began to fade into the background.

Then, in addition to his successful businessman self, there was his beloved self. It too was insufficiently registered to compete with his essential unintelligent self. He was able to recount many things he had done for people: He had given large bonuses to his employees, he had taken a couple into his home when they were having hard times, he gave another couple the down payment for a house, he enjoyed giving people simple gifts and remembered to bring back souvenirs from his trips. He received genuine pleasure from telling me about these acts, as well as from the gratefulness of the recipients, but he didn't consider them significant.

I asked Harry to stop and feel what it was like to do the things he did. In calling his attention to the details of the actual experiences, I made it difficult for him to deflect the experiences of pleasure. Attending inwardly to these sensations and realizations, which normally he would allow to slide by, he learned to savor them, and they became more and more real to him. As he came to register these experiences more poignantly, his member selves took on a higher profile.

However, when Harry ended his therapy, accepting his happiness in life, he still did not believe himself intelligent. What happened instead, as I saw it, is that he raised the value of the member selves so that the essential unintelligent self was no longer the dictator of his self composition. It had become a figurehead with a much reduced voice in the democracy of Harry's selves.

One of the goals of therapy may be to change the direction of attention so as to find new focuses more compelling. In Harry's case, his unintelligent self didn't turn into the intelligent self that was actually merited by the facts. It became merely a member of Harry's community of selves, a change in the proportion of its importance to the importance of his other selves. Thus in the process of reconstituting the self, one option is to discover that the essential self may prove not to be as dominant as originally supposed.

When the environment evokes various aspects of our selves, there may be confusion as to the dominant self. On some occasions we may feel most in touch with a "good person" essential self; at other times we may be more driven by a "tough-minded" essential self.

A measure of flux is inherent to good function—not as evanescent a sense of self as found in the early gestalt theory of the self, which postulated continuing flux, but still responsive and malleable in a continuing relationship with the environment. Even while shifting in selfness according to interactions with others, a person must also feel a dependable core, which will limit an uneasy vulnerability to contradiction. Thus the discovery that the good-person self can remain stable in the face of the tough-minded self is an important factor in coordinating stability and fresh responsiveness.

By successfully facing contradiction, retaining the essential self provides continuity, dependability, a sense of wholeness, a sense of belonging, without the blind restrictions that might negate other selves. Essential selves are always in a struggle for ascendancy with member selves that must be brought into the picture with more impact. Let's see how this works.

Member Selves

Member selves have more fluidity than essential selves and more observability in the everyday task of psychotherapy. In a sense they are more field dependent than the essential selves, responding more discriminately to the coping requirements of the environment.

The line between essential and member selves is not clearly drawn, and part of therapy may rest on being able to transform one into the other. For example, a person who thinks of himself as circumstantially kind (thus having a kind member self) may benefit from discovering how deeply ingrained his kindness is, actually a kind essential self.

One patient, for example, a widely admired public official who was troubled by depression, had many desirable member selves that were overshadowed by a sense of his essential but undefinable worthlessness. The member selves were real to him—his competent self, his admired self, his respected self, his determined self—but they registered only dimly. They felt more like other people's impressions of him.

He ascribed irrelevant motives to the people who liked him: They all have an angle. He exercises power, so people want to get on his good side. He is a husband and a father, and so naturally he is loved by his wife and children. People like him because he is clever, good-looking, and dependable. They would feel differently about him if not for these things. The absurd conclusion we could derive from his attitude is that the only way to trust love would be to have no characteristics at all.

Nevertheless, in the face of such nihilism, one day in my office he finally felt the genuineness of their high regard. He was describing a gift he had been given, and suddenly, in the telling of it, he blushed, abandoning his stoic style. When the session was over, he asked if his next appointment could be scheduled earlier than usual, and I gladly arranged it. When he next arrived, the first thing he said to me was that he had become very emotional when he realized that, as tight as my calendar was, I would give him this special appointment. To him this meant I cared. The simple act of making the appointment had made a mark because his sensations had already broken through, where previously he disregarded stronger evidence of caring. At this point it became apparent to him that the selves we had been addressing—member selves—were indeed real but he had not been allowing them to be registered.

Why not? Here we come to the appearance of an essential self. Having gone through his scenario about the phoniness of people's feelings for him, he came upon a more practical and recognizable fear. If these admiring people had known his stubborn self (which was for him an essential self) and the way he grimly exercised it with his mother, or if they had known of his adolescent criminality, from which he narrowly escaped jail, they would realize he was not the person they were admiring.

Now we were in the realm of contradictory selves. The stubborn self, suffused by a sense of bad seed, defined an enduring cluster of his experiences formed in impressionable years. He wouldn't do anything his seductive and angry mother wanted him to. Any seduction was a red flag for his stubbornness to rise up and protect him.

Elaborating the experiences that formed this defining self softened him; it was as though the telling gave this self proportion. His old essential stubborn self, formed of his rebellious experiences, when reexperienced fell into place as only one of his selves, no longer essential. What became more accentuated was that his many, less indelible selves daily created the love and respect people felt for him. He saw that through these selves, he had listened, forgiven, instructed, laughed, behaved humbly, and so forth. The resulting member selves were a composition of everything he had been, much larger than the essential stubborn self, which had hung on underground through the current substance of his life.

However, knowing how reflexively he disallowed the registration of experience, I could not assume that this new realization would register as fully as necessary. I asked him to close his eyes and tell me what he felt. He recognized a number of fresh things about his inner experience; loving tears, a chest without anxiety, and the feeling of being young again, all more essential in the marketplace of his experiences than the anachronistically dictatorial stubborn self.

This sense of multiple possibility in self formation gives breathing room for continuing change. The versatility of self formation is especially useful in relation to specific themes and their consequent selves. In order to coordinate these selves, one must first develop a clear picture of the individual selves. The blurring of these selves often accompanies the failure to give them their proportional roles in the person's life and makes integration difficult. This is where the accentuation of a person's characteristics through personification, dialogue, and accentuated awareness helps to restore vibrancy to these partially operative and contributing parts of the person. The therapeutic process is an act of restoration as well as reconstruction because much of personal expansion consists of using what one already *has* in order to become what one already *is*.

Characteristics and Selves

Very important to the concept of member selves and their fluidity is the fine line between characteristics and selves. It is easier to think of characteristics than to take the anthropomorphic next step required for seeing enduring characteristics as selves. One must not be put off by overdoing the distinction, because animating the characteristics serves some of the same purposes as the designation of selves.

Perls, for example, was masterful in animating characteristics; first with the polar top dog/underdog dichotomy, then creating quasi-beings out of any characteristic, even out of inanimate aspects of dreams or personal statements. Rowan (1990) has compiled a list of animations that Perls used, after he began to use the so-called empty chair for imaginary dialogue. Placed into the empty chair, such things as the following came alive: "your inhibitions; phoniness; your smirk; the old man you saw when you were five and a half; that memory; the dream you didn't have; the mountain trail; the car number plate; the pillar in the station; the railway station; the water in the vessel; the statue in the lake; the rug on the floor; two rooms talking to each other; your left hand; Fritz" (p. 81).

These empty-chair guests, although live players in the drama of the self, would not necessarily qualify as selves, however. They may be only momentary players rather than summations of experience. The prime contribution they make to the therapy experience and to the sense of self is the animation they contribute to whatever is otherwise given only routine conversational existence. These animations become more than transitory words when they can talk and have relationship and struggle for resolutions: dynamics not activated by stagnant descriptive words.

Furthermore, by giving anthropomorphic life to clusters of experience, selves introduce flux and fresh detail. Once the dialogue progresses, the relationship of one self to another—domination, missed connections, guilt production, exclusions—is addressed. Then the consequences of this relationship can be examined in process rather than as a stagnant conclusion. The dialogue provides options for rediscovery of possibilities foreclosed by people who come for therapy.

Markus and Nurius (1986) have added to this search for selves by proposing the concept of "possible selves," which extends the versatility of self formation. They take account of the fact that people are influenced not only by what they believe they *are* but also by what they believe they might *become*. "Possible selves are the ideal selves we would like to become. They are also the selves we could become, and the selves we are afraid of becoming. The possible selves that are hoped for might include the successful self, the creative self, the rich self, the thin self, or the loved and admired self, whereas the dreaded possible selves could be the alone self, the depressed self, the incompetent self, the alcoholic self, the unemployed self, or the bag lady self" (p. 954).

These possible selves are unlikely to be wholly new, and they go in and out of the person's self experience. For example, one physician came in one Monday morning feeling burdened by responsibility. He had been on call since Friday and was responsible for forty patients, most of whom were desperately ill. The insecure self within him was aroused by these pressures, and the possible competent self receded into the background. He actually did well during those three intense days, though not as well as when he is less pressured. His insecure self had canceled out the actual help he had given his patients and the seemingly impossible requirements of the weekend. As soon as he took too long with a patient or got distracted by interruptions, his competent self was no longer real to him, remaining only a possible self, overshadowed by his annoyance and cynicism.

Only when I asked him to describe in detail his experiences over the weekend did the amazing quality of the work break through.

Then he saw himself differently. With a small smile, he quoted the poet William Blake: "When I feel bad, I can only write prose." Not bad, to be a Blake writing prose.

Naming of Selves

Naming is an important arm of the process of self formation, since names give selves brightness, recognizability, and implications for likely behavior and feeling. The process arises naturally as therapy progresses. If we don't get the right name, the error inserts a jarring note, much as would an error in interpretation. We are cushioned, however, against the worst consequences of error by coordinating with the patient's own judgment of what name to give the self and by the openness to change the name as the facts call for change.

To illustrate how the naming of selves is affected by the fluctuations in the formative process, let us imagine a person who has the following four characteristics: he is careful in his choice of words, noticeably obstructionistic about things he is told to do, passive in conversation, and insufficiently interested in his work. Given this cluster of characteristics, we might name it a procrastinating self, or a lazy self, or a diffuse self, or even a grandfather self, if he associates laziness with his grandfather.

Then, too, this formation might change according to the chemistry between these characteristics and others. For example, if this person were to show nonchalance about getting the job done rather than worry, we may name this self his who-cares self. If he seems quite confident, we might call it his biding-my-time self. If he is grimly slow to move, we might call it his begrudging self. If he is tuned in to the needs of others, we might call it his respectful self. If he is successful in his tasks we might call it his striking-when-the-iron-is-hot self.

Furthermore, not only is it therapeutically vital to provide an apt name for the self and the options to change it when circumstances change, but we must also ask the accompanying question: At what point do discrete *characteristics* cohere to such an extent that we prefer to call them a *self?* Suppose a person pretends to trip over your feet, tells funny stories, turns serious conversation upside down. You may laugh with him or ridicule him or stiffen against him—all simple reactivity to his behavior. That is how most relationship goes: simple engagement of one person to the other. At a certain point, however, these behaviors and the person's evolving characteristics may be so enduringly interwoven and so clearly recognizable as a cluster of experiences as to warrant designation as a self—in this case, let us say, a clownish self. This clustering, named or unnamed, creates a dynamic within the person and will incline him to clown, sometimes irrespective of his current needs.

In a sense, therefore, the self has a life of its own, a configuration that guides the person, often without his awareness. This is a familiar function of underground personhood, reminding us of the functions of the psychoanalytic unconscious. An important difference is that this underground is more personalized and is more recognizably formed from conscious experience. In therapeutic work, there are three primary ways for the therapist to use this population of selves: dialogue, accentuation, and orientation.

Dialogue

The therapist will often recognize these influential clusters of characteristics before the patient does. He may then take an integrative step, identifying these clusters. By naming them as selves, then evoking the stories behind them—with their struggles, climaxes and, hopefully, resolutions—the therapist breathes life into these isolated clusters.

When there is psychological disturbance these selves are alienated from each other, leading to fragmented living. By restoring the identity of these multiple selves we can recognize the alienations that occur when contradictory messages, needs, and actions are too difficult to harmonize. This range of selves represents a mosaic of personal characteristics, each self vying for ascendancy in a complex system of internal characters. With these multiple selves as our focus, we may say that when we are working with an individual we are, in a sense, doing group therapy (E. Polster, 1987).

Let me illustrate this form of group therapy with the story of a patient named Alex. He was a contractor who had taken on a difficult and unusually lengthy project. He was angry with several people who advised him to take the job and especially his client, who lied to him. But he was still blaming himself heavily for his "mistake" even when the project was almost over and he could have felt relieved.

I asked him to play out a conversation between his conflicted selves, and we started by discussing the naming of these selves. He felt that the original bad decision was a function of his naive self. He wanted to name his current behavior—anger, helplessness, stuckness, and victimization—his bitter self. He took on the role of each side alternately, switching chairs as he spoke. The two selves spoke very carefully to each other, the bitter self with cool anger and the naive self with cool apology. But the conversational momentum grew, and soon the bitter self became increasingly angrier. Frightened by the anger, the naive self became verbally entangled, trying to find the right thing to say while at the same time skirting his fear of the bitter self's anger.

Why Alex would skip over the fear soon became evident. Trying to help out in the dialogue, I suggested that the naive self, instead of remaining immobilized, simply tell the bitter self how afraid he was becoming. Then, while the naive self was telling of this fear, the story took a surprising turn. He remembered a terrible experience. A neighborhood boy had continuously taunted him with insults, until he could no longer take them. One day, the naive self said, he just lost it and attacked the other boy, mindlessly banging his head on the cement. The naive self, getting less naive and less fearful, said he believes he would have murdered him if the fight had not been stopped.

As Alex went on telling of other memories of his rages and temper tantrums, the previous boundaries among selves dissolved; it was as though the naive self was now speaking for all his selves. By chronically blotting out this other character—the murderous self, as he called it—he had veiled his street savvy, becoming fair game for exploitive people, who had in his current business cheated him badly.

However, in blotting out the murderer's violence, he had overlooked the spunkiness of his retaliation against the childhood bully. This is where the fluidity in self naming becomes crucial. Alex's spunky self had been contorted by his dreaded, probably premature, assumptions that he was a mad murderer.

Now I turned again to the bitter self, who was also frightened by the murderous prospects he had just heard. He spoke about his own fear that his bitterness could be escalated by the dissociated murderer within, apparently ancestor to both Naive and Bitter. Naive and Bitter now had a common ground in their murderous undercurrent self. When I asked Bitter what he might do, he went on to say that if he were not careful to block out this murderous self, he might throw his chair into my computer, break my statuary, turn over my desk, and generally tear my room apart. He was both scared and excited.

I knew my patient well enough by this time not to be afraid of him. For his part he, not surprisingly, was greatly relieved just to be able to say these things without being swept into doing them by this dreaded internal self. He experienced two primary effects. One was his discovery that he did not reflexively go berserk, and the other was the reconnection among his alienated selves, Bitter, Naive, Murderer, and Spunky, who had more in common than one might have thought.

The reconciliation we see is that first, the naive and bitter selves managed to talk to each other; they reconnected in new dialogic potential. Next, they unearthed another member of the group, the even more seriously alienated murderer self, madly uncontrollable. Though undoubtedly it was present underneath, my patient was also able to rise beyond this murderer self. Then, discovering the spunky self, who was now restored as the one who was no longer going to take guff from the bully and who also lived under the shadow of his murderous self. This added one more member to the group, a key participant whose voice now merited attention.

Accentuation

Naming of selves has a value as a selective therapeutic tool that goes beyond experimental dialogue. Excessive dialogue may interfere with the necessary conversational engagement between therapist and patient. Naming of selves, even without ensuing dialogue, is also a means for accentuating characteristics and experiences that might otherwise easily slide by. The therapy situation is a corrective for the squandering of experience, spotlighting it instead. People do take their therapists' words earnestly, but the designation of self magnifies the reception through the inherent drama. The designation of self adds a personal stake to characteristics with which the person identifies more intensely.

One patient, for example, told me of a new attitude he developed after we named a part of himself the A-student self. He had shunned this self in childhood because it got him into trouble with other students, who saw his academic achievement as arrogance and rejected him for it. Or so he thought. Possibly they rejected him for being a know-it-all, but he attributed the trouble to the good grades. So he gave up being the A student and just got by in school.

Now at forty he was still doing it. He was trying to pass an upcoming licensing exam by preparing as little as he could get by with. Not only did this cause him anxiety in the moment, but the habit of just getting by had stunted his learning process generally. As a result he chronically felt as though he might any day get caught in faking both knowledge and skill.

Naming his shunned A-student self was a spotlighting act. It helped bring back his early memories of school success as well as his memories of having been shunned. These stories amplified his A-student self and gave him a new motivation to revisit and accept this self.

Orientation

The third role of self naming, taking its place alongside dialogue and accentuation, is the background orientation it offers to both therapist and patient. This orientation is a silent partner to accentuation. By itself, it doesn't have the drama that dialogue or accentuation has. Nevertheless, it plays an extremely important role in the therapeutic process. The unannounced recognition of certain selves may serve to increase the therapist's own understanding of the patient, providing informed guidance in the therapeutic interaction.

The actual designation of selves must be only a small part of a therapeutic repertoire. Otherwise, to overplay either dialogue or explicit naming of selves loses subtlety and direct engagement with the wide variety of content that therapy evokes. Too much naming may result in excessive vigilance and self-consciousness, impairing ordinary communication. To talk to a patient about his kind self, for example, might represent a stilted way of just saying how kind he had been. The technique, valuable though it is, must not be permitted to take over from the ordinary communications that guide people's relationship. Any technical developments must take their place as an improvement of ordinary engagement, not a replacement of it.

In the following case, the recognition of selves was largely an orienting aid. In two years, there never was a dialogue among selves; in fact, in only a few carefully chosen times were the selves named out loud. But I was continuingly oriented by having recognized these selves, and when they were named, it was with great impact. The recognition of this patient's selves helped me to understand him better, but the details of our conversations were by far the primary therapeutic substance.

My patient, Jason, was hired to conduct community outreach for a large corporation. His humane attitude often contradicted the purposes of his corporation, and his defiant tone made me wonder whether he was more interested in showing up the corporation than in trying to accomplish his own ends. When therapy began, he felt altogether an outsider in this corporation. He believed his job of merging corporation and community needs was only a token rather than a serious concern.

After his many antiestablishment pronouncements and his resignations about his powers to change anything, I proposed that Jason had an antiestablishment self within, so rigid that it was damaging his life. We did not spend much time talking about his antiestablishment self, but instead we dealt directly with the many unhappy experiences it represented. They were subsumed within his struggle against an authoritarian and distant father, a frequent theme in our conversations.

Jason had also moved frequently while growing up, and talked in detail about his lifetime of confusing changes, going through a revolving door of new communities and never becoming a part of any of them. Although he was an executive in the corporation, his ideas were often set aside—just as they had been with his father and other kids in the neighborhood. He expected, as always, to be excluded. At the same time, he wasn't going to be co-opted by corporation policies, which he believed excluded community interests. All of this and more we talked about, with rare reference to his antiestablishment self, which I think he would have experienced as too technical.

This designation, however, oriented me. It helped me to see that Jason's antiestablishment self geared him to plunge ahead with little hope in what he saw as an impossible job. He felt so disregarded by the organization and angry about the expected failure in his work, we had to face the dominance of his antiestablishment self over all the other selves he housed. This essential self was a form of self dictatorship, squashing all other selves, which were also internal representatives. He had missed the point of his diversity within, as well as the actual values of his corporation.

However, not surprisingly, this dictatorship was loosened by the registration of other selves. He also had an ambitious self, actually bordering on grandiose and requiring him to succeed irrespective of the clash of values. On the one or two occasions when I spoke to him of this self, he recognized it immediately. What he had not seen, however, was that this ambitious self was a servant to the anti-establishment self and kept him tilting at windmills, dreaming the impossible, sulking when thwarted, ignoring establishment priorities and habits.

After a while Jason began to see his ambitious self more broadly, not simply as a servant of the antiestablishment self trying, against the grain, to change the most fixed positions of his company. When this ambitious self started serving his own overall good sense, he found doable tasks to serve his humanitarian purposes. One of the things he did was to create a film on the use of company day-care centers; he also saw to the problems of needy workers. Eventually he allowed himself to be friendly with his peers and developed respectful relations among them. His ideas were more frequently welcomed into the corporate decision-making process. He soon became busy doing the things he could do rather than concentrating on what he could not do. Cracking through his sober ways, Jason let himself enjoy his success, a pleasure previously forbidden by the antiestablishment self.

These new experiences and successes called for revision of the sense of his self. So one day I told him that I now saw him as a corporation man. He seemed insulted for a moment, but then laughed at the truth of it. Nevertheless, corporation man or not—corporation *self* would be another unspoken way to put it—Jason is clearly his own man. Bright, diligent, kind, and cooperative—he had always had these characteristics but had subsumed them within his dictatorial, antiestablishment self. Now they were real to him. Now they were released to have their own fresh applicability within his corporation self, a new composite self that belonged where he worked.

Again, to talk about selves seems a strange way to talk about a person, as though these selves were his tenants or employees or internal sprites. Why not just say here is a person who hated the establishment but he was also ambitious and he had overestimated how much he would have to sacrifice his values in order to do his job? Isn't that enough? Often it is, but the repertoire that includes the naming of selves will be enriched by the option to broaden and accentuate the workings of the person's mind, to animate the mind at both the conscious and unconscious levels by personification and to foster a special form of human drama.

In Jason's case, we discussed many things other than the named selves. We discussed his plans for films and the complications of production. We discussed his relationships with his colleagues and how he could orient them and elicit their cooperation, especially in funding. We discussed the slights he experienced, his excessive vulnerability to criticism, his tendency to end conversations prematurely. We discussed his feelings of superiority, his impatience with others, his expectations of rejection, his misperceptions in trying to get help from people not empowered to help rather than those who were. These and other experiences and their relation to the context of his life and the relationship habits that were no longer applicable—all these were coordinated to give him the new orientations and skills necessary to set his mind to the task at hand instead of reproducing his earlier deprivations.

With the naming of each self, the self becomes an agent of the person—brightly organized; a spotlight on otherwise ephemeral existence; a banner, so to speak, around which the person rallies his psychological energies. Just as the novel creates human images that echo in the minds of its readers, the image of selves also comes alive, giving membership and coherence to otherwise disconnected parts of the person.

The therapist uses the device of the self to give life to his patient's experiences, registering them so vividly that the abandoned aspects may be more fully reexperienced and the fragmented person made whole. Thus the self or selves provide an animated sense of the individual's qualities. These qualities, either inborn or developed, are a foundation for the continuing challenge created by the events and feelings of everyday life.

Part II

Therapeutic Pathways to the Self

4

Attention:
The Basic Personal Energy

Only one event from the fifth grade sticks out in my mind. Every now and then, the battle-ax teacher would suddenly leap on a friend of mine when she caught him staring out the window, daydreaming. She would grab him by the jaw and bellow, "Pay attention, Andy!" I thought she was stupid because I knew he was paying attention, though not to her. Furthermore, he was never going to pay attention until she said something worth his while.

Three things registered: my compassion for Andy; the realization that what you pay attention to in this world is going to make a huge difference, maybe the greatest difference of all; and my enormous relief that she never caught me. It is therefore a strange homecoming for me now, sixty years later, to say that regulation of attention is a key source of distortions in a person's self formation process and that the renewal and redirection of attention are key focuses of all therapy.

Here is a small example of the self realizations that result from regulating and directing attention. A certain patient, having had many experiences of failure, felt an inadequate self within; for him, it was an essential self. In spite of his misery, the enduring nature of this self made his feelings of inadequacy strangely more acceptable than having to face what was quite obvious to me in listening to him: that he is actually a very stubborn man. But because he was preoccupied with his inadequate self, his attention was not directed to his stubborn self.

When I gave him examples of his stubbornness, he was stunned at first but later intrigued. Once his attention was focused on this self, its existence seemed obvious, even to him. But his misdirected attention had served him the same way misdirection of attention serves a pickpocket who bumps you on the shoulder while removing your wallet. Although my patient had been brutalized out of attending to his stubbornness, like Andy out of daydreaming, it was still always there.

Though he couldn't shift his attention right away, he soon became fascinated with his stubbornness and able to recognize it. First he could see it in his familiar behaviors: refusing instructions, silence, coming late, stiffened body, forgetting assignments. Then when he took the stubbornness on, he let loose with a stream of critical analysis of his boss's dominating style: mimicking his staccato instructions, describing a neck that couldn't turn toward his listeners, asking for suggestions but going on with his own ideas. Actually, this brought attention to his critical self, which was an active accomplice of his stagnant stubbornness. By now, feelings of inadequacy became, instead of an essential self, only one part of his self structure.

Such constrictions of attention are found in obsessions, depression, paranoia, and other diagnostic entities. Whenever a person continually focuses on particular classes of experience—severe criticism from people in authority, for example—such narrowed attention imposes a narrow self structure, making the criticisms seem the essence of his existence. The abstractions that form around such narrowing—lazy, rebellious, cowardly, inventive, talkative—create a fixity of self rather than allowing an active self formed by versatile attention to continuing experience. The opportunities for fresh tests of the abstractions are consequently spurned, and attention dulls.

The fixed selves that remain may be said to be dissociated, alienated, fragmented, preoccupied, distracted, repressed: all the many things therapists will say about people whose attention is not directed well enough to provide full motivation, function, or knowledge. Whether to their benefit or to their loss, they are operating from a position of selective attention where they cut off experiences and certain related selves.

This dissociative operation often leads to a single-mindedness that sets aside indispensable personal characteristics and experiences. That happens because the configurational reflex, responsible for the coordination of diverse parts of the person, will, in times of stress, break down. Through such breakdown, there will be dissociated shifts in attention; that is, the individual simply removes a part of himself from his attention. Often, though this attention is cut off, the self may still function. It may even be a governing influence, but always isolated from the total person, who doesn't quite know what is going on.

The selves, be they essential or member, may coordinate well with each other or compete and be alienated. They may be cunning or resigned. They may each go through periods of being favored or neglected. And they confront stimulation, accepting it or fending it off. With such a mosaic of characters, some selves will have greater influence than others. One of these selves may make its agenda the one that gets primary attention, becoming a governing force that operates somewhere along the continuum from dictatorial to democratic. Its influence, often causing preoccupation, directs attention, but in the long run the person must take account of the excluded or distorted selves, which will have to be coordinated. Democracy is the goal.

The governing self has some characteristics of the old-time ego, but it is not simply the dealer in a poker game, handing off to id, superego, and reality. It is itself an active participant, having its own directions and relationships to other selves, winning or losing power in the marketplace of selves. Sometimes this force is quite conscious, as in the person who is driven by his governing ambitious self to run his own business and become a millionaire at forty or a full professor at thirty, subverting much of his attention to this ambition. At other times this governing ambitious self may be quite unconscious. Through indirection and misperception, the person may be concealing this ambitious drive, even from his own aware-ness, behind a more innocent laissez-faire persona.

The individual who reaches his goals with limited representa-tion of his variety of selves risks dissatisfaction because the subdued selves or the skewed selves may either sabotage his purpose or not participate in the satisfactions.

This is an old story to psychotherapists, though dressed in new clothes, more brightly visible when the old language of unconscious, repression, fixation, repetition compulsion gives way to the sharp personification options of therapeutic action. The exclusionary attention represented in unconscious processes has been well doc-umented by psychoanalysis as a source of pathology. Similarly, the exclusion of certain selves by excessive narrowing of attention to other selves can handicap a person, much as though he had had a part of the body amputated.

Nevertheless, this narrowing process, harmful though it may be, brings us to a key therapeutic point, to which we must not allow troublesome consequences to blind us. That is, the awakening of attention is paradoxically achieved in therapy by narrowing atten-tion. The disease and the cure can both be created by the same ingredient—narrowing attention. With this in mind, dissociation, the sine qua non of narrowed attention, may become a therapeutic ally as well as the source of personal devastation it often represents.

Dissociation may be healthy when it temporarily narrows atten-tion in order to serve the general purposes of the person, as it may in single-minded dedication to a cause, or when one can readily, after narrowing attention and upon the right arousal, return one's attention to other needs, as does the writer who shuns all social rela-tions until he completes his book.

The therapeutic session itself is a major example of the benefits of narrowed attention. It joins with those mind-altering procedures that dissolve the broad range of the person's concerns and focus sharply instead on a thin band of experience. Meditation, hypnosis, drugs, brain washing, and the here-and-now emphases in psychotherapy all wash out the complexities of social pressures and personal contradiction (E. Polster, 1987, p. 163).

When the patient enters the therapist's office, he is freed of many of the expressive restrictions in the world at large. To the extent that these exclusions are dissociative, therapy provides a setting, outside the ordinary stream of life, where the person can say anything he wants about his feelings and behaviors. It creates a new context of openness to a thin slice of experience. In addition to providing the new atmosphere, therapy also offers many procedures and values that create an incitement of spirit, where new experiences are invited. This funneling of attention gives the therapist considerable leverage; in the world outside the office, the contradictory messages of a lifetime and the current community complications can be paralyzing to people trying to solve problems.

However, in traveling the dissociative route, what is learned in the narrowed therapeutic situation must be transferred to the actual situation in which the person lives. A great therapy session does not necessarily become a great therapy, one that brings observable positive change in the life of the patient. Many patients are experts in dealing with the dissociated therapy experience, operating freely and seemingly productively. They and their therapists produce works of art: discerning observations, bright turns of phrase, rewarding new function, commentary on how the human condition can win out over the oppressive forces of the world we all live in. But they can't necessarily take these benefits into the real world, where responses may be disharmonious.

Drugs, of course, also create greatly narrowed and compelling attention. The difficulty in both cases is that the person can repeat the new experience of full attention only by addictively going back to drugs or to the therapist's office. One leader of a drug rehabilitation center said he could cure anyone of drug use while they resided in the center, but ten days after returning to their regular environment they would be back on drugs.

This is not news to therapists. They know that new therapeutic realizations must be followed by testing them in a world that won't sit still. While the patient tries to apply the changes achieved in the narrowed atmosphere and support of the therapy setting, the whole range of troubles present before therapy may still represent an obstacle course for the patient.

Therefore, in spite of the important contributions that dissociation may offer in creating optimal openness to new experience, it is only a counterforce to disastrous consequences of earlier dissociations. The therapist is paradoxically required to attend to the patient's old dissociations as well as to focus new directions of attention. The task is complicated by the childhood experience of immense receptivity with poorly developed skills for handling complexity. The child cries out for simplicity of attention, which is exactly what dissociation offers. Oversimplification follows, building on the child's requirements for simple solutions unavailable in a complex world.

One form of this dissociation is the development of a highly specific criterion of acceptable living, like being loved by father or getting straight A's in school—a kind of criterion self. Nothing else will do, even though many other sources of satisfaction may be available, because the obsession, often outside awareness, has determined what is absolutely required for good living.

A primary intent of psychotherapy is to introduce seepage into the dissociated self through attention to the other selves within, as well as through contact with other people, especially the therapist. When these contacts are strongly experienced and attention is restored, the impact has its greatest chance for registration. The drama of selves is an aid in increasing attention, as any drama would be.

With the added accentuations, new experiences have a better chance to compete with the old dissociations for influence in the forming person. The unloved self, for example, created by experiences with a scornful father and dissociated from love from current friends or teachers, must be met again. When the person allows new love to feel real—through recognizing bodily experience, replaying fantasies of love, reporting current loving experiences in detail, changes in language, and so forth—the unloved self will dissolve. The new love will soften the dissociative wall, seeping through into the unloved self. No longer walled off by the dissociated self from the fresh experiences he now also attends to, the person is better positioned to be guided into the new directions for a change in self.

Variations in Attention

To restore new channels of attention, there are three important variants that merit special recognition: concentration, fascination, and curiosity.

Concentration

Perls (1947) gave an early boost to the recognition of attention with his emphasis on the concept of concentration. He employed concentration, along with its accompanying awareness, to form a strong advocacy for therapeutic pointedness in what he then called concentration therapy. He said: "As avoidance is assumed to be the central symptom of nervous disorders, I have replaced the method of free associations or flight of ideas by that antidote of avoidance—concentration" (p. 8).

Furthermore, in writing about the simple attentiveness created by focusing on the here and now, I have previously pointed out the satori-like power of highly focused simplicity (Polster, 1990). The temporary escape from the total background of the person's life opens the gates for fresh entry into the narrowed workings of the person's mind. Without disabling contradictions there are increases in clarity of perception, arousal to action, and the new challenges of testing out disabling fears (Polster, 1987).

The simplicity that concentration fosters is generic. One sees it in the eyes of a baby examining a new toy, in the focus of a worker for whom nothing exists but the job at hand, in the baseball player who keeps his eyes on the ball until it meets his swinging bat. But there is probably no better example of pure continuity of concentration than we observe in the person who meditates, keeping his mind focused on the mantra, swept into union with the mantra, losing a sense of subject and object and becoming absorbedly integrated with an objectless perceptual simplicity.

Even among meditators, that level of absorption is mostly reserved for the masters of meditation; one would expect such purity of concentration only in exceptional therapeutic moments. Thematic variations and contradictions create perceptual complexities, as does continuing self/other interaction between therapist and patient. Yet there is a relational counterpart of the purified meditation, as when the therapist drinks in his patient and everything he says, incorporating his purposes and conflicts, his words and movements, developing a resonance of finely tuned responsiveness. The therapist, while concentrating, is aiming his mind with pointedness. By getting this clear directedness of attention across to the patient, the therapist induces the recognition that the patient's words count—a counterforce to the patient's habits of dismissal.

The therapist gets this concentration across in many ways, not always easy to identify. Some therapists are masters at making disarmingly casual observations while noticing even the smallest detail of what is going on. Most concentration is more intense. For one thing, the therapist looks totally absorbed in what the patient is saying and seems so undistractable that external noises would slide right by. Better evidence of the therapist's concentration is that he is tuned in to the details of expression, responding not only to implications of statements but also the individualized style of the patient. His observations, such as "You tell your story carefully," reflect this individualized focus. His accuracy, pertinence, and understanding all reflect strong concentration. Each patient seeks such concentration from his therapist. At the same time, being listened to and understood create increased attention by the patient as well. Thus each multiplies the impact of the other.

Perhaps the tradition of therapeutic concentration is already built so deeply into the therapist's frame of mind that he will take it for granted. But it must be honed continuingly, as all concentration must, because it is a fragile asset in a world of distractions. Athletes, musicians, diamond cutters, and sculptors sharpen their concentration powers through practice and through incorporating a sense of emergency and personal investment. Concentration is so important a factor in therapy that its commonality must not belie its profundity. It serves as a fulcrum for therapeutic leverage.

A significant consequence of concentrated attention is that the patient, when either receiving it or exercising it, temporarily dims the debilitating context of his life, including prohibitions against having opinions, inculcated goals to be a business success, demeaning criticism, physical beatings, and a whole range of internal tyrants evaluating each move he makes. Even when the patient does talk about contextual matters, including old painful experiences, the fixed aspects of his life may loosen and he may speak of old wounds with a new freedom. The mutual concentration of therapist and patient is like opening the window in a room of stale air. They can experience the therapy room as a place where they can be as freshly attentive as they might be when totally absorbed in a movie or a conversation or a physical exertion.

This refocus of attention from the context of a person's life to focal experience was a momentous methodological innovation. It opened the way to the expanded self-awareness of individuals and societal groups, "experience-near" therapies, immediacy-oriented techniques, brief therapy, the recognition of altered states, and the incorporation of hypnotic phenomena, long viewed only as esoteric, into regular therapy interaction. These all contribute to the growing recognition that profound attention is not to be taken for granted, and that it is a key factor in creating openness to new experience.

One of the unfortunate accompaniments of this shift was the overemphasis on the here and now, elaborated at length in my earlier book, *Every Person's Life Is Worth a Novel* (E. Polster, 1987). The value of the here and now was widely misunderstood. I believe it was useful primarily because it emphasized the importance of function and attention. Determining whether something happened here or there, now or then, is only a way of locating the person's function and attention. But when the attention is so intensely guided in the time/space dimension by the here-and-now technique, it is more difficult to slide off whatever one is attending.

Since such concentrated focus is more commonly associated with awareness than with interpersonal engagement, I must emphasize that it is also especially important in the enhancement of contact between people as well. High concentration, focally maintained, strengthens engagement. It is both preparatory and energizing; preparatory through tuning in sharply to whatever is happening, and energizing through the stimulation of incisive meeting. This heightening of the current engagement is a valuable contributor to reconstituting selves, since in therapy the intent to change selves competes with the powerful impressions created by the person's early contacts, strongly imbedded into the original self formation.

Fascination

Since concentration has no implications of personal feelings, by itself it lacks the required humanization that fascination contributes. Fascination is a value component of attention, not in the sense of moral or ethical biases, but rather in representing personal interest and its extensions, such as in being charmed, captivated, enthralled, awed— all words that carry a special sense of personal caring.

Because of the risks of excessive involvement, fascination is a concept not much heard in therapeutic methodology, where dispassionate accuracy is more commonly sought. Yet the magnificent luxury of receiving continued and unwavering attention through weeks, months, and even years of discourse is the grounding on which much therapeutic work is accomplished. To be able to give the patient such necessary attention, the therapist is much aided if he is open to being fascinated by what the patient is saying.

A misunderstanding about fascination is that only certain favored and compelling people are fascinating. However, fascination is not so exclusive. It is not such a big deal to be fascinated when someone comes into your office feeling that his life is on the line and open to revealing the most intimate experiences, many of which would make an intriguing plot for a movie. The only surprise would come if one were not fascinated. Yet this failure to be fascinated occurs often, either because the therapist is not open to such feelings or, more likely, the patient is not up to being fascinating.

A professional challenge for the therapist, therefore, is to be fascinated in simple natural reactivity to patients, many of whom have made a life work out of being uninteresting in general or in the particular arenas of their trouble. Under those circumstances, where the patient is greatly experienced in being uninteresting, the therapist pits his own openness to being interested against the unwillingness of his patients to be interesting.

Many patients are masters at being uninteresting, a mastery carved out of a multitude of preparatory life experiences, all geared to take the heat out of their existence. In fact they are only excluding the selves that are dulled by pain or too dangerous to be let out of the house. Yet it must be said that nobody is so skilled in maintaining a completely colorless quality that he doesn't have loopholes through which the therapist may see. As I have previously written, "Patients may appear linguistically sterile, morally neuter, visually plain, or depleted in energy. However, these are all camouflage, intended to deflect from what is actually interesting" (E. Polster, 1987, p. 4).

One of my patients, Giaccomo, is thoroughly convinced of his uninterestingness. Giaccomo is obsessive, devoted to seeing himself and the world of people around him as uninteresting. I find him extremely interesting and am glad to see him every time he arrives.

He is a complex man who always gives me a good argument. Among his many selves, he has a strong alienation between a superior self and a klutz self. The klutz is his rider and driver, crowding his mind with his difficulties in managing his world. He will not go into gatherings of people because he has nothing interesting to say. Nor is there anything interesting to hear, as his superior self readily reminds himself and me.

Probably most people would find him uninteresting, in his current constricted state, though not as unreservedly as he portrays it. Although he thwarts my interest every step of the way, he can't succeed in getting rid of it because my fascinated eyes see beyond what he thinks he is showing. His perceptions about the world and the people he runs into are excellent, though grossly overgeneralized, and I would agree with his values if he did not caricature them, as he does in describing phony party behavior, people trying always to make the grade in work, selling out on principles, and all the many other traits that we humans exhibit.

His cynicism is actually interesting, but he turns it into a nihilism that allows nothing to be truly interesting. I glory in his mountainous, chaotic, three-hundred-pound physique; he sees himself only as misshapen and blubbery. I once told this Gargantua of his Rabelaisian self. He was momentarily delighted to be seen altogether differently, but then quickly decided I was just playing therapist. But my greatest opportunity to allow my fascination full play is that, as a therapist, I don't have to make party conversation with him. I know, and I think he does also, that everything I say to him is as close to the truth as I can get it. I take his entry into my office as his invitation to be seen differently from the way he would be seen elsewhere. We speak vigorously all the time, something he would not permit socially. Although he thinks I am very smart, he agrees with nothing I say. Is that his klutzy self speaking or his superior self? There is always a loophole in every remark I make, and he goes for the loophole like a moth to the flame.

At this point in our therapy, he has a lively time with me.

Though he was originally severely depressed and in unrelieved misery, a function of his klutzy self, his pleasure comes from the exercise of his superior self as he duels with me—his version of a possibly admirable person. I have to be careful that he doesn't come simply to have a lively time rather than to actually experience himself anew and so change his self configuration. To counteract any temporary pleasures and make sure his therapy represents growth, not merely entertainment, I explained I did not want to be his drug of choice.

I see him changing outside of therapy only slowly. He has trouble seeing it at all because of his high requirements, but when I explain what I mean, he grudgingly accepts the increments that are beneath his superior self. He tells me of new experiences in his life when previously practically nothing was worth mentioning: a new person met and visited, the purchase of a car and all the details of his frustration and dissatisfaction, a weekend with his sister, a work assignment. All these are small in terms of giving him satisfaction, but they promise he may move out of his agoraphobic confines. I am quite convinced the restoration of his fascination with the world he faces and with himself, as well as my fascination with him, provides a significant chance for change, one small step at a time. If I were to let him imprison me in his own sense of dullness, we might as well not do therapy.

When I write of people camouflaging their interestingness, I not only refer to people who manage to be boring but also to people who are generally interesting. Either they are unaware of how interesting they are, or they actually become uninteresting when they are in danger of revealing an unwanted self that involves troublesome memories, purposes, values, and inconsistencies. When they succeed in becoming uninteresting, they defeat their therapists.

In supervising therapists, I have often seen them defeated by their own loss of interest. When they offer difficult cases for examination, they have already lost interest in the patient. They are discouraged with their failure to make progress, and also their patients make it hard to be interested in them. The patient's unyielding characteristics—repetitive complaints, unwillingness to register the therapist's observations, dangers of suicide or madness, hopelessness they feel about therapy and their futures—all become unremittingly burdensome. When these therapists can bracket off questions of success and failure and concentrate on what is indeed interesting, it is always there: a chance meeting with an old friend, a new pressure at work, a thought about travels. If we loosen the tight therapeutic format, these could all be interesting even though they offer no immediate payoff. These topics may initially be no more interesting to the patient than to the therapist. Yet the elements of interest are there, and tapping into them successfully will increase the chances of relieving tension and returning to the fundamental fact that each person is a miracle of diverse selves.

Curiosity

The third variant of attention, curiosity, was proposed by Michael Miller (1987) as a fundamental human function, prior in urgency to Freud's primordial sexuality or Rank's creativity. He cites evidence for infant curiosity and the primitive prohibitions against curiosity—Adam and Eve, for example—as indicators of the primordial quality of curiosity. He ranks it with libido in its guidance of behavior and underlines the rigidity that follows its suppression, resulting in fixed beliefs, distortions, premature knowing, abstractions, and assumptions. Accordingly, neurosis can be seen as a consequence either of generalized deficiency of curiosity or of a specialized deficiency limited to the patient's problem areas.

Let us compare Miller's view of curiosity with Freud's. Miller (1987) said: "Curiosity can be a rich theoretical category: It can connect self and other, emotion and intellect, the empirical and the innate, the impact of early personal history and the immediacy of present contact. It represents active desire without being overly abstract and intellectual" (p. 22). Freud (1957) said: "The true technique of psychoanalysis requires the physician to *suppress his curiosity* and leaves the patient complete freedom in choosing the order in which topics will succeed each other during the treatment. At the fourth sitting, accordingly, I received the patient with the question: 'And how do you intend to proceed today?'" (p. 312; italics added).

Freud equates therapist curiosity with intrusion, but some patients may welcome it. It is a way of inviting new information and may be enabling for the patient who is excited and warmed by the therapist's curiosity. For Freud to have asked his patient how he intended to proceed could well have been a function of Freud's own curiosity, rather than a way of hanging around while his patient proceeded. As Freud elaborates this case further, it is evident that his curiosity about the unfolding of events was a contributor to the excitement with which Freud wrote of these events.

In trying to explore the patient's experience, the therapist's curiosity represents a mutual process of discovery in which therapist and patient join. Questions asked because the therapist is curious and actually wants to know the answer will have a stronger ring of mutuality than questions asked technically, so that the patient can experience the answer he gives. For example, a patient speaks circuitously about the absence of love from his mother. The therapist thinks he knows what the patient means and knows it must be said more clearly. She asks, "What did you miss from your mother?" This is a technical question, giving the patient a chance to say "love" or something comparable. On the other hand, the therapist actually may not know what the patient missed from his mother. Asked because the therapist genuinely wanted to know the answer, the same question would express curiosity rather than technique. Though the technique-directed question may be selectively useful, the absence of curiosity will probably be felt and the sense of joined endeavor diminished.

Each of the three variants of attention I have just described provides its own special focus on the world of experience. What is common to all three is that they should be easy for therapists to use to their advantage because the therapeutic situation is made to order for the heightening of attention. Four forces combine to overcome the professional ennui, technical neutrality, or personal need for distance that may dull the therapist's attention.

First is the force of the natural drama of therapy, the life crisis that brings the patient to therapy. The drama itself raises attention levels. Second, the therapist is commissioned to devote close, almost unwavering, attention to the accounts and experiences of his patient; this has a contagious effect on his patient's attention, each party enhancing the attention of the other. Third, therapeutic perspective provides a sense of microcosmic significance to all experience, giving greater importance to each experience than the everyday experiences that might appear to stand only for themselves. Fourth, there are specific procedures that foster high attention: the creation of safe emergencies, focusing on tight sequentiality, and the evocation of dramatic storyline. All these procedures directly foster attention and will be described in later chapters of this book.

Paradoxical Attention Options

When attention is impoverished, the therapeutic task has two contrasting options: tuning in to the patient as he is and redirecting his attention.

Tuning In

Tuning in to the person just as he is, without requiring change, is part of the gestalt paradoxical theory of change. Getting over fear, anger, confusion, inferiority, degradation, and so forth is said to happen when the patient experiences these states freshly. Beisser (1970) described this theory by saying that "change occurs when one becomes what he *is*" (p. 77; italics added). This is a statement of faith—if a person accepts himself as he already is, without planning or looking ahead, he will become the self he needs to be.

There is an important element of truth to this belief, since what one *is* is always the starting point for the path one might take. But

the faith that this starting point will impel one to become the self
he wants to be banks on a difficult step-by-step therapeutic process
during which it is easy to lose sight of the pathway traveled. If this
trip is aborted, one may then be stuck with inflamed pain where previous distraction served as neutralization.

Thus within the complexities of choice between tuning in to
what is and redirecting the attention of the patient, it is important
first to tune in to the patient's existing experience, fostering
vibrancy in place of staleness. One example of this therapeutic
option is evident in the case of Franklin, a forty-year-old man who
lived a carefully controlled life, managing relationships with colleagues and women very tightly. He frequently spoke about severe
obsessions in early adolescence. His noisy neighbors had loud lawn
mowers and raced their car engines while working on them. The
noise cut into his mind and left him feeling, not distracted or
invaded, but humiliated.

We explored the details of the noise: when it happened, how
often, who the people were, what he said to them, what he thought,
how his parents handled it, what kind of lawn mowers and cars—
every bit of information he could produce. Then I conducted the
same search for the details of his shame.

When Franklin described his experiences with noise or with
shame or the many other ingredients out of which his humiliated
self was composed, he spoke in a routinized manner. That emptiness
helped keep the obsession in place. Replacing the emptiness with
fresh attention—through fleshing out the details and my clear interest in the details—helped loosen his obsession. At the heart of such
meticulous attention was the full focus on his actual experiences, dis-
placing his empty abstractions by accentuating actual events.

Redirecting Attention

The second option, equally important, is to redirect attention to
that which is being avoided. This is a departure from the gestalt
paradoxical theory of change. Contrary to those with the greatest
faith in the "naturalness" of growth, I believe guidance through

explanation, instruction, or other forms of influence is therapeutically valuable. For example, if it is accurate, why not tell a woman who was repeatedly derogated by her mother that most parents would be happy to have her as a daughter. Some therapists believe such influence counters self-discovery, but to me it is evident that reliable learning is not limited to uninfluenced learning. Careful and experienced perception of a truth may alter the sense of self, whether or not the person discovers it by himself during a purified step-by-step process.

The psychotherapeutic fetish for self-discovery rather than for being told is a good concept only up to the point where help actually helps. Let us look into our own experience: Haven't all of us at some point been enhanced in our sense of self by a trusted person confirming a desired but unclear personal characteristic? As Kohut (1985) has said, "You need other people in order to become yourself" (p. 238).

An example of redirecting attention is another session with Franklin, the patient obsessed with noise. He had begun expanding his relationships with people at work, and they had begun to show him increased attention and respect in return. He was just beginning to focus on his relationships with women when his neighbor's dog started barking all night long. He was enraged. He found himself unable to concentrate at work, partly because of this replica of his old obsession about his neighbor's noisiness and partly because of lack of sleep.

I wondered whether he was using an old device, obsession, for avoiding his expanding relationships with women. This time, instead of tuning in, I redirected his attention. Rather than talking about his obsessions, I asked him to tell me about the relationships he had been developing. He was able to do this, telling especially about some new sexual options. Then, after considerable conversation, I asked him what he now felt about the barking dog. He was surprised to realize that the barking dog was no longer of any interest to him. The "problem" of the barking dog had not disappeared, but he was able securely to shift his attention and not let it run his life.

We must realize, however, that even though such redirection of attention may well prove to be a counterforce to stuckness, it may also sometimes be taken as a disregard of the patient's concerns. One patient, obsessed about his wife's failure to show him love, at first strongly opposed my redirection. He could not understand why I would want to know more about other parts of his life. To him, anything but his relationship to his wife was trivial. When I managed to convince him temporarily that his life mattered, he would deign to tell me—more for my sake than his—about his music playing, his colleagues, his work, where he lived, his recreational activities, what he and his wife talked about, the books he had read. He would then return to the repetitive complaints, presumably after getting me off his back, but always with an increase in liveliness and detail.

Then, after a while, he began to get glimmerings of the importance of his diverse concerns. At last, feeling less pressure about his wife, he began to take seriously the fact that he had a choice about staying with her and that if he did he would do so because in his full appraisal it was best to choose that route. The key opening to feeling his choice came when he said, "I no longer feel afraid to be alone." This implied that in increased attention to the range of his life, he palpably realized he would not be alone, irrespective of whether he left his wife.

To succeed in coordinating between tuning in and redirecting, the therapist must be flexible and have good timing. Strongly focused attention on the part of the patient, whether it is obsession or lively absorption, is a delicate state. To ask a patient to talk about something outside the range of his absorption may shatter the absorption. Even as simple a question as "What are you thinking?" when he is not thinking, may interrupt his direction of attention.

While being open to the range of what merits therapeutic attention, we must also be alert to the distractions created by poorly verbalized or untimely shifts in attention. Any skilled work has its contradictory requirements, and this is no less so in psychotherapy, where the choice to tune in or to redirect is never-ending.

5

Therapeutic Sequences:
The Passage of Self

Now let us consider how attention may operate during the moment-to-moment sequences of a person's experiences. People come for therapy because they are stuck with the same old selves that plague them. Their behavior and feelings bump around like a broken record. Once a broken record gets into a new groove, the music will be restored. Similarly, our patients need a way to restore a movement that is naturally available but not exercised. In this chapter I will present some ideas about how therapy can be used to get the movement going again.

The selves that people feel stuck with are fixed into position when continuing experience is, for whatever reason, not registered. People stay the same because they don't let new experience teach them differently. Since selves are configurations formed out of experiences, reconnecting isolated experiences helps also in recovering a fluidity of the selves within. These experiences are reconnected not only by the general understandings these connections provide—their overall meaning—but also by the simpler connections of moment to moment. From these simple connections, the person becomes ready to take the next step and release the fluidity required for up-to-date self formation.

For example, consider a child who was frightened by a teacher threatening to sew up her lips. This experience might stick her with the sense of a terrorized self. It could also reduce her continuing attention to teachers, thereby diminishing her chance of getting new experiences with teachers and releasing her from the teacher's earlier threat. Only new experiences will change her terrorized self, yet the child's stuckness makes it difficult for her to get those new experiences. For this to happen, it is necessary to reestablish the leverage that each new experience has for subsequent ones. When continuity is restored by tapping into the natural surge to move forward—by speaking of the fear, for example, or by understanding what the teacher meant or by crying—rather than to go blank when the teacher asks a question, the child becomes unstuck and may proceed fluidly to answer the question. She is then on her way to a more masterful sense of self.

Difficulties in taking these sequential trips raise the question of resistance (Polster and Polster, 1976). In classical application, resistance often represented an unwillingness to take the steps called for by the therapist. Diving into underground experiences for the reasons for resistance became a vertical path to meaning, dissolving the so-called resistance by piercing translations into the deeper regions of the person. What I am proposing here is an *alternative horizontal avenue* for arriving at these deeper regions.

It starts with a no-resistance premise: Every event has its own validity and takes its place in the accumulation of experiences. With this limited role for each event, the horizontal, step-by-step connection of simple events to each other does not move immediately into insight. When people are restored to openness to their ongoing experience, these experiences will represent voices in the chorus of individual events, emotions, and movements that are naturally directed to their unfolding meanings and that become synthesized into selves.

Usually both therapist and patient understand the value of getting this movement going in the larger concerns of life, such as marriage, job, or social acceptance, or in changing symptoms, such as depression, obsession, or anxiety. These areas are the definitive ones for therapy, but to get unstuck therapists and patients must also think smaller, taking account of the simple, step-by-step process they must traverse. The sequential flow of words, ideas, and actions is the spring from which smooth movement begins. Without the experience of the natural sense of nextness inherent to this flow, the trip to the larger goals of therapy will be choppy and the odds on resolving the problems will be reduced.

Selves form and get tested by moving through the experiences of life: conversational exchange, problem solving, language choice, school progress, confusion, anger, mystery, sorrow—always accumulating evidence for and against their acceptability, for and against the creation of new selves. The release of this simple continuity of experience is, therefore, the triggering mechanism for the fluidity of selves. If they can't move through these continuing moments, selves remain fixed.

If, for example, a person feels a decent self within, the validity of this decent self may be overturned by the most simple contradictory experience if the continuity is interrupted, as it may be by confusion, implication, fear, and the like. When this person's decent self is poorly established, it can be easily disconfirmed even by the common failure to contribute to every homeless person. Without further continuity in the experience of decency, the person is prematurely stuck with the "failure" of his decent self. To open up the continuity will offer new experiences that may revalidate the decent self.

Another way of thinking about these gaps in continuity is that they create *psychological slippage*. This concept takes account of how these gaps lead to a loss of personal momentum. In mechanics, slippage refers to the loss of motion or power through inadequate connection between gears. When gears mesh properly, the rotation of one gear impels the other forward; the resulting movement is fluid, powerful, and directionally assured. When the gears are poorly engaged, power is lost and movement is sluggish and uncoordinated.

In human terms, people's experiences must also mesh properly, each connected with what follows. In therapy we pay special attention to reconnecting those experiences that are sequentially disconnected. The influence of one experience on another is like two hands; when they are firmly engaged with each other, the movement of one hand will influence the movement of the other. When the hands are only loosely engaged, the movement of one may have relatively little effect on the movement of the other. By the same token, one moment of personal experience will not have influence on the next unless the connection is firm.

Insight and Sequentiality

I will soon describe procedures for a moment-to-moment tightening of connections, but first a few words are necessary about a classic tool of reconnection—insight. Rather than connecting moment to moment, the concept of insight takes account of connections among widely scattered experiences, which are given meaning through insight. Sequential connection and insight are interrelated, since important insights may light the way into the next moment. For example, when a patient is given the insight that her reluctance to talk is related to her father telling her to shut up at the dinner table, that insight could free her to say the things that her sense of continuity would require her to say now.

The highly interpretive language of psychoanalysis, which depends on such insights to close the gap among experiences, is different, however, from the sequential language I speak of. Donald Spence (1982), a psychoanalyst, helps form a bridge by recognizing interpretation not so much for its explanatory contribution as for offering "linguistic and narrative closure" (p. 137), that is, contributing to the completion of what has been begun. His perspective on interpretation, similar to what I am proposing, is that it helps flesh out the story of people's lives, filling in gaps and making sense of both the succession and complexity of events. For him the interpretation is more than a causal explanation because it takes events as the core of what the analyst coordinates, thereby providing closure and creating an aesthetic sense of completion. Attention to the aesthetics of the continuing line of events implies that interpretation must move events forward, impelling the person to new behavior and feeling rather than stagnantly explaining why they happened. To Spence the interpretation given to the person about why she is reluctant to talk would be another event in itself, as well as an explanation of why she is reluctant.

The shift from the causal to the evocative is subtle. Without tackling the philosophical intricacies of causation, it is enough to say that from the evocative function of interpretation, it may more easily be seen as inside the patient's narrative structure, rather than standing apart. Thus the primary function of interpretation would be to fit into the sequential development of the storyline. Otherwise, without a sense of sequence, some patients may wander, session after session, alluding almost absentmindedly to their life's complaints, struggles, and confusions.

The loose connections may be episodically tightened by interpretations, which are especially useful in creating a sequential fit between large arcs of experience. But the danger in making interpretations is that the therapist, if not also oriented to tightening the immediately sequential connections, may collude by offering sequentially distant explanations without observable consequences, often feeding new material to the wanderer.

The import of the discontinuity created by these gaps in experience has often been overshadowed by a restricted image of the unconscious, not so much as the source from which to reclaim experience as a reservoir from which new meanings are derived.

Freud tangentially recognized the importance of gaps in continuity by describing the lost material as forgotten and dissociated, unhinged from current experience. He said the forgotten events remain in the mind, not very deeply removed from whatever is happening, lacking only the linkage. Though Freud's most recognized route to linkage was the larger meanings offered by insight, less recognized in his writings was his concern with directionalism and the step-by-step process by which this meaning is established. For example, in giving interpretations, he calls for the therapist to hold off his understanding until "only a single step remains to be taken" (Freud,

1949, p. 71). Thus it is evident that, though he gave insufficient attention to this sequential imperative, he plainly recognized that the road to be traveled is paved with a succession of experiences.

Moment-to-Moment Continuity

Three concepts can help the therapist identify poor sequencing and restore continuity: tight therapeutic sequences, sequential inevitability, and loose therapeutic sequences.

Tight Therapeutic Sequences and the "Arrow" Phenomenon

A key factor in developing continuity is getting down to business pointedly by creating tight therapeutic sequences, a concept I introduced not long ago (E. Polster, 1987, chaps. 3 and 9). In contrast to leisurely paced therapy, where patients may wander aimlessly, tight sequences are those sets of experience where the perceived consequences of any event happen right away, or at least very soon. To develop such consequentiality the therapist must focus, not on the here and now, but on the transition point between now and next.

In a therapy session this means that the therapist sees each moment as a springboard into the future. The patient will announce that future in sometimes clear, sometimes cryptic signals; the therapist reads each of these signals, edging forward to discern the hints for what is going to be next. When, for example, a patient rambles unhappily about the death of her mother, only touching briefly on her sadness, the signal for sadness, unexpressed, lights up the therapeutic options for what is next. The therapist may impel the patient forward, compensating for her tangentiality by attending keenly to the sadness and amplifying it in any number of ways. For example, she might guide the patient by observing that the loss must have been more poignantly felt than what she is expressing. Or she might ask her patient to say what she missed in her relationship to her mother, perhaps even to talk to her imagined presence. Or she might direct her to localize the feeling of sadness in

her body, where she may discover tight muscles or restrictive breathing or an urge to cry.

Such sharp focus and consequentiality create attention to the
connection between successions of events, like sadness and expression or sensation. The recognition of those gaps in continuity—psychological slippage—helps the therapist give direction and
coherence to what might otherwise feel to the patient like a life
filled with disconnection and incompletion.

Rather than settling for chronic and unsatisfying allusion, in this
example the connections between sadness and the range of possible consequences—crying, anger, resolve, remembering—are
restored. In leading the patient into a connecting next expression,
the therapist must discern that each moment calls out for a number of possible directions. They are, in a sense, arrows, each pointing to a different nextness. These arrows are complex directors of
movement because there are always a large number of them, offering a number of possible nextnesses. Different therapists will experience different priorities among these arrows.

If, for example, a patient were to say she has been wanting to
call her mother for a long time, the therapist might respond to any
of a number of arrows that may point to this patient's nextness.
Depending partly on what the therapist already knows, she might
respond to the unlikelihood of her patient actually wanting to call
her mother; to what she had been afraid of in calling her mother;
to what it is that she might want from her mother; to the shift from
shunning her mother to seeking reconciliation; or to wanting to
tell her mother of a particular grievance or a particular pleasure.
This choice requires the therapist to be well tuned to what she
already knows about the patient and to the nuances of the patient's
expression. When the therapist picks a suitable arrow and com-
municates in the patient's frame of reference, she develops a maximal chance for the patient's directed continuity to lead to a
relevant sense of self.

If, however, the therapist is not tuned into the patient's frame of reference, she might mistakenly ask this patient what she has been afraid of, when all the while what is on the patient's mind is the grievance she wants to speak about. This will make the continuity choppy. Following the wrong arrow will, first, retard continuity, requiring the patient to try to figure out the answer rather than to smoothly ride with the therapist's questions or observations. It can also skew the patient's mind to a different self; in the present example, her afraid self rather than her angry self. To take another example: If a patient is telling of a quarrel with her boss and is absorbed in that, to bring up her father may distract her from revealing a self better revealed in talking about her boss. Or to bring up her whiny tone of voice in talking about the boss when she just wants to tell the story of her boss's treatment of her will create further gaps rather than tightening the sequences.

Of course, the therapist may not have been wrong in believing that father is important or that her patient's tone of voice is important. Accuracy, however, is not the only thing that is important in following the patient's arrows. Timing also counts. If the therapist has speculated accurately that father is an important element in her patient's relationship to her boss or that her whiny tone of voice is important, sooner or later the patient will probably present an arrow pointing to father or to tone of voice, for which the therapist's alertness will prepare her.

Yet, though this synchronicity between therapist and patient is basic, it must not represent a hard and fast rule. There must be more than accommodation by the therapist to the patient's own preferences. Her sensitive and purposeful discernment may be more timely than the fixed habits of sequencing by which the patient is rigidly living. Though the major orientation is to ride the patient's arrows to where they take her, it is also always necessary to keep tuned to the rigidities that *prevent* people from moving forward. The therapist should not be held hostage to continual synchronization of her priorities with those of the patient. The patient, after all, may self-defeatingly care more about other matters, just like the paranoid person preoccupied with fixed expectations or the anxious person who braces her muscles against new sensations. The therapist is always alerted to the reconstitution of selves even when the patient's habits of noncontinuity interfere.

Here is an example where my sense of nextness jarred against a patient's current self-image. This patient always spoke very rapidly. To me, the rapidity of speech implied that he wanted to get through his contacts with me and others quickly. At first, when I asked him to experiment with speaking more slowly, it seemed an insult to him. I thought I might have followed the wrong arrow. He objected, but humored me by slowing down anyway. When he did speak more slowly, he was surprised to discover a feeling of intimacy against which he had desensitized himself all his life. When the intimate feelings appeared, he was warmed, adding an incremental support for this warm self.

Sometimes it may seem as though the therapist is not following the patient's arrows because they are not the ones the patient prefers, even though the arrows are very evident. One patient, pointedly task oriented, could not bear the moment of silence that arrives in any unpressured flow of communication. Although she had told me she had nothing to say, she balked at my asking her to try silence. Her opposition made it seem as though I had not followed her arrows. To me, however, having nothing to say was a clearly evident arrow pointing to silence. The natural consequence of having nothing to say is to say nothing. Though I realize that anything anyone says is more complexly motivated than that, I nevertheless tied this arrow with my previous sense of her need to take some of the pressure off from her drive to produce.

She did allow a moment of silence, and her response was fear. She was afraid that if she continued to be silent, she might be faced with an unknown explosiveness inside her. This explosive self lurking in the background was an old interpretation of her unusually high energy. But her silence did not lead to explosion. She simply emerged from the silence and began talking easily of many interesting but unthreatening thoughts, without further concern with exploding. Her fear of exploding was too fixed into the background of her mind and had not been put to the test of experience. Though she might be sufficiently occluded in some areas of her life, so that only through explosion could she express herself, in this particular sequence what she said was smoothly expressive.

Such a fear of nextness will make people wary about the most simple expressions. A person may be afraid of her vicious self if she has scathing things to say about mother, her lazy self if she relaxes, her selfish self if she stands up for her own needs. The interruption of the most simple manifestations of continuity is a prime way of preventing these selves from appearing. By creating sequences that don't connect implied directions together with actual actions or feeling, or by expressing one's self diffusely or by becoming mute or repetitive, or by exercising any of an infinite number of ways of interfering with fluid sequence of either behavior or consciousness, the person can stop the music. Whatever is feared will not happen.

For example, if I were to ask a person diagnosed with a borderline personality to close her eyes and visualize the father who terrorized her, this might put her in danger of feeling a sense of chaos or uncontrollable rage or of experiencing severe tremors. Although there is merit to the fears of some people, for many people the fears are overgeneralized, interfering pervasively with continuity rather than appearing only when the danger actually exists. When such fearful characteristics are pervasive enough to qualify as a self, they are no longer glancing experiences; they become sources of overgeneralized personal identity, highly threatening, and their authority often overshoots the mark. Thus a person with a vicious self may see the danger of her viciousness everywhere rather than only when she is specifically aroused.

The need to follow the patient's sequences through tracking the arrows imbedded in each step of activity is not an unfamiliar orientation to therapists. However, these intervals have often been distantly disconnected areas of experience, such as childhood and adulthood, premarital life and marital life, life with father and life with boss. It is important to add the small "betweennesses," and they must also be explored in smaller units of the therapy session itself. They are in the immediate expressive flow, where easily recognizable examples of discontinuity may affect the person's sense of self.

It is important to emphasize the value of recovering the betweennesses simply because they are so readily devalued. Sometimes that is because the larger goals of therapy, like symptom removal, crowd the therapist and make her impatient. But the patients' own ambitions for reaching the ultimate change they seek also make immediacy of sequential connection seem either too gradual to be interesting or too frightening to be tolerable. Sometimes, the betweenness may be devalued because it does not move in the expected direction or is only indistinctly connected to what the patient has said. The aim, however, is to make each step felt, a part of the unfolding drama that sequential connectedness produces.

Here is an extended example of a series of sequential steps in a session where the sequence between one statement and another was dogged by interruptions. It will illustrate what I mean by the tightening of sequences, showing several steps in the tightening process and showing how in this case a gentle increase in the spiciness or directness of the language tightened the sequences. What will be evident is that each of my remarks, small though its force may have been, tightened the connections between one statement and the next until, at last, the sequences grew in momentum to form a moving story, one that embodied and clarified hidden selves.

The patient, Kevin, started the session by talking in his characteristically meandering style, hemming and hawing, reversing his field, self-deprecating. Veiled within his formless verbiage were a number of arrows, each appearing in its turn. First, he alluded to his innocence about life. For me the word *innocence* was a promising first arrow. It was a more than usually self-revealing word for Kevin to use, reflecting an innocent self that I saw as depriving him of pungency and confidence. His response to my pressuring him to specify his innocence was to hem and haw and use anemic language. Yet hidden within his deflections, he was actually saying something pungent. His words amounted to a second arrow: he pretends to be innocent and to need my advice or leadership more than he really does. I highlighted this pretense as a stronger sentiment than innocence would imply. By veiling the pretense with muted language and tone, he had kept the sequences looser than they should have been. Still, these were arrows that pointed to a new implication of self—his independence of me plus a vocal tone of superiority, another arrow.

I followed the superiority arrow by wisecracking with Kevin about building me up, emphasizing his generosity in protecting me by pretending to be naive. Both content and wisecrack must have encouraged him and made his sequencing more fluid because he excitedly replied, "Yeah, yeah, yeah."

His excitement was a sign of good continuity. He was now unafraid about the simple truth of his protection of me. This surprising truth was prophetic of what was to come later, as many arrows are. He became somewhat bolder, saying he was thinking last night about something, presently forgotten. But he had decided anyway not to tell me because it was too assertive.

Convoluted though this was, I took forgetting as the next arrow, as well as the dismissal of me reflected in deciding not to tell me. I teased him, saying, "How quickly they forget!" He laughed at being caught in further superiority, as well as at my lightheartedness about what he would have expected to be heavy. He went on, still hazily, not yet catching on fully to his freedom to move on. But again his words further represented a strength he was beginning to enjoy. Apparently changing the subject, he said, self-congratulatorily, that on the way over he had thought that he is being a good friend to himself these days, though not yet to others. But he still didn't remember what he had wanted to tell me.

At this point I simply accepted his forgetting and I took his fear of being too assertive for my next arrow. I guessed he was forgetting because he didn't want to hurt me with his assertiveness. He demurred, however, unsatisfied with my guess. He seemed to be puzzled; I think he felt he could not hurt me. Nevertheless, he remained careful. His superior self, which I guessed was lurking in the background, if fully accepted would have believed he could hurt me.

Wanting to maintain the sequential connections to his assertiveness and recalling an earlier confusion he expressed about similarities between me and his father, I next took up that arrow. I asked whether his father could handle his assertiveness. Now the gears meshed perfectly, and from then on it was a smooth ride forward with no interruptions into his unfinished business.

Kevin remembered his father's anxiety about assertiveness and he told me about it now, with little sequential slippage. With increased consequentiality, clarity, fluidity and drama, he said: "Yeah, sometimes when I do get assertive . . . oh yeah, times where I have been assertive, it's felt like I've defeated him. I can remember one time when we were . . . myself, my mom, and he were sailing. We went for a week on a sailboat up into the coastal islands. And there was one very windy day where we had the big jib up—do you know about sailboats very much?"

"Not much," I answered.

His voice became instantly more animated and he continued to describe the events with great excitement. His authority was not only greatly increased as he lucidly instructed me but he did it with animation and color.

"The jib is the forward sail. And you can have different sizes of jibs. And the bigger the jib the more wind it catches and the faster it makes the boat go. But the bigger the jib you have, the more unstable the boat can be. Particularly because it pulls right from the very front of the boat. So we had a huge jib on that day. We got up in the morning when the winds came up and it was really rough. But we were screaming along with this huge jib and I loved it. And the boat was kinda shaky. And my dad wanted to take the jib down. And I really wanted it up, I wanted to cruise. So we got into a fight about it. And he finally just said [he imitates his dad's angry voice and also smiles, having found his own angry voice], 'Okay, take the jib down. Do what you wanna do, I don't care. Leave the jib up.' So we did for a while. At one point, it got caught in something and I had to crawl up front to undo it, and I cut my finger kinda badly when I did it. And that just made him feel worse. He just said, 'Oh god, now you cut your finger. This is awful.' And I just felt tremendously guilty after that point. Like I really usurped his authority."

And so went a marvelous story, told with fluidity and energy. It reminded Kevin of his own authority and his freedom to take an exciting chance. One never can measure the exact effect of any particular therapeutic event, but this one clearly made his relationship with me more vital, and soon he made a career change, a decision that was his own rather than one dictated by the family program.

Sequential Inevitability

At this point in the creation of Kevin's tight sequences and the resulting smooth flow of communication, it is important to note a valuable component of fluidity. Once Kevin's momentum got going, the "of course" quality of his sailing story caught on; he rolled from one incident to the other, fleshing out the story and accentuating his victory over his father and the defeat that his guilt had registered. Though no sequences are actually inevitable, there is a point at which the of-course phenomenon takes over and the sequences *seem* inevitable.

Kevin's story was lubricated by the sense of sequential inevitability, and it primed him to continue his movement forward. He enlarged on his father's fragility and the assumptions Kevin now makes about the fragility of others, including me. Though he exaggerates the fragility of others, it is better than feeling fragile himself. Then, in his of-course mode, he unhesitatingly said what previously would have seemed unspeakable from either his lively superior self or his guilty usurper self: that there were some things he didn't like about me. But, not surprisingly to anybody but him, that turned out to be just another lively statement from someone to be reckoned with and I turned out not to be as fragile as he would have thought.

Sequential inevitability rests on the premise of simple consequentiality—that is, the realization that words or acts have immediate effects. What in ordinary conversation may proceed airily, with little notice, in tight sequencing is propelled forward. When successful, each statement becomes a leverage-creating moment, swinging the patient into a sense of newly possible directions. Clearly, for the therapist to evoke such a fluid directionality, he must exercise an artistry for which his entire therapeutic work prepares him. The more resonantly the therapist is able to segue into the patient's momentum, the more likely will his remarks bring on the organic next behavior.

Therapy in its greatest moments provides masterful examples of a sequential imperative, the sense of the irresistible sweep into nextness. Experience appears to be seamlessly and inevitably interconnected, forming a sequential fit. The sense of sequential fit, through the seeming inevitability of events, has a quasi-hypnotic effect and offers relief from the vexing questions and contradictions that alienated selves impose and that immobilize the mind.

Under such conditions of hypnotic-like openness to new experiences, the plaguing interferences of such questions as "Am I going to anger people?" "Am I going to get promoted?" "Am I going to end up sick, fat, or in jail?" fade away. Without the absorption created by the sense of sequential inevitability, the patient's preoccupations will disconnect whatever he is doing from feared prospects; by repetitions, gaps, obfuscations, silence, changing the subject, abstractions that do not get fleshed out, confusion, circumstantiality, and the like.

If the therapist helps the person out of this choppy existence and into experiences where one follows the other, the patient will soon enter into the stream of what seem to be inevitable next moments, accompanied by profound absorption and open-mindedness. When the therapist sensitively develops this sequential fluidity, the patient slips into a mental groove where she becomes hospitable to thoughts and feelings that would previously have been unacceptable. Under these conditions, the patient has less need for the tailoring aspect of the introjection triad. It is like the guileless receptivity of early childhood, and it is crucial for the reforming of the self configuration.

The paradoxical movement backward, inspired by sequential inevitability, is evident in the following example. Mark, thirty-five, referred snidely to his mother's effervescent way of speaking although it was evident that he, with his heavy voice, could benefit from her lightness. One thing led to the next and then the next, and as he spoke of her lighthearted voice, I asked him to imitate it. By this time in the sequential buildup, he was beginning to think his mother's style might not be as awful as he had thought. Where he would have previously disdained my suggestion to imitate her voice, it now seemed the naturally next thing to do. When he did imitate her, he felt his own lighthearted self and he became more intimate, like his mother.

In the of-course mode, he was soon telling me what he wouldn't have told me before. At five, he had sexual feelings for his mother. He had been able to smell her and feel himself against her clothes and he adored her. But they called him a mama's boy. Because of the stigma, he stiffened against the intimacy with his mother, never giving it up but also never at ease in closeness to her. He believed his sexual feelings might betray his mama's-boy self. When I jokingly added, perhaps more freshly than normally acceptable, that he had really been mama's little fucker, he got red and laughed, reexperiencing a long-lost intimate self that esteemed warmth and lightheartedness. Neither he nor his mother had ever known what had happened to their relationship.

Through the simple sequences, one of-course after the other, my patient had swung into a mood where each next statement or feeling felt right, untailored. The pieces just fit together, and he absorbed the validity of an abandoned self, giving new context and proportion to the mama's-boy self.

It may help clarify the primitive predisposition of people to be swept into the stream of continuing nextness by placing it in context with a number of mind-influencing procedures such as hypnosis, meditation, drugs, and brainwashing. Each reduces the interval between stimulation and reaction, between what has happened and what will happen next. Each also invokes high attention, a feeling of heightened emergency, and confidence in the inevitable succession of events.

This reduction in the interval between stimulation and reaction is reminiscent of the old stimulus/response psychologies that saw this simple interconnection as the rudimentary human experience. Whereas they went too far in reducing human behavior to such simplicity, the stimulus-response mechanism is a good model for a mind unencumbered by competing selves. The presence of an inevitable complex of selves, providing indispensable depth and variety to a person's life, may also be a key source of personal distraction.

Though the person's perspectives and options carry the indispensable burden of assessing a very complex world, there is much for the therapist to learn from the special advantages of simple stimulus/response sequences. Among the high-focus methods that reduce complexity is hypnosis. In hypnosis, the sense of sequential fit is set up through a series of highly narrowed cause and effect sequences and a highly narrowed focus of attention—like counting, giving easily resonant suggestions, or watching a predictably moving object. These experiences are each small in momentary impact but in series they soon add up to the of-course feeling. The individual may ride this of-courseness into the most surprising consequences (Erickson and Rossi, 1979).

Meditation is comparable. The repetition of the mantra creates a sense of ultimately welcome choicelessness, a release from the individual's thought processes or other background influences that interfere with absorbed attention. Once this narrowing occurs, the sequence of awarenesses seems altogether natural and conflicts recede into the background.

Some cautionary observations must be made, because the sense of sequential inevitability, freeing though it may be, also has some harmful prospects. Without the interferences presented by what *should* be next, people may be in for some rude awakening. To be unmindful of consequences can be, first of all, dangerous. While the feeling of safety is advantageous for movement in therapy, one should be mindful not to mislead patients by inducing a greater sense of safety than circumstances merit. Bosses do fire assertive employees, sexual fantasies can create debilitating panic, rejection is often severely depressing, and all of these experiences will translate into selves that cannot be happily assimilated. Furthermore, the sense of sequential inevitability may make some people opinionated, naive, single-minded, and other states of mind that will make the cure worse than the disease.

However, at its best, sequential fit represents the simple, unmediated grace that comes with an organic progression, within which all the parts fit beautifully together. It is a therapeutic mandate to induce appropriate confidence rather than wild license in the sequential progressions; only with this carefully in mind can the process work. People may receive great benefit from restoring a hospitality to the disconnected aspects of their lives, often renewing freshness and zest, lost to responsiveness because they are too complex.

Although tight sequencing helps to directly create the of-course phenomenon, much as one sees it in hypnosis and meditation, it does so in a more complex engagement, a closer replication of the actual everyday living engagement. When the discontinuity that plagues most patients is reduced, the tightened sequence helps momentarily to wash the slate relatively clean, leaving a short span of hospitality to new messages.

Loose Sequences

While sequential tightness and the continuity it highlights are crucial to unveiling the experiences from which the self is formed, they are only part of the story. Loose sequences are key counterpoints (E. Polster, 1987, pp. 63–67). They contrast with tight sequences by giving the person freedom to establish a necessary pacing and thematic development. Though these experiences are not always located immediately in the line of problem-solving sequences, they are valuable because they offer unrestrained opportunity for patients to acceptably continue the habitual style that is the core of their lives. Therapy is, after all, not only a drive for change but also an opportunity to experience one's self as one already *is*.

From this foundation of an existing self structure, the person may find his own verbal pathway for exploring diverse, sometimes chaotic, wisps of experience. Free association is one technique that offers very loose constraints on purpose or communicative style. Historically, free association helped to create expressive continuity in a strangely paradoxical way. Though on the one hand these chaotic associations may have seemed choppy, they also circumvented common linear standards. When these linear standards were eliminated, every statement qualified as a natural consequence of what was previously said.

Even the most surrealistic shifts of subject became sequentially valid. If the patient, for example, were to remember falling off a swing in the playground, followed incomprehensively by his annoyance with a co-worker, the analyst would see those manifestly disconnected statements two ways: first, as an example of mental freedom and second, as the untranslated unconscious bespeaking secret connections. In either case, the person, shedding normal standards of sequence, flows innocently ahead through seemingly disconnected thoughts.

The importance of continuity, both supported and contradicted by free association, has been challenged nowadays by oversimplified understandings of the nonlinear experience. Surrealistic artists, for example, scramble time and space perspective, creating strange juxtapositions of events that have little immediately apparent connections with each other, as though ordinary connectedness is a prison from which they escape. But the therapist wants very much to restore connections, to reveal what goes with what. In spite of the marvelous expansion of psychological potential that is offered by surrealism and other nonlinear thinking, the therapist cannot rest with connectionless existence.

To place nonlinearity into therapeutic perspective, it is important to realize that acceptance of nonlinearity broadens the sense of what is sequentially permissible. To get there from here, either in time or space, we need no longer feel as compelled as we once did to move in a straight line. The mind is an unruly instrument, and it will readily take strange routes to where it goes, sometimes unexplainably, sometimes whimsically, sometimes dangerously, sometimes mystically. But it is clear, nonlinearity notwithstanding, that the mind is always going where it is going. If we want to find the self in this inexorable movement forward, we must loosen the normal measure of sequence in order to follow the person's arrows into her forward movement.

Loose sequences also exist when the therapist listens but inserts little of her own thought into the stream of therapeutic interchange. Acceptance and understanding of what the patient has said in the form that she said it also permit loose sequences. In loose sequences, inevitability and pointedness take a vacation. In their place come freedom for trial explorations and the tentative meandering that allows new thoughts to catch on. Loose sequences and the unpressured, soft, open-minded attitude of the therapist allow the mind to roam. Thus the patient can gather her thoughts together, say what occurs without having to make it work therapeutically, leave room for false starts, and through the pruning process sift out the key elements of her life instead of being stuck with a jungle growth of thoughts, feelings, and memories.

The therapist uses the loosely formed sequential requirements to appreciate the unstudied human engagement, to prepare her mind for the therapeutic task ahead, to try out ideas without having to make them work, to assimilate what she has learned, to give time for opportunities to appear for the application of new knowledge, and for getting a bird's-eye view of one's life.

One patient, for example, was talking about an old boyfriend who had once treated her cruelly. She was emotionally distraught and suddenly felt a pain in her chest. She became anxious when, in tightening the sequences of her experience, I asked her to concentrate on her chest and to tell me about the pain. This threw her into a state of anxiety and she began to cry, seeming immobilized. Though I could only speculate about the source of her anxiety at the direct focus on the pain, what was clear was that the deflected experience of pain was more bearable than the pointed experience.

I don't know what would have happened had I continued to guide her into a tighter sequence in this session. Perhaps she would have moved through it with important new expressions and insights, discovering a feared self. But I didn't think so. I thought I had just rushed her and that tightening through internal concentration was premature. I already knew that as a child she had been stimulated beyond her capacities, but her effervescent style moved nobody to let her have her own pace. So, loosening the sequencing, I asked her to drop the internal focus, giving her support and orientation to the probability that as time went on she would become ready for more pointed experience than she was ready for now.

As time passed and she grew more at home with her life story and with her relationship with me, she began to allow gradual increase in attention to her inner sensations. Then, six months later, she fell in love with a man with whom she became ready to experience her sensations more poignantly, a man who, for the first time, she could trust not to rush her sexually, to allow her to feel her inner experience with no demand from him. I think the change in pacing that her immobilization had pressed on me and the consequent allowance of internal ripening were prophetic of her later experience.

Nextness

The concept of nextness must also take account of the amplitude of the sequential arc. The arc may involve the relationship of moment to moment, of today to tomorrow, or of one phase of life and another. It may involve the chapters in a book, segments of an athletic event, one friendship followed by another, and so on. What one person may experience as "next," if she is dissatisfied at work, may be her next job rather than something she might immediately say to her boss. This sequencing may be just right for her, as she plans ahead; or it may be an enormous leap ahead, foolishly disregarding necessary immediate needs.

While there is no escape from the simple reality that one thing follows another, the mind's versatility will not be imprisoned by any one person's view of what follows what. If I ask you where you went for dinner and you give me your commentary on the quality of restaurants in our city, I might be intrigued by the shift and prefer it to a direct answer to my question; on the other hand, I might feel disregarded, even bored. At a particular bakery, when I asked the warm, motherly person behind the counter what kind of kuchen they had, she answered, "Delicious." That response was sequentially strange, but I felt a good flow rather than a gap and simply pointed to a particular kuchen. If not for the woman's warmth and the visible presence of the kuchen, I might have felt a gap in continuity instead of the pleasurable resonance I actually felt.

For those with full confidence in their stream of attention, loose sequences, unexpected, even unexplainable, may not feel like a gap so much as an invitation to a mysterious sequence, giving it a welcome place in a natural, though ambiguous, flow. Some may call this ambiguity nonlinear, but in terms of sequence the nonlinear is simply the linear without the requirements for familiar connections usually imputed to linearity.

In surrealistic sequence, strange relationships are projected by the unreined mind. Thoughts may follow one another in a seemingly gratuitous manner as though quite disconnected from one another, torn out of normal context. Yet they occur through adjacent time units and have their own unknown interconnectedness in the absence of syntactical sequence.

This experience of the interconnectedness of all is often inspired by meditative and religious explorations, where people are released from the constraints of ordinary sequencing. These experiences of transcendence of boundaries demonstrate an indomitability of the mind, unwilling to be limited to the provable, and a testament to the fact that we know only a minuscule proportion of what can come to be known.

Every experience is fated to be transformed into the next one. We cannot wipe out sequence, but we are free to experience it in our own ways or even ignore it. Where disconnections are experienced, they are judged to have created gaps rather than mystery, choppiness rather than fluidity, dissatisfaction rather than good feeling, and fragmentation rather than unity.

6

Storyline: The Eventful Self

A s we saw in Chapter Five, the restoration of sequential connectedness results in increased fluidity of expression. An important by-product of this fluidity is that it will produce key stories revealing important selves. What I am proposing is that the connectedness of the experiences engenders a momentum that leads the patient into stories that fit the patient's therapeutic needs.

In Kevin's case, for example, the sequences of his therapeutic interactions with me resulted in his climactic story about the sailing trip with his father. Through this story he revealed his fear of a usurper self within him, a fear that kept him hesitant and sapped him of a measure of his vitality. This revelatory experience is an expected consequence of any freely developed therapeutic impetus.

Humans, as storytelling animals, are impelled to animate the events in their lives, to organize them, and to identify with them. In the particular forms of concentration represented in therapy, these stories always reveal important aspects of the storytellers, especially when they are the lead characters.

The telling of stories is so natural that its central role in psychotherapy has been largely taken for granted. Instead of prizing the stories for their elemental contributions—the experiences they report and the lives they replicate—therapists often place greater emphasis on the conclusions that stories lead to and the understandings they provide. While these understandings are vital, they do not stand alone, grounded as they are in the story's events, which are the signposts of a person's lifetime. The events reveal personal qualities, replicate previous experience, accentuate conflict, communicate a connectedness among people, and evoke the drama of the experiences from which the self is formed. Selves that are revealed in the patient's stories are themselves the characters in a small work of fiction.

It may seem odd to see the formation of selves as a work of fiction, since our patients are real people telling us about real events. But the reality that they are building through their stories is a malleable reality, carved out not only for descriptive accuracy but also to make personal sense out of their lives.

The mind's animating function, so evident in primitive peoples, is particularly important because of the role that stories play in constructing personal self images. The therapeutic problem reflected in stories our patients tell and the selves they identify is this: though the stories make lively sense in portraying the selves within, the casting directors that people become often typecast selves or wrongly cast them. My obedient self may no longer play the major role I have previously assigned to it. Such errors influence a skewed view of reality, providing flawed maps, which much be redrawn. So even though the fictional function of the mind is compelling, like many fundamental human functions, it is vulnerable to error. The stories we tell do not provide assurance that they represent up-to-date function.

Through the pivotal role of the story in replicating our lives, it seems evident that humans are generically storytelling animals. Not surprisingly, the storytelling function, vital as it is, appears in the earliest years of communication. Witness the research of Jerome Bruner (1987), who reported the recordings of Emmy, a two-year-old chatterbox. Her bounteous soliloquies, an indefatigable self-record, helped her, as Bruner says, to "locate" herself in the midst of a profusion of daily events.

Here are some examples of her biographical wanderings. "Daddy did make some cornbread for Emmy" and "Sometimes Daddy, some-times Mommy put Emmy down with home" (her word for *diaper*). Another time, apparently concerned with her diaper privileges, given the recent birth of her brother, she says, "Sometimes Mommy, some-times Daddy put Emmy down with home, sometimes Mommy, sometimes Tanta puts Emmy down with home. Sometimes Jeannie and Annie and Tanta and Emmy and Mona and my Daddy and Carl, Daddy and Carl, Mommy. Comes Tanta and Jeannie come over and sometimes Jeannie take off my changing table at home and might get that diaper and put it on. Sometimes Jeannie change my diaper."

We can see that Emmy knows what her priorities are. By telling stories she is keeping those priorities alive, playing the scenes over, registering their value and intuiting the self that is composed of these experiences. There are certainly a lot of people around to influence her sense of self.

Emmy's experience of stories filled with people attending to her is very different from the experience of a patient of mine, plagued by a disregarded self. Her father, a well-known man, was the subject of a recent biography. *His* sense of self was very important to him; he was less concerned with his daughter's. When my patient read the book, she became furious. She felt betrayed by what she read. She should have been one of his closest intimates, yet she was learn-ing things about his life at the same time as thousands of strangers were learning about them. She felt betrayed in other ways too. Her father gave huge donations to community organizations while she tried to save the money to buy the house she wanted. Still, with-holding his story was more painful to her and a greater insult to her sense of self than withholding his money.

The freedom to tell therapeutically valuable stories does not come easily. Evoking the ingredients of storyline and realizing how they fit together require all the skills, knowledge, and timing that therapists spend lifetimes developing. To evoke or to tune in to the stories people live through is a fragile process requiring that thera-pists always have their antennae raised to see the relevant storyline.

These antennae must be sensitized to the infinity of hints people send out. The potential for stories has roots in the most ephemeral experiences, most of them lost, left behind in a lifetime of uncountable events.

Think how much has happened in any patient's life, even today alone—connecting the safety belt on the car, a casual greeting at a newsstand, dinner with a cousin, a surprise phone call, almost getting hit by a car, and on and on. A million events like this actually happen every day, and we take most of them in with only passing notice, not feeling how they might feed the sense of self and reality. But they are the vitamins of our existence, and the therapist in full homage for these idiosyncratic lives knows there is always a story there.

Yet, paradoxically, we would not want to be, nor could we be, continuously aware of the infinity of these experiences. But unfortunately, the surfeit locks out many important experiences along with the trivial. Consequently, people often pass through life with insufficient realization of the important events they live through. They can't remember what they are angry about, how adored they were, when they drew important conclusions about themselves, whether they have forbidden thoughts: the whole repertoire of lost experience psychotherapists have long been describing. The failure to register these experiences leads to flimsy grounding, with resulting stereotyped meanings, empty rewards, and unregistered presence.

Functions of the Story

The story, well told and palpably experienced, is an essential therapeutic tool for countering the emptiness of experience. It is a way of organizing specially selected life experiences—sometimes reflexively, sometimes deliberately—by verbally replicating them. Telling a story is taking a verbal picture that records events. It sets down the markers for how the selves formed.

When the sense of self is grounded by only a narrow view of one's lifetime of experiences, it is made vulnerable to new experiences of rejection, attack, ambiguity, and failure, each of which in the absence of a large range of experiences becomes disproportionately representative. The registration of events is a vote for one self or another; without such votes, the self is an unsupported construction. Therapy, therefore, is the process of getting out the vote for one self or another by restoring the events of the person's life story.

The analyst Alice Miller (1986) pointed out the importance of seeing the patient's storyline by telling of two analysts who were both called in the middle of the night by the same patient. "The first analyst did not understand the *biographical* context of this so-called acting out. The second one *listened to the story* contained in the reenactment, and this helped him to devote his full attention as a spectator to the drama, jumping onto the stage and joining in the act" (p. 16; italics added).

The therapy office is a hothouse of storytelling. But patients tend to squander experiences, growing them like unwanted weeds or untended flowers. The events need the light that the therapist offers when he turns a dry experience into a vital story. Let us say, for example, that a patient, speaking in dry monotones, tells his therapist three things: that his mother died when he was seven, that from then on his father would periodically mope on a dining room chair, and that his father would repeatedly say, "It can't work." He may, through identification with his father, be branding an inconsolable self into his mind and squandering the richness of these events. This terrible sequence of discrete experiences is only one part of his story. Though he may see the inconsolable self as personally definitive and hopelessly imbedded, he is surely dismissing other experiences—relationships with teachers, experiences at a circus, books he read, life at the playground, neighborhood fights. These could be important connecting links to other selves, revealed in his full storyline, offering competing views of himself.

I am not suggesting the therapist turn away from the key symptom of inconsolability. What I am suggesting, though, is that narrow symptoms are only one side of the story. By adding new events to the patient's repertoire, the therapist reintroduces struggle between conflicting events and conflicting selves, replacing the one-sidedness that has gotten the person stuck.

A good story gets depth and directionalism from the conflicts that are contributors to the person's life. When the story expands further, as it usually does when more light is brought to the events, this particular patient may tell about his rage at his father, not forgotten but disdained. Then he may remember making up his mind right then, at seven, never to feel like a failure. He had put down a signpost in his mind. That signpost had been forgotten, buried by too many failures, but originally it pointed him toward finding his own way.

As he tells these thoughts, his buried indomitable self sends out a new signal and is nominated by these new experiences to be a player in his complex of selves. Will he accept the nomination? The campaign has begun. In addition to whatever understandings these events point to, the storyline now has two characters, inconsolable self and indomitable self, and they compel attention to the incipient struggles in the dynamic of these selves.

How can the therapist help?

The therapist is commissioned to see the propellant energy of these events and not let them be squandered. A boy's mother died when he was seven. His father falls apart. The boy makes a remarkable vow. The devastation, the sadness, the terror, the indomitability, the insight, the scope of mind—all these are fulcrum experiences, and the therapist honors them with his keen interactions.

He may ask gentle questions, he may point out what is skipped over, he may cajole, expostulate, suggest, even occasionally command. He may show the patient how to have greater empathy with himself and how to be an open-minded witness to the remarkable experiences he has lived through. No level of deadness in the patient should distract the therapist from the true story values of a person losing his mother at seven.

Story Guidelines

In this coordination of reciprocal impact between therapist and patient, there are many useful conversational stimulations, including the tightening of sequences that was discussed in Chapter Five. A few general, though overlapping, guidelines are: hospitality to events as well as meanings, expanding fragments, transcending fixed beliefs, and recognizing life themes.

Hospitality

Keeping professional acumen while being enthralled is no small feat, but unless the therapist is willing to be immersed in the storyline itself, what is left may be all too routine. Since the patient often cannot realize the incredible reality he has lived through because it was too painful and because patches of his life have been torn out, the therapist must be a guardian of the merits of the events of his life.

In his story den, the psychotherapist has been active witness to passages of hundreds of people who have shown him the most idiomatic selves. These experiences help him to be skilled in noticing the inclusion and exclusion of events. When he is devoted to the events people live through and when he infects his patient with this devotion, the patient has increased motivation to resurrect his own lifetime of events.

There is, however, a dilemma to be faced: trying to accentuate storyline while needing to work toward valid conclusions and definitively summarize the person's problems. Freud's writings are defining examples of this dilemma. Underneath his theoretical elaborations, Freud described his patients' experiences much as a novelist might. He told of event after event, satisfying many qualities of good storyline, including suspense, contradiction, strangeness, imaginative situations, and lively language. In tackling the dilemma between medical acceptability and good storyline, Freud did not give up the drama of the case history, but he allowed it to be overshadowed by the theoretical and technical conclusions that could be drawn from them. As Hillman (1983, p. 7) notes, Freud was concerned more with why things happened than with what happened, more concerned with explaining motives than relaying the elements of plot, which direct the patient's interest to what happens next.

Part of Freud's reserve about reported events was that he didn't believe them. Whether the events were real or not is arguable, but an unfortunate casualty of this gap in credibility is the actual drama of the events. Freud's disbelief placed him in a considerable dilemma because he understood that, believable or not, the stories had to be taken as "real" if they were to serve analytic purposes. At one point Freud (1963) says about his therapy with the so-called Wolf Man: "Many details, however, seemed to me myself to be so extraordinary and incredible that I felt some hesitation in asking other people to believe in them" (p. 192).

More important than his distrust of the Wolf Man's accuracy was his general distrust of manifest events (Freud, 1963, p. 237). He took account of these reservations by giving the stories a special technical role within psychoanalysis, one that would implicitly raise the importance of meaning well above the inherent drama of the stories. He called for an oddly conditional acceptance of the stories: listening carefully *as though* they were true. Then, at the end of the analysis, he could point out that the stories were only products of the imagination, diversions from the patient's real problems.

This is not to say that Freud thought no stories to be believable, for he is speaking only about those that stretched belief. Nevertheless, believability became suspect under Freud, triggering the sense of the therapist knowing more about the patient than the patient knows about himself. Though there is obviously a large magnitude of distortion in anyone's perceptions and memories, I believe this attitude of disbelief is excessive and leads easily to the nihilistic expectation that nothing in life really is as it is, a cynical accompaniment of therapeutic disbelief.

Freud was thus not only deflected from the value of storyline itself but was a harbinger of the current constructivist positions that amputate reality itself, turning everything that we perceive into nothing more than a mental construction. Since I am taking a highly personalized position with respect to the formation of selves, it is important that this does not get confused with the antireality position of constructivism.

Constructivists differ in the degree to which they believe the individual may create and organize his own world. Some, like Heinz Von Foerster (1984), deny any evidence of an actual reality: "When we perceive our environment, it is we who invent it" (p. 42). Watzlawick's (1984, p. 330) view is similar, though somewhat moderated by his identifying the advantages of living *as though* there were a given external reality. On the other pole of the constructivist dimension are those who take a more open view about the existence of a real world, recognizing a universe of reality objects while emphasizing the vicissitudes of knowability (Mahoney, 1991, p. 111).

The self compositions I have been describing share ground with constructivism by crediting each person with great configurational freedom uniquely to organize his experiences into selves. But for me, even though composition of these selves is highly idiomatic, it is nevertheless based on what has actually happened.

The registration of personal experience is a very difficult feat, and we must respect its artful requirements. But with variable accuracy, the pictorial and anthropomorphic substance of selves is trained on the actualities of a person's life. The dialectic between actual events and highly personal self composition, always uncertain, contributes drama and clarity to a suspenseful organization of experience.

When people tell me stories in therapy and they have formed characters that I have called selves, these selves are fictional only in the sense that they are personally arranged accounts of their lives that have evolved from actual experiences. To explore this phenomenon of the self as a work of fiction, synthesizing actual experiences, I, unlike Freud or the constructivists, take the stories people tell me as the more or less factual materials that are the more or less dependable substance of the self. It is my job to struggle with the discernment about what is more or less substantive.

Fragments

When do a person's verbalizations become a story? Surely, Emmy's verbalizations at the beginning of this chapter are slim story fare. All she was doing was remembering a succession of events. Usually, with stories we expect more elaborate interweavings of events, with suspense, revelation, character development, implications of underlying human concerns, clues to how to face issues, and so on. But these conditions are important for judgments about the *quality* of the stories, the attraction the story has for readers or others who are not direct participants. In psychotherapy, everybody is a direct participant. Since we are not dealing with vicarious experiences, the standards for the value of a story are looser. Just as a parent may enjoy his daughter's school play as much as a great Broadway production, our patients give us firsthand experiences and we therapists are listening person to person.

To recognize the value of the story in psychotherapy, we must include even the simplest series of events. For me, the story is any sequence of events that, in the telling, are connected to each other. Therefore when Emmy says, "Daddy did make cornbread for Emmy," the nouns *Daddy*, *cornbread*, and *Emmy* are interconnected by *did make* and *for*, and these interconnections form a storyline, no less so than if she had been anxious that Daddy might not make cornbread for her or that this act did or did not reveal love for her. The more elaborated storyline, including conflict, is what we often associate with the creation of a story, but the story itself exists even in the absence of these complications.

However, if Emmy's story were aesthetically or therapeutically minor (which in Emmy's case it is not, since it is miracle enough that she recounts her experience), it would be the joint task of therapist and patient to make a "better" story out of it. The therapist must help the patient to take account of weaknesses in storyline and improve them. I will give a case example of one way to do this in relation to the awakening of selves. But first, a few thoughts on some general indicators of what the therapist looks for.

Some key elements that often call for improvement are: whether the story is tightly enough contained; whether it is well organized; whether it is interesting; whether it gets to the point; whether it include characters who are calling out of the blank spaces; whether it is repetitious, mechanical, impersonal, flowery, undependable, or distracting; whether it includes conflict and development of a theme.

This is a big order. Stories that meet all those criteria are better handled by masters in storytelling, people who are not only highly talented but also can work over the storyline at their own pace. But therapy provides two advantages that make the storytelling assignment somewhat easier. First, only the patient and therapist need to be interested. Second, the storyline is always going on, so there is never a final version that stands forever in completed form, ready for a critic's review.

A typescript of an entire therapy, even though it would contain elements of breathtaking drama, would soon become boring to a reader. The storyline moves by fits and starts, often fragmented and unskillfully presented. It is studded with events that do not tidily conform to fictional standards of directionalism and unity, but nevertheless they represent extraordinary experiences and characters.

Though they all move forward toward some unidentified conclusion, unfortunately the therapeutically relevant stories are episodic in nature, often interrupted or with serious gaps. A fruitful therapy will contain many sessions that reveal surprise, suspense, deeply moving feelings, lively language, clarifying moments, contrasts in habits and attitudes, representations of human fate and survival. These experiences, episodic and often painful, may not be so clear in storyline that the patient would register them as a coherent experience. Patients, in fact, commonly squander events that offer little coherence or direction until the work of therapy takes effect.

Now for an illustration of how the storyline may unfold and its relation to the emergence of selves. Hubert's main reason for coming to therapy was the difficulty he has had in establishing continuing relationships with women. The therapy experience moved from session to session, each separated in his mind from the other. Even though themes did reappear, he did not immediately remember from week to week what we addressed in a previous session. In the first several sessions, he told me about a number of experiences with different women, describing each experience at some length. But to improve his storyline, it was necessary thematically to tie those events together. Otherwise they would be isolated events, each one starting over again without any experience of the movement so crucial to therapy.

I articulated the primary theme: Over and over he appears to be having an excellent relationship with a woman until a problem arises. From then on, nothing works no matter what he does, and the relationship ends. Hubert is surprised to hear it put that way, even though he knows that is what has been happening.

A corollary theme, which I pointed out with only moderately illuminating effect, is that he is peremptory in his reactions. Where others might see alternatives, he immediately knows that there are none. Though his points of view are valid, they do not leave much room for any other point of view. This phenomenon we came to know as his intractable self. An example: Hubert, forty, took in the twenty-year-old daughter of a friend who needed a place to stay— no sexuality, just generosity. His girlfriend at the time protested vigorously, but Hubert wouldn't toss his friend's daughter out, and that was the end of that. He may have been quite right to stick to his guns, but there should be more compelling reasons to end a relationship.

Hubert's story was incomplete. When I asked him whether any important people in his life had made up their minds right away, he started out by remembering his opinionated father, a story of its own with many fascinating details. Then he told me about himself and his alcoholic mother. When he would come home from school, he knew right away that if she was drunk, the game was over. When he could see in the first moments that she was drunk, he would simply yield to everything. Here the story identifies his yielding self. Hubert experiences himself either always giving in or having unshakable integrity.

In fleshing out a promising storyline, the therapist must make up for the natural deficiencies in ordinary storytelling. Whereas the novelist would have been able to write the scenario of his character's adamant behavior at his own artful pace, in therapy the patient's revelatory process may be sluggish. The therapist is required to remain interested whether others might be or not. At first there are only hints, but they don't immediately lead anywhere. Habit interferes with freshness.

As Hubert's story unfolded, session to session, together we filled and patched as we went along. Eventually what seemed to be only a peremptory style became revealed as a larger unresponsiveness, unhearing and overbearing, combined with a poor facility for supporting his own position with anything but impenetrability.

I wanted to see firsthand how this rigidity of response worked, so I designed a role-playing experience for him and me. He had related an experience about an argument with some dinner companions over educational policy. Hubert was adamantly convinced that the education problems in the United States can only be solved by federal pooling of the financial resources of all schools and dividing these resources evenly among all schools, poor and wealthy alike. His friends, who were affluent, were tired of taking care of the poor, whom they felt should take care of themselves.

Hubert and I began the role-playing conversation, with me playing the composite character of several of the friends. Very quickly I discovered firsthand how Hubert alienated me. He was basically asking that I reduce the quality of my children's schooling so that schooling in poverty areas could be improved, and he displayed no consciousness of the sacrifice I would be making. He could not address my concern, take account of the flaws in his argument, or spell out the flaws in mine. So there was no place to go except repetition of his position and an alienated digging in of heels. This time, though, he could see what he was doing.

Then I asked him to play the other side and I would play him. Acting as Hubert, I was able to show him how to be incisive without alienating people, without making a fool out of the other person. Suddenly it was clear that his yielding self, the source of a lifetime of sacrifice, could coordinate with these people without his intractable self dominating the relationship.

This time the role playing was the freshening instrument, providing greater faithfulness to what actually happens in his relationships than his deficient reports had. The fresh behavior and its new meaning gave coherence to the otherwise mysterious alienations Hubert was repeatedly facing. The relationships with women and his childhood experiences with his parents thus fit together, the flesh and bones remodeled into recognizable shape. When meaning evolves, the experiences become spotlighted as well as summarized, registering new events and new selves that, unwelcome to the fixed mind, would be squandered.

Incidentally, months later, Hubert was in the company of these same people, and once again the conversation turned to a passionate topic. Even though the potential for alienation was there, this time the exchanges went well and they enjoyed each other. They had a good laugh when one of them said to him, "The last time we were together, I really thought you were an asshole."

Fixed Beliefs

Not only did the development of Hubert's storyline unify fragments of his experience, but it also unmasked fixed beliefs. The role-playing events, revealing his intractable self, adamant and ineffective, and his yielding self, responsive but exploited, gave a much clearer view of his argument with his dinner companions than the fixed beliefs he was originally guided by. I do not actually know which version is true, since his companions may actually have been the ones to rigidly block out Hubert's arguments.

The new picture of Hubert having fixed beliefs would, however, better explain his pattern of making abrupt changes in relationships. It just fits better than to see him only as a man of integrity, who out of faithfulness to his principles always get into trouble with a recalcitrant society. Furthermore, I saw what seemed a key sample of his fixed beliefs right in front of my eyes. Thus the new view fit better into what we knew of his life. It provided what seemed a more dependable light to guide us.

Thus the evolvement of storyline must take account of signs of fixed beliefs, because they will interfere with the appearance of certain significant stories. Premature assignments of meaning already made by patients are a major distraction from the aesthetically right storyline. Patients are either already living their lives according to mistaken meanings or they shun those they have long dreaded. The blushing person, for example, may feel in danger of having his boyish inadequacies found out rather than feeling the radiance of the blush. The energetic executive may not rest because the rest means passivity. The silent person will be careful not to show those inner strivings that once got him into trouble.

Though aesthetic fit yields to the elusiveness of truth and settles for approximations, this is nothing to weep over, even though exactitude would be preferable. Approximations are a natural part of everything we do and an essential part of the therapeutic role. One patient's stories about his father portrayed him as grotesquely hateful, probably a skewed perception. After the parents separated, my patient's father violently threatened him and his mother, trying to break into their house with a gun. We spent considerable time talking about his unrelievedly hateful father.

The fixed view of his father, though I thought it to be approximately accurate, was too airtight. I wondered for some time how the lovely man who was my patient could have a father so unremittingly bad. So I asked about exceptions to his belief, and he began to send out glimmerings of his father's possible attractiveness. He referred to his father's buddies, to the respect his father had achieved in his work, to new attempts by his father to seek him out.

All this exploration was sporadic because other themes were more immediate. Then one day he told me that he remembered taking baths with his father when he was three. Two things about that memory stood out: the playfulness in the bathtub and the mightiness of his father's testicles. Here is my patient now telling me of being in the bathtub with this terrifying man and he is awed, not frightened, on seeing his father's testicles.

The truth grows. His new story of bathtub pleasures *fits* as the type of experience previously incomprehensively absent from his life. Something else helped create the sense of fit: my patient's style of telling his story—his surprise, his flushed face, his language, the inclusion of detail, his lively sensations, his past accuracies, his imagery, and his acknowledgment that the bathtub experience was important. These were as telling as the results of a lie detector test, not proof positive but a worthy guide to the actualities of his life.

Details are especially telling. When my patient told me not just of the generalized awe he had had of his father but also of the mightiness of his testicles, that detail had greater convincing powers than any abstract statement would. In searching for the actualities of a person's life, it is commonplace to honor poetic truth, the misshapen creations that point to greater truths than the narrowly literal. Selected details may communicate an artful truth, not as a capriciously developed storytelling trick but as a native reflex to extrapolate a detail into a larger, throbbing actuality.

Though I can never know the historical truth with exactitude, the story of my patient's bathtub experience reminded him more clearly than ever that his father was not always his enemy and in fact was, at one time, his friend. He didn't have to now love his father, as I doubt he ever will, in order to be reminded of what we identified as his manly self, long in the background.

Thus the burden for accuracy is lessened. The literal actuality of my patient's bathtub experience is not sacrosanct. The details of his original experience may not have highlighted the very same factors that his memory now highlights. The chances are great that, given sensitive attention to the congruence of this story with his previously reported experiences and also with his currently convincing reactions, his story will restore a greater reality of his father's character than the extremely narrow image to which his fixed beliefs had previously limited him. The family drama branded in his mind has led him to so narrow and compelling a view of his father that it interfered with his sense of manly self. Loosening the images of father and manliness drew attention to the suspenseful future, giving continuing drama to what might otherwise be a foreclosed future, changing embittered, dispassionate, fixed expectations into we do not yet know what.

Life Themes

How, though, does his memory of playing in the bathtub with his father qualify as a story? It is a mere fragment if we use the criteria that any reader or listener would ordinarily associate with a story. Though the event is dramatic, one must flesh any fragment with antecedents and consequences and with a thematic structure. Any particular memory takes its place in the stream of memories told over a period of time. The bathtub story's breadth is expanded when it is interwoven with all the current personal relationships this man has recounted and when placed in the context of his repeatedly expressed ambivalence about being intimate.

From the perspective of such fragments, the therapeutic storyline may be seen as a sequence of events tied together by a theme, providing implication and mobilization for the patient's continuity and orientation. In fulfilling this mission of elaborating storyline, the therapist becomes coauthor and editor, not only of the storyline itself but also of his patient's developing sense of self.

Therefore, a key guide to the evocation of storyline and its accompanying remodeling of the self is careful attention to the thematic structure of what people talk about. Any single person contains an infinity of possible stories. How is a therapist to choose which are relevant? Without thematic guidelines, the choices might bypass therapeutic purpose, becoming irrelevant, repetitive, incomplete, boring, hyperbolic, tangential, or exhibitionistic.

Identifying a theme lights the therapeutic path and helps keep the therapist alert for the particular selves that form out of these themes and for ways to create therapeutic movement through ambiguous directions and dim purpose. There are many generalized themes, experienced broadly by people at large, and there are also many individualized themes to guide the therapist.

Generalized Themes

Generalized themes are commentaries on people at large in that they are themes that touch all of us. Because these themes are common to everyone, it is especially important that they not be transformed from empathy with the human condition into trite and premature understandings. It is almost unnecessary to say that common though these themes may be, they are never carbon copies and must be recognized in their idiomatic character.

Perhaps the most common theme in psychotherapy has been the family story, sexualized in Freudian work but also central as a nonsexual, interactive set of relationships and events. It is almost reflexive for therapists to seek the source of current difficulties in the patient's early relationship with parents and siblings, who form the major part of anyone's felt early community and who therefore are seen as prototypical source of storyline and self formation.

The classic Oedipal scenario has so many variations, however, as to be almost unrecognizable in the life of any particular person. Dominance may come from either mother or father over both sons and daughters. Rejection has an infinite number of sources: subtle requirements unmet, snide remarks, favors given to others, unavailability for conversation or instruction, the absence of acts of endearment.

Thus most therapists will see the theme of early familial interaction appearing over and over in the stories their patients tell. In fact the process may become contaminated by therapists' preset readiness to see this theme and directly evoke it. They may wonder

almost reflexively about similarities between their patients' reactions to them and their reactions with their parents. Or they may
quickly call for elaboration about even casual remarks about parents. Or they may discount the centrality of current events and redirect patients to talk about their parents instead, as though the
current events were only stepping stones to further elaborations
about their parents.

There are many themes commonly addressed by people at large,
and they may or may not be directly related to their relationship to
their parents. Themes of envy, for example, though perhaps first evident in the familial situation, may be more pertinently told in relation to other people, such as a colleague, a spouse, a friend, people
in different social groupings. Therapists must be alert to these depar-
tures from the familial, as they broaden the scope of the person's life.

One of the goals of therapy is the discovery that there is a
life beyond childhood, where development of options and attitudes is permanently available. To reduce nonfamilial envy to the
status of a derivative of the familial experience is to dilute independently lively material from the patient's storyline. Bringing some
currently acute issue back to the family may be like inviting a person who has fallen and broken a leg to make a discourse on gravity.

Other generally experienced themes are such key feelings and
characteristics as shame, guilt, resentment, confusion, stupidity, greed,
powerlessness, ugliness, unworthiness, gullibility. Any of them could
be a basic source of therapeutic stories and the selves that result.

These are all negative themes, and the negative selves formed
around them are the most commonly attended in psychotherapy
where both patient and therapist contract to solve problems. However, equally important are the positive common themes, such as
beauty, generosity, sensitivity, endurance, sexual liveliness, surviv-
ability, determination, uprightness, honesty. Each of these is also
vital as a source of stories and the self formation that results.

The positive elements in any person's self formation are commonly overlooked since therapy is geared to the troublesome. But
the solution of problems is facilitated by the realization of enabling

selves as well as disabling ones. For every story that reveals the enabling qualities—intelligence, uniqueness, endurance, charm— the person is creating a more equalized competition in the struggle with the demoralizing selves that may have dominated his life.

Not only are key characteristics and feelings a source of personal stories, but key events serve the same purpose. All of us experience key events, important turns that are worth spelling out. We have all had memorable surprises. We have all known times when our lives were literally endangered. We have all either stolen something or wrestled with the prospect. We have all had our own unique introduction to sexuality. We have all cried, screamed, or otherwise vented strong feelings. We have all had memorable people in our lives, and also moments when we knew we were having a major impact on someone else.

The list goes on. The more alert the therapist is to these fulcrum experiences, the more quickly he is likely to unearth them in the lives of those patients who have set them aside. The broader the therapist's orientation is to the immense variety of themes people naturally live with, the more alert he will be to recognizing story-line possibilities and to evoking them. A slight grimace in a patient's reference to a co-worker may tap into the theme of envy and the consequent story, which may spell out the envy. A blush in telling about a return from a vacation with a spouse may tip off an embarrassment about privacy or sexuality. Pallor in speaking about a mistake at work may evoke the theme of severe punishment.

Individualized Themes

In addition to these common themes, experienced by almost everyone, there are also specific themes that recur in the lives of any particular patient. An obsessional patient, for example, will not allow anything but his obsession to matter; it remains a persistent theme. The challenge to the therapist is to take the stale obsession and give it lively story form. Another patient may be principally concerned with his business, another with his marriage, another with his phobia.

A key factor in individualizing these themes is to expand abstractions and ferret out the storyline details that the abstractions either introduce or summarize. Sometimes the relationship of abstraction to detail is either self-evident or not worth exploring. A man says, "I love fruit, eat it three times a day and that's why I am so healthy." There is no reason to investigate the kind of fruit he's talking about or the manifestations of his healthiness. The danger in therapy, however, is that both therapist and patient may be geared to communicate on an abstract basis and lose the restorative powers of storyline, often settling for the empty and distorted understandings that abstraction offers. Abstractions are the containers of life experiences, and they offer rich signals for the stories that would reflect the person's self structure.

Consider my patient Robert, an architect who was bothered by his laziness. This is so common a complaint it would have been easy to take its meaning for granted. People assume they know what it is to be lazy. That would have been fine with Robert, who wanted to talk about his laziness with a shapeless assumption that we both knew just what he was talking about. But his characteristic laziness was pervasive enough to be a definitive self, and it begged for detailing. Through this self, instead of doing what he is supposed to be doing, Robert may daydream about doing something else, he may converse with his secretary, he may go to the bar for a drink, he may endlessly go over what he has written, he may forget what he wanted to do, and so on.

When I pressed Robert for details of his lazy self, he first felt misunderstood. Then he answered by mechanically telling me what he does when he is being lazy: he stares into space, he turns business phone calls into social visits, he reexamines design plans blankly. But he was just warming up, and soon he remembered a more lively detail, one which thirsted for the future.

He told me that, as he whiles his time away, he feels his father sitting on his shoulder, a metaphor with a promise of development. Then he fleshed this out in story form, telling chapter and verse about how his father debunked everything he did, drove him to accept his values, inveigled him to become an architect, and continued to live his own life through Robert's work, kicking and screaming all the way about Robert's failure to do it right. Life with father thus reopened, the anger was revisited, and Robert's stale abstraction about his laziness was jogged into energetically told stories. His sense of his father sitting on his shoulder becoming a wrapping for fresh details about the self he previously abstracted.

Abstraction is like substituting a title for a story. Patients commonly abstract the problems they present, referring only in general terms to rejection by parents, frequent moves during their school years, sexual molestation. They color these experiences with only spare detail, enough to point to disturbance but missing the rekindling effect of storyline. This is a common result of the summarizing mind. The novelist Flannery O'Connor (1974, p. 48) sees this problem among fiction writers as well, who are also drawn to the "bare bones" of abstraction. She sees them taking the easy way out, neglecting to flesh out their ideas and emotions and trying to reform the world rather than to tell a story of the simple experiences people live with.

It is as true for therapists as for fiction writers: As long as they neglect the story options in the events underlying their abstractions, they will be stymied by patients who are guided by fixed self configuration. Abstractions deprive the self of detail, animation, and action. They often stop the music, giving an unyielding picture of the self into which the events have been unidentifiably fused.

Where these abstractions are used as orientation for movement and for a clarified designation of self, they develop a dynamic function, pointing the way forward. But they are often used as a substitute for such movement, supporting the stagnancy of a prematurely completed self picture. The restoration of pulsation between abstraction and detail is thus a major guide in creating the storyline, which continuously freshens up the individual's self.

The simple focus on the nextness of detail where abstractions have dominated helps turn the extreme complexity in anyone's life into manageable simple sequences of events. The story creates a recognizable and bounded stream out of a complex diversity of events. While neither unaware nor disrespectful of the complexity of anyone's life, the therapist evoking the story whittles life down in size to the point where the human mind can register movement and continuity. He selectively sets aside the complexities buried in abstractions, giving them human scale instead of dealing with the sweeping understandings they may represent. The loss of the scope that abstractions provide is often painful. The events they too broadly encompass are often dear as part of the range of events for which the person might otherwise cry out.

Many important events never survive the passage of time as life markers: the death of a friend, a key decision, a physical injury. Even more elusive are the less important markers of a normal day: a conversation at work, a golf game, an argument over homework. Without the narrative detail of these stories, the linkage that thematic realizations might provide in the chain of life experiences is lost.

Since abstractions are the mind's housing for the stories that furnish it, one may be said to be living in an empty house in the absence of these stories. But thematic alertness will help make stories abundantly available. When, in therapy, these stories are evoked, they will newly spotlight the patient's selves and help him to recognize that he is the central player in his life's drama. With each realization of this centrality, he is enabled to restore connections among previously disjointed parts of his existence.

Thus the themes of life may be thought to spotlight what is happening when there would otherwise seem too much to handle. The rediscovery of unclassified experience does nourish the individual's identity with thematic structure, often without awareness. Yet there is so much to take account of, and the thematic identifications of this large variety of experience serve as an aid to evoke stories that will serve as a filing system for a lifetime.

The thematic structure not only helps us to select the experiences that matter, but it also provides a trail of our existence, much like the bread crumbs Hansel and Gretel dropped to guide them back home. Just as they got lost when the crumbs were eaten, our patients lose their selves when they lose the stories that mark their paths.

7

Contact: The Relatedness of Self

Now that we have seen attention as an energizing background, sequentiality as a force for personal fluidity, and storyline as the organization of life's events, we come to the key ingredients from which the self is formed. These ingredients are contact, awareness, and action. Each has long been a guideline for gestalt therapists, and each plays an important role in the formation of selves. In this chapter we consider contact and its primary role in the therapeutic reconfiguration of selves.

Some stunning studies in midcentury confirmed the truth of the old concept that man does not live by bread alone. Babies who were profoundly neglected were found to just wither away, not because of physical trauma or deficiency but because of the absence of contact (Spitz, 1945; Bowlby, 1953). The findings were noted with interest in the psychological community, but that interest was only modest in proportion to the profound implications for the existence of an inherent need for contact. It became clear not only that contact was a social bonus helping people live good lives but also that people are directed into contact with other people by a generic, even biological undercurrent.

Only gestalt therapy among the therapy theories has described the phenomenon of contact as a simple organic hunger and included it as a moment-to-moment element in therapeutic procedure. Freud (1957) came close when he wrote of cathexis, a profound attraction in which the energy from one person is bonded to another. But this view became excessively sexualized and its place within the person's libidinal energy was esoteric. It faded from the core of psychoanalytic orientation and was never used in therapeutic procedure.

Perls, Hefferline, and Goodman (1951) took a commonly held view of an indivisible relationship between the organism and the environment one step further. They said that contact was a primary human function, preceding the more complex relationship between self and other. To them the contact boundary was an "organ of a particular relation of the organism and the environment" (p. 229). To call it an organ constituted a metaphorical leap that gave contact a primary role in a person's development, as fundamental to psychology as lungs are to physiology.

Simply defined as the meeting between ourselves and what is not ourselves, contact is going on all the time. It is as ordinary as breathing or blood circulation, as easily overlooked as the air around us. We are natively bonded with otherness by simple givens such as seeing, hearing, touching, moving, tasting, smelling, and talking, the elemental contact functions. We don't do these things to *make* contact; they are inherent processes—they *are* contact. Since they are basic to our existence, our task in life—and that of the therapist helping patients—is to make the contact functions work as well as possible.

From our earliest moments, the contact we have with other people tells us whether we are good or bad, careless or careful, loved or not loved. We become suffused with the messages people convey to us about who we are. The selves that form from these events, feelings, and meanings are the result of simple experiences of the things people say to us or do to us. Thus in the therapeutic reconstruction of selves, the therapist aims for new experiences of contact so that they will become composed into new selves, better connected with actual experiences and better integrated.

If a person gets beat up by an older brother, the self-image as weak and cowardly or rebellious and bitter must be changed by new contacts that will provide up-to-date data. Perhaps through contacts reexperienced during therapy, this person will, instead of these fixed selves, discover his angry self, his rising-above-it self, or perhaps his cunning self. To this end any therapy must find a means for restoring, improving, and expanding the person's contacts so as to feed new material into his psyche, necessary for the remodeling of the self.

There is an abundance of opportunity, since people create contact in all circumstances of living: when they talk to a friend, get into a fight, eat, look at the stars, make love, thread a needle, read a book. The formation of self will be unhappily skewed by the harmful ingredients fed in by negative contact experiences. Therapy helps to create a new balance among a person's selves by recognizing and eliciting beneficial contact experiences.

Particularly important in the therapy process are the intertwined roles of technical and common contact. Because therapy is preponderantly technological, it is important for us therapists to remember not to overplay the technology, which must always be coordinated with contact as it may occur in everyday living. Therapeutic learning must be applied in everyday living, and the contributions of common contact can be a bridge between the technical therapeutic sessions and the ordinary environment of the patient.

Because a great many gestalt therapists (including Perls, Hefferline, and Goodman, 1951; Polster and Polster, 1973; Zinker, 1978; and Yontef, 1993) have written on a broad range of contact principles, including the contact boundary, the contact functions, contact episodes, and the therapeutic experiments that foster improved contact, I will not repeat that material here. Instead I will address the distinctions and overlap between technical contact and common contact. The overlapping quality is evident in everything the therapist does, and the restoration of the common in what is primarily a technical enterprise will help to increase the humanization of psychotherapy technique.

Technical Contact

Technical contact consists of contacts that are specially reserved for the therapeutic situation, contact that would be quickly recognized as therapy. These contacts enhance the therapeutic potency of engagement, by accenting behavior, feelings, and memories and finding a place for them in the up-to-date context of the person's life.

The therapist gives clarifying explanations, designs experiments, provides special supports not commonly available, directs specially focused awareness, asks pertinent questions. These and other forms of accentuation, familiar to all therapists, would be seen as altogether unnatural and even intrusive in everyday life. Some people, irked when an acquaintance makes a therapy-like observation, will say, "Stop doing therapy with me"—presumably instead of just talking to me—emphasizing that what is acceptable in therapy may be intrusive in everyday life.

Unfortunately, the way people ordinarily talk to each other is not sufficient for changing selves. Our habitual ways of talking frequently register too little that is novel, impactful, or deeply relevant. Ever since Freud's technical innovations—hypnosis, free association, and transference—ordinary engagement has been overshadowed in therapy by technical innovations. So new and powerful a form of relationship was created by these techniques, and many more that have been developed over the years, that many therapists would find it amateurish to be an ordinary person with their patients. Why come to therapy for just another dose of ordinary engagement?

Freud recognized the inadequacies of ordinary engagements that provide experience after experience of skewed visions of one's self. He made historic attempts to remodel ordinary engagement for a more incisive and accurate illumination of the self. First he went far afield from common contact by using hypnosis; eventually he abandoned it, partly because the effects he wanted didn't endure. Even though he could technically induce surpassingly powerful experiences of memory and emotion, necessary though this seemed, these hypnotic experiences often failed to connect with the person's ordinary life and his sense of self.

Trying to get closer to the person's ordinary experience while still technically increasing the leverage for new experience, Freud next introduced free association. He saw it as a contrast both to the highly technical hypnosis and to ordinary conversation. But free association turned out to be a first cousin to hypnosis, similar for two reasons, each of which is still beneficial for psychotherapy even today. First, it created high focus on self experience; second, it created a disengagement from the broad context of the patient's life. While free associating, the patient could set aside everything in his life but the associations he was concentrating on, except for selected observations by the analyst about the meanings of the associations. The patient was directed away from ordinary engagement and was offered expressive innocence instead.

A further reinforcement to this form of concentration was Freud's introduction of the transference phenomenon, which came a step closer to common contact than free association. The technical and theoretical implications of transference guided the therapy relationship into a microcosmic representation of relationship. Expressions to the therapist achieved transcendent registration and generated a powerful intimacy both symbolic and experiential. But the heavily symbolic quality of the relationship blurred the more directly experienced aspects.

For an appreciation of the contrast between heavily technical transference and the less technical concept of contact, let us look at them as two poles. At one pole—contact—the patient talks to the therapist as the person the therapist actually is, a representation of common contact. At the other end of the pole—transference— the patient talks to the therapist as though he were someone from his past, often father or mother. These polar markers were evident in the case of Kevin, described in Chapter Five, who blurred the differences between me and his father, reducing the quality of our individualized experience.

The psychoanalyst and the gestalt therapist have historically approached this gap between past and present from opposite ends of the pole. The analyst has used the anachronistic contact to understand the patient's stuckness, accenting the point in the past where the distortions of contact began, expecting the insights to improve contact. The gestalt therapist, on the other hand, accents immediate contact with the therapist, trying directly to improve the quality of this contact. He expects this sense of immediacy will impel the patient forward step by step into new experience. This movement forward often paradoxically takes the person back to unfinished business from the past. We'll see how that works shortly, in an illustration from a session with one of my patients.

Though the procedures are significantly different—more interpretation for analysts, more focus on immediate experience for gestalt therapists—psychoanalysis and gestalt therapy hold one goal in common. They both try to restore the patient into the moment-to-moment stream of experience, rising beyond the stuck past into the evolving stream of current contacts.

One psychoanalyst, in trying technically to incorporate more current contact into his transference work, said about his method, "Though the tone is always gentle, the language is extremely confronting, giving the patient no chance to escape from the impact of what he is saying" (Davanloo, 1980, p. 106). *No chance to escape* is an apt way of heightening the contact between him and his patient. The theoretical implication is clear: for his patient's words to have impact, they must be part of a sequential progression that leads to improved contact. While giving high emphasis to the transference phenomenon, this analyst, by accenting current experience, corrected a common source of slippage in the psychoanalytic system. Merely interpreting the past provided too many escape hatches and allowed the person to avoid good-quality contact.

To clarify technical contact further, here is an example of a designed experiment where the accentuation of contact was achieved. Claudia, a forty-year-old patient, had just told me about a panic state when she had experienced sexual feelings for a friend during the previous week. This panic reflects the ups and downs of therapeutic change. She had originally entered therapy because her life was lusterless, governed by a dulled self. By this time she had become enthusiastic about her life, but now these sexual feelings had suddenly erupted, like a tic, from what I saw as a carefully controlled sexual self.

Getting at this combination of selves involved two processes: first, a new view of her sexual self, filling out some of the lost details; then, introducing some new contact that could have the vibrancy she needed without being taken over by the sexual.

The elaboration of her sexual self came through eliciting stories about her troublesome sexual experiences. When I questioned her, she remembered a time when she had to drop out of a course because she fell in love with the instructor; the feelings were unbearable. She told also of experiences as an adolescent when she had been followed by men. In addition to the deep sense of danger, she also felt puzzled: "Why me?" She also told me about other sexually driven relationships that were never actually sexually consummated. Her sexual pleasures with her first husband were the primary reason for marrying him, and it remained their only bond during the marriage. She made this bond through her vibrant sexual self, which was free within the limits of actual intercourse.

In listening to her stories, while she was giving greater recognition and registration of her sexual self, I came to the second requirement, of eliciting a new contact. Part of the problem seemed that her tight packaging of her sexuality made her vulnerable to overplaying natural moments of sexual interest. Over the time we had worked together, she was quite energetic and warm with me without any sexual overtones. I thought this unthreatened freedom to be enthusiastic was playing a part in changing her life from lusterless to enterprising and exciting. But, while this liveliness was quite evident, there nevertheless were certain deflections in her contact with me that could have been due to sexual fears. I had not addressed these because she was doing well in the way she was already relating to me.

Now, though, when she spoke of her panic at sexual thoughts about a friend, I thought it time for her to face me more directly. So, in the service of technical contact, I asked her to make up sentences beginning with the word *you*, directed to me. I hoped she would get either a more clearly registered sense of her safety with me or face whatever danger she might feel.

Not surprisingly, this usually verbal woman could not think of anything to say. As the session ended, I asked her to think about it. At the next session, she came with a list of fifteen short sentences. Simple as these sentences were, they did accentuate our contact, expressing new things to me and leading to key memories, which helped place her panic into context and enabled her to experience a new self. Here are a few samples:

> You frustrate me by asking the question [to make up the sentences].
>
> You do it intentionally to create my anxiety.
>
> You do it because you want to help me.
>
> You do it because you know the end result will be of benefit to you. [She meant "benefit to me." This slip of the pen was a lead-in to extensive discussion of how everything in her relationship with her mother was for her mother's benefit, even though her mother pretended it was for Claudia's—a good basis for distrust of anyone's motives.]
>
> You might feel sorry for me—but I don't think so!
>
> You remain solid regardless of my own place and I like that.
>
> You use words and feelings in a way that pleases me.

As she read these rather mild sentences to me, her contact became increasingly more vivid, as though the rheostat had been turned up.

Her face became flushed, but she was looking at me more confidently than ever. She seemed altogether at home with me, deference and deflection gone. Once she released her radiance into direct engagement with me, she felt upright and straightforward. Not only did the experiment uncover the difference between the glancing contact she was accustomed to and the direct contact she was now feeling—a new reference point for her adult womanliness—but it also opened her mind to tell me the story of when she started loving people only from a distance.

She remembered her grandfather, whom she adored. When she accompanied him on neighborhood errands, it seemed to her that he drew others to him like a magnet. What was so magnetic was not clear to me, since she described him as a very finicky man and one whom everyone feared, even as they admired him. He was quick to find fault with goods, people, and services. In spite of her adoration, she never actually got close enough to experience the togetherness that she had always craved and of which she had been deadly frightened.

After realizing this, she started to cry softly, with a sense of both the dearness of her grandfather and her deprivation, not the least overwhelmed by her emotional state. Then, when she was done crying, the psychological prize came—a new self realized. She said she felt equal to me for the first time. What a new thought!

This equal self—something she had always felt underneath—did not succumb to superficial manifestations of inequality, as with her dominant grandfather and my position as therapist. Our human positions joined together. The positions were not identical, of course, since there were all sorts of difference between us. But the equality is what mattered. It came from a simple meeting with me, without the prejudice or fear that had made her deferential and wary.

The major bonus was that the intimacy of equality had no implications for her of the explicitly sexual. In facing me she was no longer governed by her distant, powerless, inferior grandchild self, from which position she adored but was overwhelmed by the object of her adoration. As an equal she would not be swept away by me or dominated by me. The chances were increased that from a sense of equality, she would be less likely to feel swept away by some future sexual arousal.

Lest it seem that a designed experiment, obviously a technique, be the criterion of technical contact, I want to point out other technical factors not so easily distinguishable from common contact. My questions probing for Claudia's past sexual experiences were technically directed. My expectation that her panic came from a surge of unfinished business was theoretically based. Her safety with me was heightened by the boundaries of therapeutic engagement. Her ability to relate with me trustingly was enhanced by the continuity of our sessions, wherein she could do at one time what she could not have done at another. Clearly, though common contact is a large factor in therapy, technical contact is the dominant mode.

At its very roots, therapy's primary technical condition is that the patient's interests are given the highest priority. This is in contrast with everyday life, where the interests of people who communicate with each other generally have equal priority. Furthermore, the heavily studied understandings of the patient's dynamics and needs overshadow the spontaneous engagement of everyday living. Notwithstanding the rightful primacy of these technical considerations, I believe they have historically been a source of therapeutic rigidity, stiffening the nature of engagement so thoroughly that it has kept many therapists as well as many patients from saying the very things that need to be said. Technical contact thus sometimes stifles the emergence of rich new data for changes in the person's self structure. It is therefore valuable for us to recognize the key role of common contact, influential enough to make a significant difference in the therapy experience.

Common Contact

In spite of the century-changing therapeutic impact that Freud's innovations for technical contact produced, Freud himself did not .

always take the technical path his followers did. For example, among other reports of his common contact, he invited one patient, who had been loath to depend on her husband for money, to borrow the small amount necessary from him. She promised to do so but actually never did, preferring to pawn her jewelry rather than take money from Freud (Freud, 1957, vol. 2, p. 144). He also writes of giving another patient "a word or two upon the good opinion I had formed of him," which gave his patient "visible pleasure" (vol. 3, p. 316).

In a later writing, it must be added, perhaps burned by the complications of common contact, Freud pointed out the limits of ordinary relationship, particularly as to granting satisfactions. Not only were sexual relations with the therapist excluded, but he also said that other more subtle means of satisfying patients with favors and intimacy were to be only "sparingly granted." These restrictions have subsequently been interpreted to apply to such simple things as giving a patient a special appointment time, answering personal questions, or discussing topics not directly related to the therapy.

Part of the wariness about common contact is that the therapy experience requires a higher intensity of focus than is required in everyday life. The intense level of concentration can be quite fragile. The technically created focus may be corrupted by experiences that are too commonplace, overblown, and sentimental to be useful. Even so simple a distraction as a patient's mundane discussion with a secretary in the waiting room might siphon off the intensity of focus, which is a great asset for therapy.

But as with most human phenomena, common contact has both a positive and negative face. We must be careful to recognize not only the disruptions it may create but also the benefits that come from its discerning use. The necessary tension buildup is not invariably fragile. Including common contact may not only complement the technical, facilitating important therapeutic developments, but may also help to strengthen the transferability of changes in self from their occurrence in the therapy office into the situations of everyday life. Technical stylization may seem too unreal unless joined with the common contact of the world to which the patient must return and where she must find her therapeutic learning to be applicable.

Since common contact is more recognizable as a "natural" engagement, available at any time in everyday life, it would be important for therapy to include some easily recognizable contact qualities. Among them are kindness, curiosity, colorful and clear language, radiance of attention, endurance, gentle strong-mindedness, and many other interpersonal considerations that people seek in their everyday lives.

Each time the patient experiences the ordinary qualities of the therapist, this experience becomes a bridge between the extravagant awarenesses of therapy and the patient's own everyday experience. Except for certain therapists who are extremely talented technically, the overweighting of the technical may turn therapy stiff and mechanical. The common contact may come from something so simple as the use of ordinary rather than technical language; moments of sharing common values; references to local or national news events; an exchange of jokes; digression about a concert or a movie; opinions about the office decor; and the like.

Recently, I had a special experience of common contact. It was more extravagant than usual, but it serves to symbolize openness to the common. Even though it was strangely fortuitous, it also had clear therapeutic relevance. I had made a special appointment for a couple who could not come at their usual time. I arranged to see them early on a morning I normally do not see patients. My office is in my home and the office entrance is to the rear of the house. When the day came, I had forgotten about the appointment. So when the front doorbell rang, I answered in my robe. I was as shocked to see my patients there as they were to see me in my robe. After a brief delay while I changed into street clothes, we proceeded with the session.

At their next session, they both arrived in their robes (worn over their clothes) and we had a hilarious laugh. This is a couple who normally had a heavy relationship with each other. The woman was just emerging from a severe depression and the man had strong blocks in his sexuality. The robe caper was a marker of a new lightness they were developing and a signpost for continuing to enjoy their fun selves, too long in the background.

In recognizing the deeper therapeutic factors, so important and well known to therapists, it is easy to overlook the simple moments of contact, which may prove to be the fulcrum around which the session unfolds. All of these humanly common experiences happen every day in the work of therapists, and they should be given merited endorsement. These ordinary exchanges, which are often taken for granted, warm people into the more nuclear issues of living. Therapy does create incisive focus and it is indeed serious business—it must not be mistaken for an ordinary conversation. But the ordinary conversation is often an important introduction to the main event, perhaps even a major player in the event.

Here is a simple beginning of a session with Claudia. She greeted me by telling me she was recovering from a cold and then went on to tell about her experiences at a Colorado ski resort. She was chatting with me much as though she were talking to a girlfriend on the telephone. I joked with her, wondering whether her cold made her nostalgic for her original home in Switzerland.

The boundaries between technical and common contact are undiscernible in this session. It began with an ordinary conversation, showing no sign of the therapeutic event that was to come. My response to her had not been technical silence. Instead, by my casual remarks I implied I welcomed her talking about whatever she wanted to. Yet my casual reference returned her to Switzerland with significant effect.

Hints of storyline often appear uncannily in seemingly insignificant exchanges. The most ordinary remarks can prove to be seeds for pertinent thematic development. A few such experiences of fortuitous, unexpected therapeutic benefits will encourage us therapists to remain alert to the natural unfolding of important events.

We would do well to selectively yield to the common contact and not blindly assume it is a waste of time or an evasion of the serious business at hand.

At this early point in the session, however, none of these possibilities was evident. Claudia just went on talking further about her skiing trip, about the beauty of the mountain and the pleasure of physical exertion. With little guidance from me other than my focused interest and assenting attitude, she began to talk about a lifetime of neutralizing her experiences. Then her next words showed her to be transcending her guilt about pleasure and success and drinking them in.

"It was just breathtaking. We were sitting on this chair lift. In our group of learning-to-ski people was a young Dutch boy and the three of us were on this little lift and we were going up and I was going 'Oooh, oh, ooh' and we were all like 'Oh, ooh' as we were looking around us we were you know just in awe and I said, 'Isn't this incredible, I feel almost . . .'—I don't know if I said 'guilty' or like 'do I deserve to feel this good' and he said, 'This is how I want to be all the time.'"

At this point I spoke and said lightly, "If that's up for election, I would vote for it."

"That's right," Claudia responded, "this is how it should be all the time."

Through this common exchange, Claudia's own extrapolation system was facilitated. She built her story step by step, each one leading to her next thought. She went on to heavier stories about her struggle with her mother, who had always blocked her pleasures. Claudia had made a momentous choice when she left a miserable marriage to marry a man in America, leaving her children behind. She has had a happy marriage and the children are doing well, but her mother dug into her with disapproval.

After speaking about various ways her mother had blocked her pleasures, Claudia went on tell about a particular time when she returned to Switzerland on one of her frequent visits. She had arranged to pick her daughter up at school but the plane was late and she called her mother to tell her there was a good chance she would not get there in time. After accusing Claudia of typical inconsideration of others and emphasizing her own martyrdom, the mother begrudgingly agreed to pick the child up. But Claudia did arrive on time, and her daughter greeted her gloriously, clambering all over her and very proudly giving her a pin she had made in school.

Claudia then said to me, with a full flavor of her equality with her mother and no taint of victimization: "Well, my mother had a heart attack. 'Oh, yes, she gets a pin and she's not even here.' It's like she just went mad, I mean completely mad. Because, in other words, I [Claudia's mother] remained in this bad marriage for you and my brother and my sister and we don't give a shit about how she thinks and look what I've done and my kids are all over me. So she just . . . uh, I mean, I just didn't say anything. I just put my arm around my daughter. What can you say?"

Of course, many aspects of these exchanges with Claudia are worth methodological attention. Especially important are the moment-to-moment sequences, a part of the therapeutic technology described in Chapter Five. These sequences were propelled forward primarily by her own confidence that each of her remarks, no matter how common, could move forward, leading in valid transition to the next remark and then the next and then the next.

This confidence was supported without much sophistication on my part. I simply enjoyed each of her remarks and built on them with my interest in her nextness. Sometimes I expressed this interest lightheartedly, sometimes seriously, but always absorbed and hospitable to her storytelling. I offered personalized assent and minimal technical interference to the flow of her mind. I believe that each part of the contact between us had a lubricating effect on the development of Claudia's storyline and on her realization of her freedom from her mother's antipleasure incantations.

The existence of common contact may sometimes be problematic because the strategy of personal improvement permeates the therapist's behavior. If the therapist praises the patient—for a phrase well put, a courageous stand at work, or generosity to a parent—how is the patient to believe it when it may be said "only" for the sake of her improvement, as a technique for positive reinforcement, therapeutic support, mirroring, or alliance with the patient's strength? This is indeed a dilemma, and it is overcome by the therapist actually meaning what she says consistently enough that the honesty and perspicuity will register.

Yet there *is* a conflict of interests. Whereas some truths have a therapeutic advantage, others might be harmful, and I must take account of the difference. If a young man tells me he is bothered because other men sometimes mistake him for a homosexual when actually he is not, I, out of ordinary respect, am free *not* to offer the observation that he looks homosexual to me as well. Though he needs to explore his own feelings about homosexuality or how people's impressions unduly bother him, he doesn't need me to add observations that may intensify an already skewed self-image. Of course, the hurtful remark will occasionally be in the patient's best interests, facing him necessarily with an unwanted truth. But that is a matter of discernment, not a license to be insensitive.

A further example of the difficulty in coordinating truth with ordinary human kindness is the following. A patient asks the therapist, "Do you think I am boring?" Sometimes a yes answer may be therapeutically best because it may stimulate the patient to take his boring ways seriously and do something about it. But such simple accuracy might be rendered more artfully if the therapist were to say, for example, "What interests me more than whether you are boring is that you yourself seem so bored." Is that an evasion? Yes, but it also may be more to the point: it is his boredom that is making him boring. This answer gives him the active role of being bored, not only boring. It is also a kindness that does not cancel out the fundamental truth of what has been said. Though the patient is wise to be wary of statements that merely accommodate, he is also wise to learn how to discriminate between what is or isn't in his best interests.

Artistry in therapy is not a tape recorder version of what happens but the individualized accentuation that takes sensitive account of the other person's sense of self and the timing, circumstances, implications, receptivity, and consequences of the therapist's remarks. This is high ambition, indeed; so high as to invite disappointment. But such gentleness of expression recognizes truth to be art form, more than simple mechanics, and it guides the patient in common contact to aspire to personal respect.

Beyond Common Contact: Artistry

There are obvious complexities introduced by the contact imperative, sometimes clashing with the technical and professional requirements of therapy. Ordinary contact may either be insufficient or it may interfere with special technical powers that therapeutic innovations have produced. Consequently, needing to tighten up therapeutic technique in the face of slippery contact requirements, we therapists often leave the glorification of ordinary experience to artists—poets, composers, painters, who make their art a kingdom of reminders of the neglected depths of everyday existence. Still, therapists and artists are both engaged in the accentuation of human experience beyond ordinary perception. We therefore share common ground, and therapists can benefit from the skillful accentuation process that is the core of artistic creation.

May Sarton is one of these artists who know how to accentuate experience. In a poem about her own relationship with her therapist, who died, she accentuates a part of the relationship with a haunting line, repeated again and again: "Now the long lucid listening is done." Here are a few lines:

> It was not listening alone, but hearing,
> For he remembered every crucial word
> And gave one back one's self to be heard.

The warm-blooded bonding of patient with therapist suffuses Sarton and accentuates parts of herself not named. We can imagine that

her therapist's devoted listening and his sensitive and deep receptivity in recognizing the beauty of her poems confirmed at least her
writer self. She tells about his overtones of silence and his face,
which had been through the mill that grinds the coarser human
experiences down. She knows he has lived a life among people like
her and retained a mind of common concern; that he confirms the
merits of her poem and lights it up at its birth.

He provides a measure of dignity, giving proportion to her
mourning, to her rage and her shame and her anguish, each of
which may have merited naming as a self and each met with respect
and recognition and mutuality. The human experience reverberates
between the two of them, and she is fortified by his grasp of so many
key things going on inside her. He is a litmus test of self, affirming
her, creating realization in a world geared to pass her by. Much of
his gift to her comes not from what we ordinarily think of as therapeutic technique but rather from the common contact that good
people will offer each other.

For many people, the kind of homage that Sarton gave her therapist might come only with death or other extravagant events, the
sort of events that inspire people to accentuate experiences that
otherwise slip by. But May Sarton is also an artist. Artistry characteristically enlarges the familiar and speeds up the slow-paced,
moment-to-moment process that makes many important experiences imperceptible.

In contrast, those who are not gifted in registering experience find
that the gradual, unglamorous, almost unnoticeable experiences of
everyday life leave them with indistinct feelings that provide a poor
measure of their selves. People seek increased sensibility for the experiences of their lives, as Sarton's therapist, from the position of his
artistry, offered it. These experiences come alive in poetic or fictional
portraits—as they also do in psychotherapy—that funnel attention
and counterbalance the insensate gradualism of everyday life.

By their freedom to describe experiences with approximation,
exaggeration, and tall metaphor, writers offer therapists important

lessons in accentuation. Although not as free as writers to bend strict reality, therapists can nevertheless benefit from an expanded hospitality to the need for accentuation.

Therefore, the therapist must see that his role in accentuating experience is as familiar as psychotherapy itself. That role has been identified by every theory of therapy since Freud's use of interpretation and transference. There is plenty of room for therapists to share common ground with artists. Indeed they must do so, or see the most accurately perceived ingredients for self formation go down the drain.

Buber was one theorist who exalted contact and abstained from stale professional language and procedures. He fathered a poetically augmented understanding of the I–Thou relationship. Many would say he went too far in romanticizing contact, that contact really doesn't matter all that much. To portray engagement as a covenant, for example, seems a sentimental stretch to therapists who are engaged with their patients for a while and may never see them again. They would say that to put contacts with patients in the same dimension as the people who are the most dear to us—parents, children, spouses, friends—is an exaggeration.

However, Buber's ardent but theoretically persuasive language is consonant with the function of therapy as an enlargement of day-to-day experiences that are otherwise often desensitized. While the I–Thou experience is limited in its most manifest moments to special relationships, it belongs to many other moments where contact is sincerely felt but disregarded. The high focus inherent in therapy raises it from a casual, normal engagement to the excitement of personal revelation for which a lifelong dedication is not required. In therapy the Buberian I–Thou enlargements of contact make the self more recognizable and enduring.

Irvin Yalom (1989), more down-to-earth than Buber in presenting the details of his artful therapeutic engagement, resonates with simple humanity in his patient's lives. In *Love's Executioner*, he tells stories of his work much as a fiction writer might. Though we occasionally recognize the discord between his personal feelings and his therapeutic purposes, he successfully walks a thin line between his common contact with his patients and the technology of his specialized knowledge and specialized procedure. In doing so he wrestles with a dilemma for which no therapeutic theory can spoon-feed professionally assured answers.

With some patients, for example, to be exhortative might be intrusive; for others it might be just the right touch, demonstrating seriousness of caring, belief in their capabilities to handle the problem, the outdatedness of their stubbornness. Or it might simply painstakingly wear the person down to see at last the bare skeleton of how his selves are interacting with each other.

Professional savvy will warn therapists to be wary of dominance or premature stripping of a person's self hierarchies. But in the hands of the artist Yalom demonstrates himself to be, his spirit of engagement frees him to do what the patient's husband or brother or even close friend might never be allowed to do. The spirit rises above the technique, spotlighting for the patient the union of his interests with the therapist's and the mutual prospects for pathways to selves otherwise obscured. In the following excerpt, Yalom (1989) relates an exchange with a female patient who is futilely in love with a man who has rejected her:

> "But, Thelma, he's just a person. You haven't seen him for eight years. What *difference* does it make what he thinks of you?"
>
> "I can't tell you why. I know it doesn't make sense but, to the bottom of my soul, I believe that I'll be all right, I'd be happy, if he thought well of me."
>
> This thought, this core false belief, was the enemy. I had to dislodge it. I made an impassioned plea.
>
> "You are you, you have your own existence, you continue to be the person you are from moment to moment, from day to day. Basically your existence is impervious

to the fleeting thoughts, to the electromagnetic ripples occurring in some unknown mind. Try to see that. All this power that Matthew has, you've given it to him—every bit of it!" [p. 33].

We see here the common exhortation that any friend might offer: the anger, the protection, the inspirational language, the disbelief of her strange behavior—all in the technical service of creating fresh impact, of rescuing a person whose obsessional obduracy has created a quicksand that is dragging her down. What stands out in Yalom's interest in contact, as well as the technicalities of his therapeutic procedures, is his recognition of both his limits and his opportunities. He is not a wild man indulging his whims but a man who has coordinated his professionalized knowledge, using it to enhance personal relationship. While at all times trying to tune in to the implications of his words and his acts, aware and careful of the powers he is exercising, he nevertheless manifests the fundamental artistry required to walk the fine line between discipline and freedom of mind. While no license is given, there is also no depersonalization permitted.

Unfortunately it is very difficult to communicate practical means for creating this level of contact. Within the enlargements of personal drama and the common contacts that are major ingredients, there are clear risks of extravagance and other forms of distortion against which the therapist is in constant struggle. But those who retain their sense of proportion in integrating the familiar and the amazing will benefit from recognizing the overlooked contacts in people's lives.

The therapist readily honors the larger contact experiences, such as trust, generosity, terror, and grief. He may also artistically enlarge the miniature signs of unrealized contact, signs expressed in an easily dismissible moment of insight, a shrug of the shoulders, the slight evasions of the eye, or a tiny quiver in the chin.

He knows that great things are going on in the background of the person's attention, and he becomes a lookout, selectively drawing these things out when it is their turn to receive greater notice. He does this by pointed responsiveness, by recognizing the struggle for clarity, by honoring key things the person is doing. If there is a scream inside, he wants to be able to hear it. If there is a flush of pleasure that may easily be set aside, he will bring it back to life. If there is a discomfort with questions, he may ask about the discomfort or speculate about it or set up an experiment about it—or he may just stop asking questions.

One patient of mine would answer all my questions, giving me good information and warm interaction. But there was the smallest trace of discomfort, so tiny that I had let it slip by for a while. Then after listening carefully to the interesting and important content of his answers, I changed our direction from this content and asked him very simply whether he liked answering my questions.

Though he was surprised at the shift, he quickly realized what he had never directly thought about. He *always* feels that revealing things is somehow wrong. He remembered his father's secretiveness. His father felt conspiracy all around him, never frankly paranoid but always feeling that he was working in the camp of power-hungry capitalistic predators whom he wanted cut out of his life even though he served them every day.

My question did what art does. It opened into a simple sketch of my patient's anachronistic fear of revealing himself. That fear was so well disguised that it might pass as only a slight, even endearing, shyness. But it held one of the key guides to his wariness about his own life and discomfort with other people, just strong enough to scribble over his pleasures. The accentuation process starts with the complex nature of experience, artistic and real, the former magnifying the latter. It accepts that everything is exactly what it is, while at the same time being more than it seems to be. Through magnification we can honor the daily path people take slightly above the amazing undercurrent of their lives; above the fertility of one hundred thousand cells in the brain each emitting neuronal pulsations just below the threshold of awareness.

Pulsating in the background of psychology is the recent discov-eries of molecular biology about the complexity of neuronal forma-tion and its possible role in the formation of selves. This field of study is beyond the scope of this book. But these explorations offer the realization that each neuron is geared to awesome coordina-tions, yet always in danger of being out of step. This will give all of us second thoughts about the routine quality of any moment in any life. The multiplicity of experiences always facing the therapist, the familiar and the amazing, all giving dimension to the other, create a larger-than-life registration of reality than any one alone.

8

Empathy: The Mutuality of Self

As crucial as the role of contact is in the formation of selves, it cannot stand alone. It is interwoven with empathy and merger, which together compose a contact triad, circumscribing the experience of full contact. What empathy contributes to the contact triad is a sense of common experience and understanding among contacting people, one person reaching out to know another person's experience.

People not only need people, they need people to be on their side, teaming up with them, supporting them, enhancing them, confirming them. When a child fails to get empathy from his parents for his curiosity, for example, the formation of the child's curious self is impaired. Though empathy is not a requirement in the formation of selves—any registration of experience will be the raw material—it is nevertheless a significant lubricant because the feeling of mutuality encourages those experiences from which the self is formed. Without the parent's empathy, the curious child would be operating under a sense of isolation, a less fertile ground than empathic appreciation.

The empathic impulse may be evident early in life. There was an illustration of this in a newspaper report about a two-year-old child in nursery school, accompanied by his mother. As time passed one of the other children, whose mother was not present, began to cry. The first child walked over, took the second child by the hand,

and walked him over to his own mother. This simple empathic act would give support to the child who is crying. We can imagine that it would also contribute to his forming selves, perhaps his crying self, his needy self, his friendly self. It might also enhance selves forming in the helpful child: perhaps the generous self, the enterprising self, the managerial self.

Interweaving Empathy with Contact

The need for empathy permeates therapeutic theories but it has often lacked a full theoretical partnership with the concept of contact. The contact priority in gestalt therapy theory and the empathy orientation in the theories of Heinz Kohut and Carl Rogers represent contrasting and potentially exclusionary positions.

Kohut and Rogers have made empathy an explicit guide in their therapeutic work, with contact an implicit accompaniment. Gestalt therapy, on the other hand, has made the opposite choice, with contact an explicit guide while empathy has been implicit. Since empathy and contact are intertwined, to make one explicit while the other is implicit skews any theory and may mistakenly credit therapeutic results to one or the other. Kohut (1977, p. 36) recognized such skewing by Freud when he observed that Freud attributed his successes to empathically guided interpretation when actually he may have succeeded because of his contactfully powerful charismatic personality.

Though Kohut broadened and humanized psychoanalytic responsiveness, adding feeling for the patient to Freud's more dispassionate interpretation, his emphasis on empathy highlighted understanding and "vicarious introspection" (Kohut, 1977, pp. 252, 306). Even though the contact factors are always implied in the concern with "empathic responsiveness" (p. 254), Kohut wraps up his position with the belief that empathy is the essence of psychoanalysis.

An example of his movement toward contact is his revision of

the neutrality factor in psychoanalysis by defining it as "responsiveness to be expected . . . from persons who have devoted their
life to helping others with the aid of insights obtained via empathic
immersion into their inner life" (Kohut, 1977, p. 252). This perspective leaves broad options for therapeutic contact and represents
a significant contribution to therapeutic responsiveness, but he
underlines other priorities when he concludes by saying, "Here
then, to my mind—in . . . the introspective stance of the observer—
lies the essence of psychoanalysis; here indeed lay the essence
of depth psychology at the moment it was born" (Kohut, 1977,
p. 303). In another context, expressing similar priorities, he said,
"The central issue . . . is that it makes little difference what the analyst does so long as he understands what is going on in his patient"
(Ornstein, 1978, p. 552).

Rogers, who originated much of the contemporary emphasis on
empathy, also prioritized understanding. Though his writings are
filled with references to relationship and the importance of reaching the client with one's acceptance, what has always stood out is a
transcendent concern with tuning in to the nature of the other person. This was one of Rogers's most valuable contributions to the
humanization of psychotherapy. But the point/counterpoint
dilemma forced the empathy factors into the foreground and the
contact factors into the background. Rogers (1961) helped draw
that proportion when he said, "Acceptance does not mean much
until it involves understanding. It is only as I *understand* the feelings and thoughts which seem so horrible to you, or so weak, or so
sentimental, or so bizarre—it is only as I see them as you see them,
and accept them and you, that you feel really free to explore all the
hidden nooks and frightening crannies of your inner and often
buried experience" (p. 34).

With these emphases on empathic understanding, the therapist
must still contactfully say or do what will *reach* the patient and
reveal that he understands. How does he do this? Is it how he looks
at the patient? Is it his selection of words, describing the patient's

experience in a more recognizable way than ever before? Is it the suggestions he gives the patient for how to speak with a sulking friend? Is it with a daring question that the patient hoped nobody would ask and now is relieved to address? Is it guidance in how the patient might breathe better?

From the empathic position alone, the therapist may clearly understand and appreciate what the patient's feelings are like—discouragement, for example—while not addressing them with good-quality contact or by saying the wrong (untimely, ill-formed, distance-creating) thing. Until empathic experience is transformed into good-quality contact through appropriate words and deeds, it is incomplete. Though empathic understanding and empathic contact are closely linked, each arousing the other, this union is never assured. In the struggle for union between the two, the primacy given to understanding weakens the role of contact.

Gestalt therapy has been responsible for the opposite fallacy, giving its greatest attention to simple contact and, until recently, relatively little explicit recognition to empathy. This priority for contact is evident in gestalt writings generally. Perls and colleagues set the tone in a description of contact, which, though it implies empathy, does not get directly to it: "Let us understand contacting, awareness and motor response, in the broadest sense, to include appetite and rejection, approaching and avoiding, sensing, feeling, manipulating, estimating, communicating, fighting, etc.—every kind of living relation that occurs at the boundary in the interaction of the organism and the environment" (Perls, Hefferline, and Goodman, 1951, p. 229). Their definition of contact incorporates empathy, as they include sensing, feeling, and estimating, but there is no direct reference to the mutuality of minds implicit in empathy.

Yet gestalt therapy, through its principle of contactful sensibility to the state of the other, has called for contact to be as exquisitely sensitive as possible to the needs of the patient. Without the empathy represented in that principle, the contact may be of good quality but therapeutically off target, as in laughing at an inadvertently amusing remark when the patient feels devastated. One might argue that someone in good contact would not do that, but laughing at someone may be a quite good contact from the standpoint of a person who is unconcerned with the state of the person he's laughing at. Unempathic contact happens commonly. To romanticize good contact by assuming it would necessarily be empathetic may not fit the experience of a police sharpshooter, an astute commodities broker, or a thought-provoking lecturer.

Empathy does require mutuality; contact as contact requires only meeting. Adding the requirement for empathy helps guide the therapist to connect with the patient in terms of the *patient's* needs. Some gestalt therapists, now with diminishing voice, have in the past misconstrued contact to imply an independence from the other person, particularly when shunning accommodation to that person. The danger of accommodation, taken as excessive in-dwelling within the other person, is that it may deprive the patient of the therapist's authentic response.

A narrow view of contact, one that neglects empathy, would be a barrier to the deeper and enduring experiences of relationship. As Perls, Hefferline, and Goodman (1951) have said, contact actually includes "every kind of living relation" (p. 229). The gestalt intonations of respect for the needs of the other person are widely evident in writings and in practice. Yet the concept of the mutuality of minds comes in through the back door, eclipsed by the centrality of contact between one person and another.

No empathy theory can assume contact will be present as an inevitable partner. Similarly, contact theory must also give explicit attention to empathy. Neither can be taken for granted. Though there is some consolation in the natural unity between empathy and contact, there is no more assurance that contact will be empathic than there is that empathy will be contactful.

The problems of coordinating empathy and contact are so important to the therapeutic engagement and the distinctions so delicate that I am going to present an extended transcript of part of a session, to help clarify the nuances involved.

This was the last of four daily sessions, conducted as part of a therapy workshop. It centered around Dahlia's yearning to have a home and her conflict about giving up her work in a large city to live with her mate on the island where this home was located. Though she was very troubled about this possible turning point in her life, she placed great value on her faith that things just work out as they must. This almost magical trust represented a self that carried within it this guiding principle of her life. We might call it a have-faith self, because it was so dominant. Now, however, this faith was wavering, and her anxiety about the seemingly hopeless task of orchestrating vocation, finances, family, and social factors was increasing.

The incongruities did not seem hopeless to me, and I observed empathically that usually her faith and her goals were more synchronized than they were now. She replied that she should only have the faith to let go, without knowing what would happen. She sounded both wistful and discouraged.

I empathized with her dilemma. At the same time, I believed that she was not registering a key conflict of this have-faith self with her accomplished-woman self. I also thought she was not registering the legitimate struggle between wanting a home, another deeply imbedded self, and simultaneously wanting her work. I hoped she could encompass my empathy with all these selves, but at this point her faith was still more important to her than the consideration of any other selves. Still, I tried to introduce her to her other selves.

ERV: One of the things that stands out in what you're telling me is your life of faith in which you, who I see as a very discerning person, don't really know what's happening, that you don't know what guides you. You know that you land on your feet but you've never measured the jump or built up your muscles. [Actually she has—very well—but does not take it into account.] I'm aware of people who do well in having faith. Yet, I personally want to know what factors enter into what. I don't want to interfere with your style. Yet, in a way you're asking me to do that. Some of the questions I would ask you don't fit into the [faith] mode you're accustomed to.

DAHLIA: Yeah, I think you're right and I don't want to be particularly different than how I am.

ERV: How do I join with you then [in creating change] when in a sense I feel commissioned [by therapeutic responsibility] to do the opposite of what you really want?

DAHLIA: *(Moves around uneasily)* I don't know. I don't know. Do you feel like I've put you in a difficult spot?

ERV: I don't mind the difficulty, but I don't really want to ignore the contradiction. Since I'm just telling you what's on my mind, I'm playing it now the way you play it, by faith, just going to let things happen even though it's not my natural style. So, you've got a convert.

DAHLIA: *(Big laugh, in which I join with her.)*

ERV: In a way what I'm doing is, through *my* faith, in a way, bringing right into the foreground the contradiction that you probably live with. The contradiction between faith and knowing, between freedom and purpose, between the noble savage and the accomplished woman.

I believed, as you can judge from the transcript, that there was no clear path to empathy with Dahlia. The struggle between empathy for her faith exactly as she states it, which is a form of fixed self formation, and my empathy for her unspoken internal conflicts taxed our relationship. I wanted to carve out a mutuality in which I respected her feeling tones and philosophical guidelines while at the same time honoring my own inferences. I felt that if I abandoned them, that might make my empathy a one-sided, even mechanical, accommodation. I am, after all, commissioned to exercise my discernments so that she may discover options of selves that she has dismissed.

Saying she did not want to change her reliance on an unknowing faith could box me in before she could even know what form my contributions might take. I could only be empathic with the faith side of her to a point, and so I trickily challenged her boundaries by joining my own faith in my flow of ideas with her faith in just letting things happen. She was suddenly caught in a paradoxical bind since my faith was that she would come to realize faith was not enough. By laughing at the sudden twist from potential alienation to my peculiar conversion to her way of thinking, we confirmed our paradoxical union.

There are noteworthy swings between my empathy with her position exactly as it is, which is often taken as the empathic stance, and my facing her from a different empathic stance, my empathy with the important role of exploration, knowledge, and accomplishment in her own life, which she strangely dismisses. Since any patient is complex and cannot see all that she is, the therapist may need to summon her valuable though unrecognized self, in this case her accomplished self. To empathize only by agreement would be an unreliable and flavorless empathy. The patient should not be treated as one-sided when she is not.

Fortunately, she forgave me for not manifestly seeing things her way. The differences between us were expressed in simple contact, which any two people might have without either position set into a definitive mold. Through this respectful contact, I believe she felt my sense of union and resonance with her while knowing also that I was not showing merely professionalized empathy. The bite that our differences offered sharpened the prospects for novelty, which any therapy requires.

At this point in the session we talked for a while about the noble savage versus the accomplished woman, the noble savage being another way of describing the self that required a primitive, even magical, faith. This led her to acknowledge many actual accomplishments and actual plans she had been working on and to talk about her practical need for money. Then, in a key development, she realized why she felt so adamant about taking her life on faith.

Her objection to knowing and examining started from her mother's overbearing insistence on knowing everything about her and demanding explanations about all of her behavior. If Dahlia had allowed this kind of examining, it might have cramped her freshness. As I saw her now—a fresh, vibrant, straightforward person—these qualities had survived the struggle with her mother. She did not seem in much danger of losing her individuality.

Nevertheless, from her chronic wariness, she was feeling this core of danger again. As she talked about this deeply felt wound, she cried out to me about not wanting to be hurt. Just referring to the wound she was crying about, she said she felt "a deep moaning pain" and an almost primordial sense of "home." She yearned for return to a home she never had, a deep self entity, and told me about her early confrontations with the absence of home. At this point, I resonated with her feelings about home, empathically expressing my own sense of home and affirming it through body similes.

ERV: And all the fun in the world doesn't eliminate the importance of being home, whatever you might do, whatever you might accomplish. Home is almost like a part of the body, like your heart or your lungs.

DAHLIA: Is it? Is it?

ERV: It is for me. I think it is for most people. It's a little easier to transplant a home than a heart but it's indispensable. You say "Is it?" in a very touching way. Have you been wondering whether you should be feeling this way?

DAHLIA: I guess I've been wondering if I've ever been at home.

ERV: Aaaahhh. So it's a longing to be home at last.

DAHLIA: But we never had a home when I was little.

ERV: What were the circumstances?

DAHLIA: My dad was a preacher and we lived in other people's homes. We'd live there for a while and then we'd move whenever the bishop told us to move.

ERV: So there were a lot of moves?

DAHLIA: Uh-huh. Four before I left. But I remember that sense of realizing that none of it was really ours and that it never felt like home and my parents never felt like home.

ERV: Which is another part of it, isn't it? Can you say more about that?

DAHLIA: I don't really know why I even said it.

ERV: But you did mean it, didn't you?

Here, except for the initial body similes accentuating her home-loving self and the primal importance she gave to home, my responses were largely background. In the rather mild questions and great interest, my empathy was more evident than my contact. When she became momentarily confused about why she said her parents never felt like home, the encouragement I gave her that she did mean it was a combination of empathy for her feelings as she had expressed them and a belief she needed simple empathic affirmation of the absence of home rather than an exploration of it. Being of like mind with me, she nodded about meaning it, that her parents never felt like home.

She then went on, without probing from me, to tell me about her feelings about home as she experiences them in her present circumstances. She develops the theme of home in detail, partly through the natural evolution of her thoughts and partly through the encouragement she felt by our like-mindedness and my specific instructions. The instructions and encouragement were built on empathy as they moved her into directional options and to the validation of her powers to get what she wants.

DAHLIA: I was just remembering what it feels like for me to drive home. Last year for my birthday I almost killed myself driving home. I wanted to be home for my birthday and it's in February and we had this horrible snowstorm and nobody drove at all during those days in. . . . Everybody stopped driving, the freeways were horrible and I decided to drive home 'cause I wanted to be home on my birthday. It took about twelve hours. I didn't make it really—my car went off the road in the middle of the night in the snowstorm. I walked home. It just felt so important to be there.

ERV: At your place?

DAHLIA: Yeah.

ERV: That's a very deep feeling—home. Your heart can create a home.

DAHLIA: But you see, my heart's only created enough space for me, really, I think. Does that make sense to you? (*She cries.*)

ERV: I think it makes sense. I'm not clear how that is for *you*. I don't know exactly where you're missing including others. You said your heart creates a home for you . . . a kind of constancy, a nest, a refuge, a dependable pleasure when everything else fails, there's that—all of that. (*As Erv speaks, Dahlia smiles and cries and laughs as if feeling pleasure.*)

DAHLIA: It's like that feels so new.

The newness is what makes her need so risky and odd, even as she suddenly realizes she is *already* doing what she still sees as a dream for the future, driving toward a home that she is already creating and reaching. Therapy often provides recognition that one is already doing what one wants to do but hasn't yet assimilated it or put it into the level of action required for fully experiencing it. Further description helps to flesh out her inclusion of home to the point of an increased sense of reality. She goes on to verbalize this increase.

DAHLIA: It's like sometimes I just walk through the house and I look at things and I think (*sobs*) that chair could stay there for years if I didn't move it.

ERV: Yes.

DAHLIA: No one's going to come and say it's theirs, and my plants, they will be there. But I dream about it not being there.

ERV: Do you literally?

DAHLIA: I dream about it all being taken away.

ERV: By "dream" do you mean you actually have dreams about it or you imagine it?

DAHLIA: Both. I guess I dream mostly about not being able to make it back. I always have these holocaust dreams that there would be a war and I won't make it back.

ERV: You've been making it back now for two years, does that not register?

DAHLIA: It seems like an incredible thing every time I do it.

ERV: Incredible meaning beautiful or terrible?

DAHLIA: Beautiful. Yeah . . . it's like whenever I get off on the other side of the ferry I go, "Oh my God, I'm almost home."

ERV: I used to feel that every day when I had my office in downtown Cleveland. I could hardly wait to get home. I could remember the feeling of knowing Miriam was going to be there and the house. . . . I still feel that way. There's never a time I go anywhere—and I go to a lot of places where I have great pleasure—that I ever feel "I wish I could stay here longer" because I always feel how good it will be to get home.

DAHLIA: And then you let yourself feel it.

ERV: I don't feel it all the time. But I feel it when I'm packing my bag, when I call the airport to reconfirm my reservations. What I'm wondering is how you might put together the deliciousness of home with its dependability and everything else you might also do as being yours to do. Were you able to hear what I'm saying now?

DAHLIA: Something about how do I hold onto the sweetness of what I'm doing and know that I have home. I think that's very important. It's so important that it feels like that's what my entire life is about right now.

ERV: They're both real. The sweetness of what you're doing and the reality of your home which you have done prodigious things to create. You created it. It didn't come out of the air or out of spirit, you mentioned a number of things you did, you did, I mean *you* did to create.

Dahlia smiles and nods, taking it in. But I want her to take it in more fully and dependably, so I go beyond my empathy with her. I give her specific instructions for expression and further opportunity to experience her home-oriented self in direct contact with me. Through this contact I expect she will more fully register her realizations with greater detail and greater retainability.

> ERV: Will you try these words? You don't have to, but let me tell them to you and see whether you want to just try out the words. "I do have a home."
> DAHLIA: (*Sobs, big sobs, no words. After a long time, she fans herself.*) Whew, that one knocked me down.
> ERV: Well, let's try again. See if you can play with those words. "I do have a home."
> DAHLIA: I feel like I could tell you the address. (*laughs*)
> ERV: Well, that's part of it.
> DAHLIA: There's fruit trees. I feel like I could describe it.
> ERV: Just go with it just the way you're doing it. It's a better way to do it than my words.
> DAHLIA: It's beautiful. Yeah. Well, first of all, there's Jason, who waits there for me and he usually walks out of the studio and he comes over to the car and he's always smiling and he says, "Queenie, I'm so glad you're home." Then he picks my things out of the car and the house is always beautiful and he's got something for dinner and he welcomes me home.
> ERV: Yes, well that makes it all the more clear that you do have a home.
> DAHLIA: (*smiles and laughs*) Does it?
> ERV: To me it does. I think it does to you too.

DAHLIA: It feels like this little mantra that I could say. I have a home, I have a home, I have a home.

Fascination, Empathy, and Boundaries

In this session, my empathy, largely inseparable from my contact with Dahlia, was manifested in the particular ways our minds met. A key factor in our meeting, never put into words but always evident, was my feeling of fascination with everything Dahlia said. She was a person of uprightness and responsiveness, a spunky child in a grown woman. Everything she said seemed to come from the depths of her with a simple directness, a sense of personal transparency. Such fascination as I felt is one of the factors uniting contact and empathy for it bespeaks both. To be so absorbed in contact, as I was, one is closest to being in the heartbeat of the other person, a resonance that is the touchstone of empathy.

Though empathy is normally identified by the substantive understanding and articulations of the other's state of mind, the nonverbal fascination that the therapist registers must not be overlooked as a carrier. His knowledgeable attention, emanating from a person of presumably good taste and dependable honesty, will credit the patient's worth.

Though Dahlia was fascinating in her own way, all patients will have qualities that are uniquely their own, and the therapist's fascination, to be dependable, absorbs these particulars. A patient who is arrogant requires a fascination with his arrogance; perhaps its vibrancy, perhaps its audacity, perhaps its role in the unfolding life story. Other patients are fascinatingly frightened; perhaps immobilized into a stare, perhaps verging on a scream, perhaps clinging to the prospect of rescue. Others will fascinatingly face the therapist with a prove-yourself attitude, cutting down his most brilliant observations, asking for the ungivable, face fixed into a sneer.

Fascination is not a given for any therapist; for many it would be an unfamiliar experience. But we therapists are luckily in a field that, like the arts, gets right to the heart of what matters to people. Unfortunately we must also overcome the interference of the complexities of therapeutic technology and make them our friends instead of our tyrants.

Furthermore, respect for the limits of the patient helps lower the risks that accompany the narrowing of attention and make it a hazardous force. The range of the empathic experience built into fascination is limited also by personally and professionally permissible boundaries for the therapist's experience. Fascination in any discipline must conform to the requirements of the job, whether it be a geological dig, an acting assignment, or international diplomacy. The more experience one has in coordinating the expansion of these boundaries of fascination with the job at hand, the less the risk.

To familiarize oneself with the expansion of boundaries, the therapist opens himself to experiences as a gourmet might to a large range of food tastes. As a gourmet of experience, the therapist remembers, registers, and savors experiences that others might quickly pass over. For me, in this session with Dahlia, to recognize her surge for a home in my own feelings of home and to increase the fascination of this meeting of our minds was simple and natural. There were no undertones of her seeing home as I saw it. On the contrary, my experience helped me to understand hers and then take hers a step beyond her misty wish into one that could be concretely described and personalized as her very own need.

Stretching the therapist's I–boundaries (Polster and Polster, 1973, pp. 107 ff.) opens him to hospitality for a large range of experience. Only within the boundaries of personally permissible experiences—those that do not violate the therapist's sense of self—can he allow the high-quality contact that is important for fruitful empathy with the patient's experience. Many therapists are already of broad mind when they enter the field, already knowing and accepting feelings and behaviors that many people would have dismissed as alien. Criminality, rebelliousness, confusion, panic, despair, laziness, lying, fear, narcissism; these and all other sources of personal trouble seek a host in the therapist. Without this hospitality, only the most exceptional person could do therapy in any but a mechanical way.

Therapists are commonly drawn more subtly than we often realize into our own previously formed I–boundaries. For example, the therapist who cannot allow silence in sessions because he esteems talking will have a harder time being empathetic with a silent person than a therapist who regards silence as valid behavior. Even though allowing silence because of its professionally understood validity, a person whose habits of mind depreciate silence will not be as likely to be poignantly empathic with a silent patient. Having been instructed to respect silence, the therapist may, without empathy for the silence, enable the silent person to emerge freely from the silence. But such permission may be empathy once removed. Such secondhand empathy has a partial impact but probably not the mind-altering leverage of a more directly experienced empathy.

With Dahlia my directly experienced empathy came fortuitously through the meeting of our minds on the thematic issue of home. Part of my appreciation of her need for a home was registered through just following the things she had said. It was a bonus, though, that the disclosures of my own experiences with home coalesced with hers. What often plagues many therapists is their understanding of others through principle when they believe they haven't had a firsthand knowledge of the other person's experience. But the therapist alerted for firsthand experiences will find that they often do arise somewhere along the road, unrecognized. A patient ridiculing his parent may not at first touch the therapist's own experience until the therapist remembers a cartoon or a friend's stories about his parents. Well timed, these vicarious experiences may carry a great sense of mutuality.

The risk in the therapist's use of firsthand experience is that he may put ideas into the patient's head that don't belong there—not faithful to the actual needs of the patient. With Dahlia, that could have been true. My intuition was that offering my own experiences only added dimension to feelings that were natively hers and that could only be sharpened and enhanced by her sense of commonality with me. That is, of course, a judgment call, something all therapists must make and live by.

There are many avenues for the therapist to stretch his I–boundaries and thereby become open to the stories people want to tell. Many nonprofessionals already have this talent naturally. We all know people in our daily lives who appear to be magnets for stories. Towbin explored this phenomenon by taking out an ad in a local paper, inviting those in whom others frequently confide to be interviewed by him. One of the interviewees said, "Ever since I can remember I always . . . people always confided in me, and I think part of the reason is that I listen to people. I talk a great deal, but I also listen to people. I'd say that over [fifty percent] of the population don't listen to other people. They just don't listen . . . but I do listen to people, and I think coupled with that I have a great understanding, because for some reason, I don't know, I have an awareness of people's feelings because I'm very self-aware" (Towbin, 1978, p. 339).

One of the most familiar avenues for therapists to tap into this openness to experience is their own therapy. They recapture some of their own diminished sense of what they have experienced during their lifetimes and they discover what it is like to be a patient. Another source is the illuminations offered by the arts, which stretch human understanding and offer a vicarious opportunity to experience the lives of a large range of people. For example, a painting by Francis Bacon may well teach the therapist something about personal terror.

Further, the therapist may engage in his own explorations for stretching his range of experience: travel, talking to many kinds of people, probing for what the people in his life think and feel, and, in general, keeping his eyes and ears open for what people are always saying about themselves. This kind of observational detail is very familiar to the writer who keeps a journal of experiences and observations, but therapists normally give most of their attention to professionally organized learning opportunities.

With all this as background, the final and most direct source of expansion of both I–boundaries and empathy is being a student of what our patients are teaching us about themselves. The patient unknowingly seeks to teach the therapist about himself and hopes the therapist will be a good student. It is a curious phenomenon that the teacher (the therapist) teaches the student (the patient) to be his teacher. Within such a learning process, empathy is natural, both as a lubricant and as an accomplishment.

Two further principles are helpful in guiding the therapist to empathy. Informally stated they are: What is, is and It takes one to know one.

What Is, Is

Gestalt therapy's inclusion of empathy has been particularly evident in its paradoxical theory of change, which proposes focusing on the already existing characteristics of the patient rather than directly "changing" him. If one resonantly accepts things as they are, this will impel the patient forward into new experience. Therefore, the therapist is called on to see the patient as he is, hear him as he is, talk to him as he is, sense him as he is, feel the effect of his actions and feelings, identify with him, and create a union.

A belief in the paradoxical theory of change is not easy to maintain. First of all, stuck people don't usually change along prescribed pathways, so it may be difficult to see change. Furthermore, when changes happen they are not as large as either patient or therapist wants, nor do they always seem like the right changes. The therapist must therefore be open to recognize change as it actually happens, irrespective of these prescriptive standards. Goals, though necessary for orientation, may also interfere with staying with things as they are, causing people to discount everything but what satisfies rigid criteria of good accomplishments.

The discounting phenomenon also reflects lost empathy with one or another of the patient's selves. The patient who is depressed has lost empathy with himself, discounting all his assets. The person who is arrogant may have lost empathy with his passive self or his grieving self. The person who jumps to conclusions may have lost empathy with his confused self or his frustrated self. The person who is repetitive may have lost empathy with his novel self or his misunderstood self.

When the patient's empathy for his own selves is restored, this will often warm him into a patience not so easily achieved where empathy is missing. Empathy when aroused has a lubricating effect. It reduces premature requirements for change, leaving the patient room and support for the ongoing process.

To stay with what is and to experience the accompanying empathy, the therapist faces another, opposite, obstacle. In resonating with what is, the complication is not only the patient's stuckness but the fact that one thing always follows another. Whatever *is* will soon be something new. The urge to move beyond *is*-ness is compelling, part of a natural surge to move from one moment to the next. This urgency makes it difficult to reside in the other person's already existing experience.

For example, if a patient is mourning the loss of a loved one, the therapist will often want to salve the mourning person instead of empathizing with his pain, thus mistakenly bypassing this empathic option. But it is not an open-and-shut case. A measure of empathy is also directed toward resolution of the mourning because the inconsolable patient does also have a need for resolution and may even be asking for relief. However, the most immediately faithful empathy is to understand that one may need time to live in pain; that one is best released from it only when the necessary intermediate feelings have had their day.

Empathy thus requires artistry in selecting from a broad range of needs and actions those that are the most prominent needs of the other person. *What is, is* runs into continuing contact, where new experience keeps on flowing. Whatever the empathic experience may be at one moment, continuing contact creates a major feedback system for keeping the empathic person on a moving track.

There is yet another consideration. Not only do the requirements for empathic engagement change from moment to moment,
but multiple experiences may simultaneously call for empathy.
Commonly, one thinks of empathy as one person seeing things as
the other does, but if that empathy is in disregard of the patient's
complexity, it might be an empty empathy. Instead of seeing things
simplistically just as the patient does, the therapist must seek a wider
path. Rather than narrowly empathizing with a patient's depression,
for example, the therapist may empathize instead with his sub-
merged talents. If this patient, mired in worthlessness, has given
hints of his musical skills, it is just as valid, in principle, for the therapist to say how frustrating it must be to abandon such talent and
to want to know more about his musical self than to understand-
ingly observe how futile life may seem.

The accuracy of empathy must be confirmed in the contact. If
the therapist believes a patient needs sympathy, the therapist may
discover, when offering it in contact, that the patient is offended by
sympathy and actually needs astute critique. In the interweaving
between empathy and contact, people build on each other's incomplete understandings, creating a mutuality that is continuously
tested and confirmed. Where the empathy and contact are not
joined, the patient is left with incomplete engagement, often
because of poor contact and poor empathy.

From this perspective, empathy is tailored to stretch the person
as well as to mirror him. If the therapist empathizes only with the
patient's manifest priority or his momentary priority, he will risk a
continuation of the repetitive thematic structure with which
patients get stuck. Thus empathy is more than routine acceptance
but calls for the imaginative entry into the broad parameters of the
patient's self structure.

Lydia, for example, had trouble talking to her mother, who was
self-centered and ungiving. Lydia's eight-year-old son was physically
handicapped and restricted to a wheelchair. Lydia's mother had
been offering Lydia her father's van, which he no longer used. Lydia

repeatedly turned down the offer, responding from the independent self into which she had grown. One day she discovered that if she had an automated wheelchair it would be advantageous to have the van. She then told her mother she would accept the van. At this point, her mother said her father occasionally needed the van, after all, and began to set conditions, including paying for taxis when her father needed transportation. Lydia, flabbergasted and furious, refused the conditions. Once again her betrayed self appeared.

In response to her mother's betrayal, tantalizing then rejecting Lydia, my empathetic reflex was to side with the betrayed self and the pain and immobilization Lydia felt. Resonating with her immobilization, I became as furious with her mother as Lydia was and expressed it with a cantorial eloquence, bespeaking her plugged-up feelings. She was revived by this and emerged beyond her betrayed self.

At that point she remembered afresh what she had actually said to her mother, surprisingly direct. When her own powers became clear again, my empathy shifted to her neglected independent self. Her independence had become obscured because Lydia can be as bitchy as her mother. In fact this bitchiness is high enough in her hierarchy of characteristics to warrant the name of bitchy self. From this position she needed to get exactly what she wanted in the way she wanted it. When she couldn't control her mother to get it, she would forget her own strength and be altogether deflated. She realized this, and she began to see how often her insistence on getting exactly what she wanted in other situations too had gotten her into trouble.

This switch in empathy—from the pain of her betrayal into empathy for her need to be independent blurred by her need to control her mother—reflects the fluidity of *what is* and calls for therapeutic judgment. Lydia was a lot more capable in actuality, as well as potential, than she could realize when disappointment took over. As our understanding developed further, to be independent of her mother meant letting her guilty mother off the hook, something she didn't want to do, even though keeping her on the hook meant weakening herself. To keep her mother guilty she had to distort the urgency of her need for the van when actually she was handling her life well. Replacing my empathy for the benumbing betrayal was my empathy for her accomplishments. This signaled her to a change of heart, from helpless bitchiness to the security of actual accomplishments.

It Takes One to Know One

The second rule of empathy is that *it takes one to know one*. Because of those experiences in my life that are relevant to yours, I feel more like I know you and understand the process you are going through. Nevertheless, as unique beings, it is plain that any mere appliqué of our own experiences to those of another person has to be partly inaccurate. It is therefore necessary that I allow my imagination and extrapolation to help ascertain how my firsthand knowledge of life may relate to your unique experience of it.

For example, having had my heart broken in a failed love relationship may help me to understand why a patient of mine avoids relationships with women, perhaps even has a heartbroken self. But it may just as easily send me off on an irrelevant track. This patient may be avoiding women because they always dominate him and cause him to grovel; he may not ever have been heartbroken. His lifetime of domination, with its potential of a dominated self, requires me to imagine the effects of domination, even though that experience may have been only a minor factor in my own life.

Clearly, authenticity of empathic understanding is not limited to manifestly common experiences. It is obviously possible for authentic empathy to exist among people who may be widely different in background. Men, for example, can be empathic with women and vice versa; an American therapist can be empathetic with a Polish immigrant; a mild person with a violent one. The benefits of empathy, similarities or differences notwithstanding, require that we carve out a common perspective. The sense of mutuality doesn't always come from previously common points of view. It may come only developmentally, from careful tracking of each remark with empathically interested inquiry or commentary.

Sooner or later, as this process of putting himself into the patient's position unfolds, the common ground between patient and therapist will become more and more evident. The reason for this is that the greatest differentiation among people exists in the more peripheral experiences. As we move deeper, the common ground is more strongly felt. Everyone cries, for example. Everyone has been defeated. Everyone is overjoyed at new personal freedom. Everyone has been in terror. Thus as the sequences of experiences proceed and the deeper experiences are met, the therapist, alert to their inevitable appearance, finds this common understanding, creating a more effective empathy.

If the therapist knows what shyness is like from his own experience of it, he is already halfway to empathy with a shy person. If the therapist knows the struggle to prevent himself from crying, he is more easily empathic with a patient having that struggle. If the therapist's father died when he was seven, he knows firsthand what the loss of father is like. But though this self-experience of the therapist is vital in the experience of empathy, in order for it to qualify as authentically empathic, the therapist must connect his own sense of mutuality with the patient's actual and unique experience.

As my wife and I have previously written, "The therapist also plays from his own feelings, like the artist, using his own psychological state as an instrument of therapy. Naturally, just as the artist painting a tree has to be affected by that particular tree, so also must the psychotherapist be tuned in to the specific person with whom he is in touch. It is as if the therapist becomes a resonating chamber for what is going on between himself and the patient" (Polster and Polster, 1973, p. 18).

The characterization of the therapist as a "resonating chamber between himself and the patient" combines the concern with commonality between the two and their individuality. Kohut (1985) has similarly addressed this resonance when he wrote that empathy is "the resonance of the self in the self of others" (p. 222).

On a closing note, I am reminded of a session where the line was thin between commonality and differentiation between myself and my patient. This woman was excessively anxious about teaching her first course in college. I resonated with her feeling and remembered how, when I was six, I believed I could not learn how to play the piano because I thought lessons were reserved for those who already knew how. Telling her this analogy helped her to experience my empathy about her anxiety. Finding herself not alone and feeling I knew her experience through my own, she thus came closer to understanding that she does not have to know everything about teaching in advance of doing it.

The extrapolation from my experience, which was actually quite different from hers, worked because of both the differentiation and commonality between us. The differentiation was experienced as contact and the commonality as empathy. But if I told of an experience that was not pertinent to hers and did not honor her individuality, it could as easily have been experienced as a sop and been a drag on her therapy.

9

Merger: The Union of Self

In our highly individualized society, it is easy to neglect people's basic need to belong. This need is evident even in the healthiest people and gnaws at the heart of those who fail to satisfy it. Yet most therapies have been private, face-to-face experiences focusing on the individuality of the patient. Therapists generally expect that if a patient's individuality is restored, she will find a way of belonging. However, in point/counterpoint relationships, as we have seen before, when one side is taken for granted, the other backgrounded side becomes diminished. If we want to handle the paradoxical needs for individuality and belonging, we have to take account of both.

I am proposing the concept of merger as a counterbalance to individually oriented therapeutic goals, such as self-awareness, self-actualization, introspection, self-exploration, freedom of choice, and personal responsibility. Merger takes its place in the contact triad, joining contact and empathy in rounding out the conceptual foundation of interpersonal relationship.

Merger is a natural function. It occurs because the contact boundary is a permeable boundary. Each person not only meets the other at the boundary through simple contact and understands the other through empathy but enters into the other person through merger. Each person is always crossing over the contact boundary or absorbing the other inside her own boundary. This is evident on the most elemental level. If I hear you, your words have entered me, with both psychological and neurological effect, perhaps micro-scopic, perhaps significant.

Such simple moments of merger are the building blocks of self formation, as people enter their influence into each other's sense of self. In merging with another person, people may learn from each other, they may form partnerships, and they may experience belong-ing. These experiences at the permeable contact boundary infiltrate into each person, creating a larger identity than what is felt by any individual alone. "I am I" and "you are you" turns into "we are together."

This merger may be only minuscule, as in seeing a stranger cross the street, or it may be deep, so deep for some people that they can't get the other person out of their system. The deep merger may be beautiful, as in the case of a great marriage or business partnership, where the selves of the merging person are being continuously con-firmed and extended in the merger with the other. The person in this happy circumstance can, in a sense, join herself with the trustworthy other, opening herself up to the partner's leverage for contributing to the self, sometimes confirming it, sometimes changing it.

This merger may also bring misery, as in a death or dissolution of a deep relationship, where the person is so intimately entwined with the other that her own sense of self goes down the drain. A key corollary of the merger factor in contact is that good-quality contact is possible only where that risk to the existing selves is accommodated. Since merger offers both risk and benefit, the answer is not so simple as would be given by a therapeutic priority for indi-viduality. It includes a judgment about the benefits of trading indi-viduality for joining functions with another person.

I was faced with this choice between merging and individuality when a patient phoned me in a panic about some emergencies she was going to have to cope with while out of town for two weeks. As we talked, she became relieved of her anxiety. But this successful resolution seemed to accentuate her merger with me because she then wondered how she would handle the time away, alone.

Did my help make her more vulnerable because she now felt she needed me? I didn't think so. She needed me anyway. I thought her new need to have me around was a restoration of trust and optimism, the only fear being that I would not be available. So I said what would have been unthinkable for me to say in my individuality-oriented years: "Think of me; that I'm with you in your thoughts and imagine how I would talk to you about the choices you will have to make. Take me along as an advisor and I'll be here when you get back."

Since I also have given considerable attention to her individualized self formation and her self-determinism, it seemed proportional to acknowledge that we were joined together in our work and that I was a factor in her life even when we were not physically in the same room together. As far as I could tell, the prospect of including me as a fantasied advisor and compatriot was not a threat to her individuality but rather was a supportive strength that enhanced her individuality. When she came back there was no observable increase in her dependency on me, only an increase in feeling joined, a stepping stone to finding these supports also in other places where she would naturally find them.

While transcendence of the primacy of merger is normally accomplished early in life, therapists have so often seen the residuals of dependency continue to impoverish people's desirable sense of self that it has been easy for them to slip past the continuously natural need for merger. Not only have we therapists slid past this need, but many of us have also actively discouraged it, even though the strong sense of connection that merger represents has been one of therapy's greatest assets. Since merger is dangerous when it is excessive, it is hard for therapists to reconcile the need to reduce dependency with maintaining a healthy merger option forever.

Merger Procedures

The gestalt therapist might ask why I am entering the concept of merger into the gestalt language when there are already several concepts that address this phenomenon: introjection, confluence, and synthesis. It is important to emphasize the merger functions as a unit because they have considerable overlap, as well as having distinguishing characteristics. Furthermore, though synthesis is usually seen as a healthy function, introjection and confluence have not commonly been seen by therapists as healthy. I have never heard a therapist say about a patient that she introjected beautifully or that she was marvelously confluent. When any therapist hears the words *introjection* and *confluence* she will understand that these words imply poor function. Nevertheless, I believe therapists would be better able to help their patients if they could sensitively restore introjection and confluence to their healthy position, as well as extending synthesis, which already has positive implications.

Introjection

I have already discussed introjection at length in Chapter Two, showing it as a basic source of merging with the world. When the child drinks the world in, she is being constantly changed by the information that she absorbs and that becomes a part of her. To a significant extent, the child becomes what the world feeds into her. Depending on what is fed in and how it is fed in, this process may or may not be beneficial. But it is a fundamental force in the formation of selves and it is also fundamental in the therapeutic reforming of selves.

One of the key offerings of therapy is new, more beneficial, up-to-date introjections than the early, harmful ones the patient has previously experienced. Therapy has always been permeated with introjections. An elemental example, familiar to all therapists and multipliable by many other examples, is the phenomenon of the patient feeling worthwhile just because the therapist listens to her.

Confluence

This is the process in which independent people coordinate with each other so fully that their separate identity is diminished. Think of a symphony orchestra playing in unison. Anyone listening would have difficulty recognizing the individual music being made by one specific violin or another. The individual violinist knows what she is doing and can distinguish her play from the others but she knows she could not make the sound alone and that her individual contribution is so interwoven within the total that it is lost in the fusion of sounds.

That fusion is no problem when the unions between self and other create something that each person individually desires. It is a serious problem when the person who is intertwined within such a system is being robbed of key personal functions, knowingly or not, and can't get out of the system. The loss may range from a diminution of general functions, like initiative, self-appreciation, and personal style, to such simple pleasures as being free to sing or go to the movies. That is a problem every psychotherapist is familiar with. As with introjection, we must discern between the beneficial and harmful effects of the confluence. Also, again as with introjection, the solution to harmful confluence may very well be beneficial confluence.

Here is an example of a therapeutic strategy based on the incorporation of beneficial confluence. It shows that the sense of shared identity may be seen as a fertile aspect of therapy, rather than an encroachment on individuality. One of my patients, Andrew, repeatedly dismissed everything he said to me, as though he had a verbal hiccup. Nothing he said was important because he "knew" these statements would not help to solve his problems. I told him I thought that he was dismissing the very observations and memories that might serve as springboards for eventual resolutions, just because they wouldn't help right away.

I thought that his impatient self was ruining him; so dominant was it in his own community of selves that it was hard for other selves to appear. With this in mind, I explained that his impatience was one manifestation of good energy, a quick reactivity and self-evaluation that could ultimately be valuable to him. I proposed that he continue to be impatient as long as he wanted to; I would be patient for both of us. No matter how impatient he would become

I promised him I would do my best to remain patient. He could depend on it.

Andrew was amused at this strange bargain but quite relieved that he could continue to be impatient. My patience, of course, had to be more than an attitude of patient nonintrusion. It was composed of substantive listening to everything he said, recovering from his dismissals of me, responding to his opposition, explaining things over and over, restoring perspective when he lost it. This contribution to our joint effort was a direct support for his impatient self but it was also an implicit support for his other selves, which were obscured by the impatient self that would nip any emerging self in the bud.

As we proceeded over the weeks and months, his own patience began to improve and other selves did appear. One was his jealous self when he discovered how much he would like to live his life as his brother did, with a good financial grounding, a wife and children, and a secure profession. Another was his obsessional self when he described the impossibility of being satisfied with any purchase because there were always some flaws in either the product or the way he wanted to use it or the price or what others may think of the product. The appearance of these selves and others began to flesh out his life, giving it more detail, novelty, and continuity.

Perhaps he might become too dependent on me, in which case the merger would be personally diminishing. But he was in little immediate danger of that. Quite the contrary, he was excessively isolated. In fact the major driving force in his life was anticonfluence, not allowing himself to blend with anyone in his life. He would have to come a long way in the direction of merger for his dependency on me to become a new issue. The time to deal with merger as a problem is when it becomes a problem.

In this case, I felt that the confluence was beneficial, an agreed confluence with the therapist. Where confluence is harmful, one of the members of the confluent team is giving up more of her identity than she can afford.

Dominance or intimidation is common in confluence, where

one member devotes her life to others without receiving the personal rewards or without having her own needs honored. Through confluence whole families may be intimidated into secrecy about an alcoholic parent. Entire families may be asked to be quiet in a house where father has a night job and has to sleep during the day.

Where confluence is strong the unruly selves of the intimidated member become dimmed, and it is the task of psychotherapy to brighten these by recognizing and naming them: perhaps a rebellious self, an intimidated self, or a sly self who finds a secret way out. The patient always alludes to these selves, and the therapist always accentuates what is only tangentially realized, bringing new experiences and their accompanying selves into the foreground. The new individuality of this realization of selves will replace the loss of identity that harmful confluence creates.

Confluence may have subtle manifestations where people don't realize their conformity until it goes over the threshold of bearability. But there are times when it is very clear what the roles are, and these may be the unspoken bargain for a division of responsibility. One person may be the more talkative and the other the listener or the responder. One may be inventive, the other may keep current activities going. One is introspective, the other gregarious. The degree of confluence in maintaining these roles may have great variance. Often the roles people have created may not hold up in the face of changes by one or the other, and these changes in the confluent relationship may cause trouble. When the listening person wants to become more talkative, it may be disconcerting to the talker. When the introspective one comes to be gregarious in surprising relationships, this may stir up conflicts.

One couple I am seeing had divided their roles only through their habitual patterns. The husband was the knowing one. He had an energetic, successful career; that was his evidence of a manly self. But he engaged in sex only occasionally and grudgingly. The wife was sexually lively but trained to obedience. She was living a little-sister self, there to be fended off and to be a good sport about her deprivations.

The husband's role replicated his lifetime of skipping out on his mother's seductiveness and domination. For him a life of winning out over temptation to save both his freedom and his virginity was his signature. The wife was sexually frustrated, quietly and with severe depression. Her role was to be what her nonsexual husband needed her to be, hoping for crumbs, which is how she had also played out her life with older brother. The result for him was a mild depression but for her it was a severe one, just short of requiring hospitalization.

Their roles needed to be shifted. After months of working together, they were able to accept a shift, one that reversed the confluent role assignments. He knew practically nothing about how to exercise his sexuality and she was a natural at it. He needed sex more than he knew and she had more potential influence than she had ever experienced. I asked her to be the teacher and he the student. At this point they could both see the value and not feel unduly threatened. He was not required to know anything about sex and she was to be a gentle but firm expert.

That was a challenge to each identity, particularly to his manly self and to her little-sister self. Giving up these familiar selves, in confluent reversal, she had to quit deferring for the sake of union and he had to quit dominating for the sake of union. Pretty soon she was no longer depressed and he, though insecure about his lack of sexual savvy, was no longer scared to death of her approach. They are each still consciously reminding themselves about the other, but now the reversal of roles represents a confluence that breaks up the old fixity. Perhaps he will grow beyond being the reluctant learner and she will revel in her influence.

In all mutuality, there is some element of surrendering choices, as when one person who doesn't want a baby yields to the other who does. This kind of sacrifice for a joint good is indispensable in relationships. Those who function well in mergers would see the sacrifice as a contactful response to the need of the other. In a society where individuality has been heavily prized, such yielding would too often be seen as weakness rather than generosity. Whether it is weakness or generosity is a discernment to be made, but made on its own merit rather than on the general assumption that yielding is weakness. The rhythm between merger and separateness, surrender and freedom, losing one's self and finding one's self, are all part of a difficult point/counterpoint reverberation that would be made easier by therapeutic and societal emphasis on the value of surrender and union.

Synthesis

Synthesis has been a key theme in gestalt therapy, which postulated a contact boundary that incorporated both separateness and union. As I have pointed out before, gestalt therapy extrapolated the Hegelian principle to apply to people. They were viewed as inexorably drawn to the contact boundary, where they would join with others, meeting in permanently successive contact moments, leaving marks within one another with each moment of meeting. They remain individual while absorbing part of the other into their own function. We become like our parents, friends, spouses, and bosses, while also operating independently of them. This portrays the strong influence that people in good contact will have on each other.

There is a constant oscillation between the simple meeting represented by contact and the more insinuating entry we all make into each other's minds. As a result of this union, every person, no matter how individualized, is the result of the influences around him.

This may or may not include the "we" feeling so common in confluence, because the individual carries the influence with her wherever she goes, adding this influence to people outside the original "we" experience. Yet the "we" may be felt anew, with others, as one feels herself belonging in her world of influence. To the extent the "we" is felt, one may feel vulnerable to losing one's self, dissolving it in the mix. "Contact involves not only a sense of one's self, but also the sense of whatever impinges at this boundary, whatever looms at the contact boundary and *even merges into it*" (Polster and Polster, 1974, p. 99).

What synthesis defines is similar to confluence. Though there is no way wholly to differentiate between them, the major distinction is that in synthesis, each person does her own synthesizing. The differences between self and other remain important, whereas in confluence the similarities are more likely to be in focus. This retention of individuality is similar to point/counterpoint syntheses, where melodies that are dissonant become heard together, united but never losing their individual recognizability.

Furthermore, in synthesis, the focus is not so much on the cooperative factor; rather, it is a meeting in which each party leaves its flavor with the other. Thus in working with Andrew, mentioned earlier in this chapter, we identified his impatient self, his jealous self, and his obsessional self, each having its own identity. Each, when freed to express itself, takes its place in a system of selves. Sometimes he will be impatient, sometimes jealous, and sometimes obsessional. The goal is to join these so that none has full dominance, giving Andrew a range of selves. They all add to his resources; so will others as he lets them in.

They are minimally synthesized by their very existence only as undercurrents in Andrew's life. When he gives up his current prejudices about them, the synthesis will become more complete. With each function restored, he will be relieved of the distraction that is created by the isolation of selves that challenge his confidence in integrating dissonant selves.

Self/Object Merger

A complementary view of the merger function is held by Kohut (1977, 1985) and others, who identify the self/object as an infant experience of merger. During the infantile phase, the child experiences the parent not as another person, external to herself, but rather as a self/object, a person residing within herself, serving supportive and confirming functions. The child, developmentally rather than through individual choice, looks to the parent as an internal appendage, undifferentiated from herself. We might imagine the vividness and intimacy the baby would feel with mother inside, unseparated and indistinguishable from the child, an isomorphic union of the internal and external, deeper than any ordinary engagement.

This intimacy, I believe, is one example of the lifelong search for merger, which restores a natural early condition that becomes more difficult to satisfy as the forces of separation make their developmental mark. Winnicott (1972) writes of a patient's ease in delving into his inner life "as long as he felt I was in this inner world with him" (p. 8). The sense of infantile interpersonal contiguity may be a lifelong touchstone of intimacy, reduced in strength as we grow more independent but never altogether relinquished. The self/object concept of indistinguishable boundaries lights up the naturalness of merger as a human imperative.

The evidence of the need to belong with others and to share destinies as well as simple experiences is widely available in every walk of life. People not only join together but seek it out with great determination and inventiveness. This need has so great a range as to include, on the mundane side, the simple declaration of a child that the toy in his hand is "mine" and the ethereal words of the Lord's Prayer: "Though I walk through the valley of the shadow of death, I will fear no evil, *for thou art with me.*"

To call the therapist a self/object, merging therapist and patient, may seem an extravagant way to put it. But it does not take long for the patient to discover—most patients know this beforehand—that the therapy combines both the dread of merger and its attractions. In this new microcosm, important personal consequences and symbolic implications are magnified, fostering personal immersion by the patient in even the simplest of exchanges and, by contrast, giving high focus to isolations within the patient as well as with the world at large. Because of these anticipations, just walking into the therapist's office feels to many people as though they are putting their very selfhood on the line, entering a domain where the prospects for inclusion are awakened while the dangers of missed connections remain anxiously alive.

For a sense of merger to develop between therapist and patient, it is only necessary for the therapist in this extraordinary context to exercise ordinary kindness, simplicity, clear-mindedness, good language, recognition of implication, and an enduring fascination with the life of the patient. Through these qualities and also through a combination of the transference phenomenon, heartfelt accuracy of knowing the patient, and wise direction into fruitful actions, the therapist is in a strong position of merger. When the merger is trustworthy the therapist may better compete for influence with the patient's lifelong adherence to harmful and anachronistic past mergers.

Transference as Merger

Contributing especially to the sense of therapeutic merger is the transference phenomenon, reformulated. As a gestalt therapist, I have avoided using the term in the past because of its depersonalizing effects. I have preferred to emphasize the actual relationship between therapist and patient, the contact experience, which is composed of telling, responding, suggesting, laughing, experimenting—everything that is actually going on. Adding to the power of this contactful engagement, however, is the symbolic component, which is represented by transference.

Historically, transference has been a prime tool of reconnection, as the experience of new relationship and accompanying interpretation served to break up old expectations and discover new contact options with the therapist. Unfortunately, transference has had double-edged implications. On the one hand, transference in its most common application has been used to take the therapist *out* of the relationship, by discounting the face value of the patient's expressions. Whether the patient is angry with the therapist or praises her, therapists have commonly dismissed these expressions. On the other hand, therapists have often assigned meanings to events, which may mistakenly discredit the patients' own experience of those events. These interpretations may deflect from the experienced contact, resulting in what I believe to be diminished connectedness.

There is another implication of transference, however, that is more empowering. The transference recognition, giving microcosmic significance to the therapy relationship, also makes the therapist a *party* to the entire life history of the patient, intertwined. The implications of the relationship insinuate the therapist into the most intimate fabric of the patient's experiences. Through the transference, given this microcosmic weight, the therapist is no longer just another person; she has elements of everybody who matters in the patient's life. The reality of these people is no longer just a disembodied concept because the therapist is a flesh-and-blood representative person, sitting right there. This unique status places her in the position where her words may come to have uncommonly large credibility, coming from a restoration of the primitive experience that is common to moments of childlike intimacy.

Such a sense of consequentiality is extremely absorbing, and occasionally it reaches hypnotic proportions. This absorption and the accompanying trust, even though often paradoxically frightening because of the intense feelings the trust has inspired, lead to less hesitance by the patient. This trust is especially enhanced by the awarenesses, actions, tight therapeutic sequences, and storytelling described in other chapters of this book. Through these procedures, the patient becomes more open to both the benefits and dangers of merging with the therapist while incorporating the new messages absorbed from the therapy experience.

It is true that this powerful leverage for change is often squandered by therapists' limitations. It is very difficult to create this level of trust in people who have already been badly burned. Furthermore, therapists make enough mistakes by pretending to know what they don't know, by speaking from theoretical fiat rather than personal sensibility, by setting goals that are either wrong or premature, by defining ambitions for success that neglect the patient's actual needs, by listening to their own feelings of inadequacy when signs of success are missing.

It is also true that this symbolic leverage can be used abusively or exploitatively by therapists. They may tell people whether to stay married or not, when the answer is unclear. They may interpret sexual abuse when the patient has no sense of it. They may be aloof and unresponsive. They may discredit observations of the patient. They may not pay close enough attention. They may take the patient on wrong exploratory paths. They may prolong or shorten therapy for personal purposes.

None of us is safe from such professional hazards. Yet, in concert with all the necessary cautionary factors, the therapist may make use of the merger opportunities provided by her special centrality to counterbalance the advantage already gained by the early infusion of society's alienating influences. The therapist as an unforgettable merging force is an antidote for the embeddedness of those damaging beliefs, which are unaffected by ordinary new experience. She does understand, she is enduring, she can go from seriousness to humor and back, she does serve as yeast for embryonic thoughts. The new experience can, therefore, be so absorbing that the patient will be influenced as though young all over again.

In the merger of minds, unions are not obvious. The term *merger* may seem exaggerated when we are actually only referring to influence, caring, cooperation, remembering, and so on. These states are part of the experience of commonality. They are only a suggestion of merger, because nobody becomes somebody else. Thus we may also think of merger as a metaphor for the inclusion by one person of another, a representation of indivisibility, perhaps subliminal but intuitively compelling.

This power of merger is pictorially represented in a novel by Barbara Kingsolver, *The Bean Trees* (1988). She uses wisteria vines, which often thrive in poor soil, as a symbol for human survival under atrocious circumstances. She says their secret power lies in microscopic bugs called rhizobia that live on the roots of the wisteria and suck nitrogen out of the soil, turning it into fertilizer. "There's a whole invisible system for helping out the plant that you'd never guess was there. . . . It's just the same as with people. The way Edna has Virgie and Virgie has Edna and Sandi has Kid Central Station and everybody has Mattie. And on and on. The wisteria vines on their own would just barely get by . . . but put them together with rhizobia and they make miracles" (p. 277).

Such mergers may be felt in relationships, where the engagements are strong enough that each person can create in another what they could never do alone. This union may be deeply linked, like the relationship between wisteria vines and rhizobia, or it might be only casual. At a minimal level, merger may include no more than a transitory memory, connecting one person with another.

The concept of merger must take account of this range of importance—from mergers that matter minimally to those so important that our very lives are at stake. Perhaps the simple memories, agreements, or common wishes seem a trivialization of the commonly grand view of merger. Actually, such small mergers show how merger permeates every corner of existence. Accumulated small mergers, developed every day, grow into profoundly felt merger. The death of a spouse may feel almost literally like losing a part of one's self. One eighty-year-old woman lamented that when her husband died, he took her brain with him. Such a loss may well feel like a phantom limb, the pain remaining long after the part is gone.

Psychotherapy in Community

Can psychotherapy, grounded in individualism and wary of merger, turn itself around and expand its response to the need for merger by working with larger groupings of people in the society at large? There are some tangential indications that it is already doing so.

Psychotherapy's influence on the development of self-help groups, formed on the basis of common characteristics, fosters both

empathy and merger. The merger factor is apparent in people joining with others to deal with the core issues that bother them. Not
only do these groups tap into a generic hunger for bondedness, but
the availability of such communal opportunities is multiplied
because they do it without professional leadership. The mush-
rooming groups, only a short step to larger congregations of people,
are addressing specific problems, such as alcoholism, gambling, child
abuse, codependency, and obesity.

The number of these groups is amazing. In his study of self-help
groups in America, Alfred Katz (1993) reported that there are as
many as 750,000 groups in the country. Richard Higgins stated in
1990 that there are two hundred types of twelve-step recovery
groups and that each week they attract fifteen million Americans
to half a million meetings. The Mental Health Association of San
Diego published the sixth edition of its Self-Help Directory in 1994,
containing the names of about five hundred self-help groups in San
Diego County alone, addressing a wide range of problems.

Self-help groups are usually small; thus they fall short of addressing the congregational aspects of merger reflected in religious experience. A representation of this need in therapeutic circles is the
creation of large groups, such as those already formed, for example,
by Jacob Moreno, Carl Rogers, Elizabeth Kübler-Ross, Jean Hous-
ton, myself, and others, each of whom created these groups for dis-
tinctly different purposes and with different formats.

More highly organized and shrewdly marketed than any of
these—also widely scorned by therapists—was the work of est,
which caught fire some years ago. That organization confirmed the
fears of gestalt therapists about introjection and confluence. The est
people used procedures already familiar to gestalt therapists: directed
visualization, the accentuation of simple awarenesses, and the creation of safe emergencies. They emphasized the paradoxical theory
of change, meaning that one recognizes and accepts "what is" in
order to, as the est people said, "get it." These groups induced receptivity to the leaders' messages through introjection and confluence.

The dictatorial tones of the leaders, isolation from the outside world and from each other, repetition of themes, inducing fatigue, and spotlighting communal example were all inductive influences.

But, as I have already indicated, introjection and confluence are also advantageous. While the authoritarian force within est, which resembled brainwashing, exploited the natural introjective and confluent reflexes, that should not distract us from honoring the interpersonal resonances and responsiveness of introjection and confluence, each of which has a continuing interplay with the individual freedom of the participant. Kindness, free choice, compelling themes, contact vibrancy, fitting experiments, laughter, music, poetry, continuity of meetings and the community, inspirational talks, relationship to the larger community, including nation and the world of nations—all these may be experienced within the introjective and confluent processes.

The merger functions of introjection, confluence, and synthesis ripen the individual for accepting those communal codes, which compel people to be as the community wants them to be. These ordained orientations light the communal path, guiding each person into communal function. Unfortunately, these guidelines may also clash with individual needs and may sometimes drive people crazy. For a psychological price—sometimes prohibitively high, other times an excellent bargain—the merger functions contribute to a sense of belonging, to a promise of being more fully and readily understood, to an easy access to substantive support, to an established and consistent sense of self, and, most compellingly, to the generic gregariousness of people.

Though gestalt theory is neutral on the health or unhealth of the merger functions, its spokespeople have commonly spoken of them in pejorative terms, with distrust of merger a natural consequence. Perhaps this negative view arises because therapeutic theory attends to disturbance more intently than normality, since that is what it is commissioned to alter. For example, though there are many references to the reduced function represented by confluence and introjection, Perls, Hefferline, and Goodman (1951) do make observations about the health of confluence and introjection. Even though they often warn against the neurotic implications, they point out the naturalness and benefits of confluence, saying: "We are in confluence with everything we are fundamentally, unproblematically or irredeemably, dependent on: where there is no need or possibility of a change. A child is in confluence with his family, an adult with his community, a man with the universe" (p. 451).

They also point out the indispensable, socially healthful qualities of introjection: "The persons are formed by the social contacts they have, and they identify themselves with the social unity as a whole for their further activity. There is abstracted from the undifferentiated felt-self a notion, image, behavior, and feeling of the 'self' that reflects the other persons. This is a society of the division of labor, in which people deliberately use each other as tools. . . . And this society . . . is the bearer of . . . the defining property of mankind, culture, the social inheritance surviving the generations" (p. 314).

We may live with nourishing introjections or poisonous ones. We may be in fruitful confluence or in a confluence that robs us of identity. Though both of these processes are indeed major threats to individuality, conversely, a monopoly of individuality is also a threat to the creation of humanly indispensable merger. As we develop our priorities, we risk getting either individuality or merger hobbled in the process. Whichever priority we follow, however, we have been dealt a hand from which we have to play both cards. Merger and individuality are not antithetical; they are like breathing in and out.

Since the merger functions are so central a psychological force, we must ask not only *whether* introjection or confluence occurs but also *what* is being introjected or joined in confluence, *how* the messages are infused, by *whom*, and *what* is being done with them. Because some of the est messages did indeed have merit, the process had widespread effects and earned many laudatory testimonials (Bry, 1976). In spite of obvious alienations from the psychotherapeutic

community, there the est people were—doing much of what psychotherapists generally support: bringing people together in mutual
psychological exploration, fostering expanded communication,
helping to find relief from shame and other sources of personal
paralysis, and guiding people to get clear about what they want and
what they are doing. When large groups such as these have unacceptable values and methods, we must distinguish the abuses of the
process from the process itself. Damning abuses should not be confused with damning the need.

Freud himself, not widely recognized for addressing communal
concerns, was nevertheless concerned about the limitations of individual psychotherapy for addressing the needs of the community at
large. He realized that modifications of method would be needed to
accommodate the larger scope of application of psychoanalysis. He
wrote: "One may reasonably expect . . . the conscience of the community will awake and admonish it that the poor man has just as
much right to help for his mind as he now has to the surgeon's
means of saving life. . . . The task will then arise for us to adapt our
technique to the new conditions. . . . It is very probable, too, that
the application of our therapy to numbers will compel us to alloy
the pure gold of analysis plentifully with the copper of direct suggestion; and even hypnotic influence may find a place in it again"
(Freud, 1957, vol. 2, p. 402).

Communal magnetism is a fact of life. When we, in psychotherapy, derogate the unruly process of creating new formats for people
to congregate and attend to common psychological concerns, they
will still be compelled to congregate, and our abdication will leave
the field to others. They will surely fill it in their own ways, often
in ways alien to our beliefs.

Awareness: The Rootedness of Self

One of gestalt therapy's most important contributions to psychotherapy was its expansion of the Freudian concept of insight into the gestalt concept of awareness. This expansion directed the psychotherapist's attention to actual moment-to-moment awarenesses. These awarenesses, in addition to contributing in the search for the reasons why patients live as they do, are relevant to psychotherapy in their own light. These awarenesses, large or small, are always going on; they range from the most innocuous yawn to an anger that has explosive energy.

As the concept of awareness brings the therapist closer to simple experiences, it stretches the supply of experiences from which the patient's selves may be discerned. Then the therapist may be more easily alerted to translate experiences into selves.

For example, a patient's tight feeling in the stomach, reflecting the person's lifelong need for carefulness, could be an indication of a careful self. Another patient's slight flush of embarrassment in speaking of a success could remind him of a time when he bragged to his friends about his performance in a high school play. Then when he fell flat on his face, this embarrassment seared him and created a modest self, overshadowing the bragging self. Another patient's private wish to be wined and dined could grow into a story about his luxuriant self. A patient's confusion about what to say at the start of a session could lead to the recognition of a conforming self, trying to find the right thing to say.

These simple awareness are like the arrows described in Chapter Five, pointing the way ahead to the identification and recovery of selves. The characteristics and experiences the patient becomes aware of are not so much direct invitations to deeper meanings as they are stepping stones to the unfolding of the patient's life and the selves that orient and guide him.

The Role of Awareness

The concept of awareness has two key advantages over the concept of insight, which it supersedes: its unity with excitement and its expansion of therapeutically relevant experience.

Awareness and Excitement

Awareness has a closer relationship to its theoretical energy source (excitement) than insight does to its energy source (libido), and therefore creates a greater sense of personal unity. A representation of this unity is the fact that awareness is more likely to be exciting than insight is to be libidinal. Excitement is the root neuronal system discharging energy into sensation, feeling, emotion, and all their derived states of mind.

Excitement represents a direct physiological underpinning for awareness, and its common meaning is easily understood by people at large. People are excited *about* something. Thus excitement immediately connects to manifest experiences, rather than being a disparate and distant energy reservoir. The merit of the particular experience is all there, including both excitement and awareness, requiring fewer interpretive or speculative connections than are necessary in connecting libido and insight.

Whereas *experienceable* bodily reality got away from Freud, Wilhelm Reich came along and incarnated libido (1949). Though his methods resulted in therapeutic experiences that were more spectacular in both sensation and behavior than would be normally encountered in therapy, these experiences were nevertheless a stepping stone toward appreciating the power of peripheral awareness. Reich tapped the inner excitements that few people recognized outside the special stimulations of sexuality, fear, and adventure. What was accentuated was the unity between vibrant psychic energy and overt behavior; it replaced the view of one's insides as a silent partner, mysteriously masterminding a person's life directions.

To show how palpable immediate and detailed awareness may be and how it registers on an elemental level, here is a report of a student in a psychology class, instructed to attend to his inner experience. We can resonate with the undercurrent of excitement at the root of focalized awareness as the student concentrated on the sensations in his body:

> "Normally—that is, before I let my 'attention wander through my body'—I was aware of my body sensations merely as a general hum, a kind of poorly defined sense of general vitality and warmth. However, the attempt to subdivide this into component sensations was a source of genuine amazement. I became aware of a series of tensions in various parts of my body: knees and lower thighs as I sit in a chair; the region of the diaphragm; the eyes, shoulders and dorsal neck region. This discovery was quite astonishing to me. It was almost as if my feeling had entered a foreign body with tensions, rigidities, and pressures entirely different from mine. Almost immediately upon discovery I was able to relax these tensions. This, in turn, caused me to be aware of a sense of looseness and even elation; a very sudden freedom, pleasure and readiness for anything to come" [Perls, Hefferline, and Goodman, 1951, p. 90].

Though this report says little about therapy per se and the complexities of using the awareness process in an actual session (I will address that shortly), it shows how powerful awareness may be in the creation of self realization and in raising the person's energy and involvement.

Such self exploration, experienced in simple personal concentration, moved a step forward from Reich, who did two things: He expanded libido beyond the erogenous zones, recognizing its presence as total bodily aliveness, and he phenomenalized libido, focusing on its concrete manifestations in the pulsating body. What was important to gestalt therapy, carried forward by Perls from Reich, was the simple and vital radiance that guides all human activity, whether it be sexual, conversational, or intellectual, whether it involved planning, laughing, crying, reading, screaming, or anything else. Perls incorporated into his own broader orientation Reich's sense of the immediacy and the vitality of the nonverbal energy vectors, the deeply personal energy streamings and their sometimes eruptive consequences.

Expansion of Experience

The second advantage of awareness over insight is that it allowed gestalt therapy to expand the range of experiences that therapists would recognize as factors in the formation of selves. The focus on awareness recognized the patient's continuum of experiences and added detail to any intellectual understandings that might evolve.

The concept of awareness led me in my own work to be more interested in how people talked, how they sat, how they chose their favorite topics, how they related to their spouses or co-workers—all the many awarenesses by which people signal their experiences. Included among these phenomena was a huge range of awarenesses, starting from simple sensation and moving on to awarenesses of feelings, of purposes, of values, of relationships, and all the personal experiences of which lives are constructed. During therapy explorations these simple phenomena expand like yeast. They are the prime ingredients for the formation of selves.

Not only does the elevation of awareness expand the therapeutically relevant data base beyond that of insight, but it also *includes* insight, which I see as one indispensable form of awareness. At the insight level, interconnection among events is revealed. Focal events are placed into perspective and may produce enormous enlightenment. But the awareness of both the therapist and the patient is not just occasional, as is insight; it is always present.

With the recognition of awareness as the generic instrument of self discovery, the simple phenomena of continuing experience move into ascendancy. This continuity of awareness and its accompanying excitement become more and more evident to the patient through the restoration and guidance of his concentration (addressed in Chapters Four and Five).

With the concept of the *continuum of awareness*, gestalt therapy also takes account of another gap—that between momentary awareness and the cumulative awarenesses that form the totality of one's life. Ultimately, we do have to organize the succession of awarenesses that occur over the course of a lifetime so that the continuity will contribute to a sense of greater or lesser personal wholeness. The selves contribute to this sense of the patient's continuity because they synthesize disconnected awarenesses into recurrent clusters of experience.

Awareness and Meaning

The organization of continuing awarenesses into selves is part of the development of meaning. These selves help us to know who we are, which is a key to creating a sense of wholeness. Meaning is achieved in two ways: horizontally and vertically (see Chapter Five). The horizontal dimension of meaning is reached through a continuum of awarenesses, as they unfold into a realization of the connections between what has preceded and followed any particular awareness. That is, meaning evolves through a step-by-step process of experience, never by isolated experience. Each step leads gradually to a new understanding of the context of any person's experiences. The vertical dimension of meaning, plumbed by interpretation and

insight, is also valuable. Vertical meaning, often dramatically realized, pierces through to the obscured meanings by relatively sudden
illuminations, often shortcutting the person's own gradual pace.

There is considerable overlap between vertical and horizontal
meaning; no meanings come either altogether suddenly or altogether
gradually. However, the awareness concept, since it encompasses
insight, offers the therapist greater choice than the earlier concept
of insight alone. I believe therapists of all persuasions should be hospitable to both. Insight by itself excludes too much of the patient's
continual awareness and requires impeccable timing. On the other
hand, step-by-step awareness could become interminable without
some revelations contributed by either therapist or patient.

You might well ask whether, in trying to close the gap between
underlying energy concept and immediate experience, gestalt therapy has abandoned the unabandonable—the basic depth of people's
existence. Might such an exclusively phenomenological experience
as is represented in the above student's report provide a misleading
sense of wholeness? Doesn't it leave out half his life, his unconscious
wishes and complex purposes? Should we not probe for a patient's
childhood experience in the dark bedroom closet where the mon-
sters almost caught him or for his schoolteacher's scorn or a childhood fistfight, and find out how these experiences might underlie
his knowing the deeper regions of his mind?

The concern with the superficiality/depth dimension is a key
requirement in the search for experience that matters. Whatever is
going on always takes its place in a larger, unmanifested, depth-
inviting context, including both the unconscious and all the other
experiences that might be available. We gestalt therapists call this
the *ground* within which all immediate experience is always positioned. Depth is commonly understood to exist when experiences
are highly significant or strongly felt or very clever or very obscure.
The depth to which I am pointing, however, is the depth one
achieves by relating any awareness to whatever context is accessible for that awareness. In a sense, depth is the undoing of the isolation of any single event from others that matter.

The cryptic unconscious, celebrated in psychoanalysis as the geography of depth, is only occasionally unscrambled. Very few of my patients have had memories in therapy that they had never had before. Usually, what happens that comes close to the fabled return of the unconscious is that people come to pay closer attention to what has been sliding out of the side of their minds. Or they suddenly see old things in a new light. The sudden emergence of the repressed is an old romanticism, which has kept many therapists frustrated and distracted from the more immediately available sources of depth, seeking in the depths of the unconscious for that which is more commonly right in front of their eyes.

Much of what is recovered from the "repressed" has been simply set aside, readily knowable but not associated with current experience. Connecting what one is doing now to early experience provides depth because it is no longer an isolated experience. To know, for example, that the fights a person is getting into nowadays are connected to childhood experiences of being beaten provides depth to current experience even though that person has always known about being beaten in childhood. We may experience the depth of a current success in college by connecting it to years of practicing the piano. We may experience our current tenderness for people in trouble by connecting it with the loss of a cherished dog.

But these distant connections, important for restoring context, are not all that is required for the experience of depth. Valuable though these connections may be and as habituated as therapists may be to believing they are the signs of depth, there are also other, perhaps more accessible, ways to the experience of depth.

An example of depth at the surface is the experience of a patient of mine who was troubled about not being sufficiently captivating at a party. She soon remembered times when she had been captivating, and these memories reassured her about herself. But they didn't create a feeling of depth. The feelings of depth came when I asked her to close her eyes and tell me what she felt inside.

At first, she found it difficult to close her eyes, accustomed as she was to shallow awareness and feeling frightened about what she would find. For some people (those heavily defended against internal experience and especially borderline patients), to focus internally would be too much to ask; it would set off terror. But she was not over her head and was able to do it.

During this sharp internal focus she told me about a number of her sensations, including the key awareness that she had a tight band of tension around her abdomen. After a further short period of focusing, she told me that her breathing had become very quiet. Then, when she continued to concentrate on her internal feelings, the tightness just disappeared and I could see that her breathing became amplified.

This new opening to her breathing led her to a direct realization and description of inner liveliness. No more guesswork about whether she was or was not captivating. She said this feeling was better than feeling captivating, and that she was surprised at how peaceful she had become. In a sense she felt the wellsprings of being captivating without really caring any more about it, transforming her self-evaluation from superficial to deep.

Composite and Ingredient Awarenesses

To expand the range of awarenesses from which selves are formed and which also provide the experience of personal depth, I propose a process of interweaving *composite* and *ingredient* awarenesses. This interweaving creates connections among the reverberating awarenesses of readily accessible experience. The interweaving also helps to expand the personal implications of awarenesses, making them all the more fruitful in identifying selves. (Also see Polster, 1970, 1987, and Polster and Polster, 1973.)

Composite awarenesses are those that are in the center of attention, the ones people notice without detailed examination: a phrase spoken in conversation, a feeling of sadness, a recollection of a visit to a childhood neighborhood, an angry reaction to bad advice, a disappointment about a canceled trip. These statements, actions, memories, feelings, and reports are valid just as they are; they may be taken at face value. But they all also contain details that would provide fuller delineation of the experience than is available in the composite awareness itself.

To illustrate, suppose you are biting an apple. That is your composite awareness. To be aware of biting the apple may be all that matters. But the ingredients of the experience, if brought into awareness, will influence the depth. Whether the apple is sweet or sour, whether you have bitten off too much, how good it would be to join this bite with a bite of cheese, whether it reminds you of the apple tree you swung from in your backyard, whether you are an apple grower—these ingredients offer dimension to the experience of biting the apple.

Or, for another example, suppose a patient says, "I drove here today so peacefully." This composite awareness has many ingredients, some of which may be brought into awareness. The tone of voice, for example, may be soft or quick or reminiscing or inviting or challenging. For the patient to become aware of the qualities that are subsumed within his awareness of a peaceful drive gives the words a greater depth than for the sentence to stand by itself, unsupported by the ingredients of which it is composed. Whether these words are spoken with a shrug of the shoulders or with conviction gives dimension. If the words are spoken with bitterness or irony, that would be quite different from someone who felt at last a moment of peace.

To the extent that any particular relationship between composite and ingredient awarenesses is relevant to the identification of selves, the depth created will help the patient become more involved in how these selves fit into his life.

The interweaving of any particular composite awareness with its ingredients—the whole and its parts, shuttling back and forth—adds individuality, directionality, and depth to experiences that otherwise may be too readily habitual, stereotyped, mechanical, and overgeneralized. For example, a patient says he is going to call the daughter he has been saying he wants to talk to. In this moment his awareness of his intention to call is the composite awareness. The therapist, exploring for the ingredient experience, says, "You don't look very enthusiastic about calling." The patient says. "No, I'm afraid." This awareness of being afraid is an ingredient to the composite awareness of intending to call the daughter, but it may turn out to be a composite experience of its own if the therapist and patient explore the ingredients of his fear. Now the original composite intention has generated novel exploratory prospects.

This process of interweaving awarenesses and the reverberations of fluctuating attention results in a throb of perceptual excitement, which makes experience fresh and vibrant. This interweaving process is the soul of knowledge, the appreciation of the continuing ramifications that one thing offers another. From these perceptual dynamisms come the roots of personal fascination, the transcendence of ordinariness that makes experience continuously inviting. Through restoration of the simple vibrancies of awareness, fleshing out the composite awarenesses, the release of the pertinent lifetime of experience will be facilitated and options for self identification increased.

Though this process may include what therapists often think of as tapping into the unconscious, it is more inclusive than that. Ingredients may or may not be within the range of immediate awareness and they do not have the causative implications that are imputed to the unconscious. They are simply elements imbedded in a complex composition.

This process of interweaving composite and ingredient experiences is one in which most people participate only reflexively. Intentional exploration may seem too self-consciously therapeutic to many people and requires considerable delicacy, patience, and creativity on the part of the therapist. For some patients the internal turn of mind is distracting; for others it seems foolish. Some are terrified to look inward; others do it but fail to make new connections and find it pointless.

The artists, gourmets, and monks of the world are only a privileged few who have created a personal luxury out of searching for their ingredient awarenesses. Still, the artist's awarenesses, more freely probed than the therapist's, can be a useful guideline for the therapist. What follows is a comparison of the levels of awareness at which the artist will work—instructive to the therapist but not duplicatable—and the therapist's own use of awareness.

In his moving book *Let Us Now Praise Famous Men*, James Agee (1941) told of the lives of migrant workers in the South during the Depression. His report provides a good example of the ingredient awarenesses that underlie composite experience. The accessibility of the ingredient experience is clear, as Agee lets his own undercurrent awarenesses come to the surface and provides a reverberation among awarenesses. Here he describes Annie Mae's state of mind as she herself never would without Agee's child eyes, man's brain, and artist's intent.

> Annie Mae watches up at the ceiling and she is sick with sleep as if she had lain the night beneath a just-supportable weight: and watching up into the dark, beside her husband, the ceiling becomes visible, and watching into her eyes, the weight of the day. She has not lacked in utter tiredness, like a load in her whole body, a day since she was a young girl, nor will she ever lack it again; and is of that tribe who by glandular arrangement seem to exhaust rather than renew themselves with sleep, and to whom the act of getting up is almost unendurably painful. But when the ceiling has become visible there is no longer any help for it, and she wrenches herself up, and wriggles a dress on over her head, and shuffles barefooted across the porch to the basin, and ladles out two dippers of water from the bucket, and cups it in her hands, and drenches her face in it, with a shuddering shock that straightens her; and dries on the split flour

sack that hangs from a nail; and is capable now of being alive, to work:

Her first work being, to build the fire, and to cook biscuits and eggs and meat and coffee [p. 88].

With such interweaving of awarenesses Agee animates the dimmed ingredients of a flattened existence and delivers to us the sense of Annie Mae's tortured self. Through his pulsating, perceptive, fluid, and fluent homage to his awareness, he raises the people and their surroundings to a deeper level of realizability than is available to their own pulverized sensibilities. How could such awarenesses as Agee incorporates be communicated to Annie Mae? By what miracle of resurrection could Annie Mae herself, as we therapists hope our patients may, develop the hospitality and the inner space to experience such a luminous sense of the struggles in which she has always been an overwhelmed victim? How might she turn her desolate, boarded sense of self into the vibrant sensibilities that Agee, as compassionate cantor, can sing out to the world?

For the psychotherapist, the writer's enlightenment, inspirational though it should be, can be only an approximation of his own prospects. The writer has the advantage of communicating to a relatively unthreatened readership. Furthermore, he is not called on to coordinate his views with those of his characters, people who, with an independent voice, might see themselves quite differently from the way the author sees them. Whether the writer can resolve these frictions between himself and his characters may affect the quality of the writing, but only the writer is injured by any failure and the reader's disappointment would be only casually troublesome.

Most patients will give the complexity of awareness only glancing attention, less than would be desirable from a literary standpoint. The therapist must understand that he cannot be as finely demanding as the writer, who may not rest until the exact word is produced, often only after a number of attempts. What is originally experienced by the patient as an unwelcome exploration may come to be welcomed. The prospect of temporary stumbling must be accommodated in the move to greater and greater clarity, for it is surprising how many awarenesses, even mediocre ones or skewed ones, can be turned to growth. I bank on this indulgence, as I grope with my patients for pathways to the experiences they are missing.

Case Example: The Dream

One illustration of therapeutic progress achieved at less than literary levels of awareness is a dream workthrough that touched one of my patients deeply, even though we didn't reach key awarenesses that *my* ambitious self would have conceived.

This patient was disturbed by a dream in which he played sexually with his mother. The suggestive composite awareness represented in the dream events fell short of its promise of primitive memories. Rather, it moved into something nearer the surface; an illuminating, releasing experience, once removed, however, from the inner mysteries into which writers dare to take their characters.

Here is the patient's story:

> [It was] a very embarrassing dream because it was very sexual. This is with Mom, with Mom as I imagine her as a younger woman. And we were in bed and fooling around sexually—naked—and I remember not liking being there, feeling like I had to be there. Feeling obligated, like she wanted me to be there and I had to be there. And I was just kind of playing like I wanted to be there. I was just being kept there out of guilt but I remember really not wanting to be there. But not showing it, not saying it, but acting as if I wanted to be there. Very strange.

The composite awareness of incestuous sex dominates the dream, Oedipus wavering in ambivalence. He recounted the dream fairly dispassionately, and since he was an obsessive person vulnerable to getting stuck with intrusive thoughts, I was careful not to get ahead of him by pressing him beyond what he brought up. This cautionary consideration, not required of a writer animating one of his fictional characters or James Agee describing migrant workers, is nevertheless a therapeutic imperative and will influence the level at which the ingredient awarenesses will flesh out the composite.

To evoke the ingredient awarenesses of these dream events, I responded to his comment about having sex with his mother by asking what aspect of the experience stood out for him. The ingredient awareness he gave was this: "We were naked under the covers and she was handling my genitals, and . . . I guess we were not having intercourse, we were just kind of lying there. As if it were post-sex. Mostly she was fondling me. Whew!"

My simple question created a strong focus. The ingredients of the sexual experience gave it a new level of excited reality. For him this was a daringly explicit acknowledgment of fondling. But this ingredient awareness was too hot for him, and he quickly shifted his attention to another ingredient aspect, the "sick" quality of the dream. He had the alarming thought that his mother might actually have initiated a sexual experience in his childhood.

He was as much frightened to think of his mother as having been "sexually inappropriate" with him as he was to face his own sexuality and his own incestuous participation, a reluctance evident also in the dream. The threat to the pure image of his mother was a major shock. Even the prospect of her impurity dismayed him, though he could not remember any actual sexual experience with her. He said he was afraid to know the truth about her and was frightened about the "sickness" of the dream. The evocation of ingredients had turned a cool report into a palpable event.

To help him finish one part of his unfinished business with his mother, I asked him what he might like to say to her. The new ingredients in his response were about the actuality of his mother's sickness rather than the "sickness" of the dream.

THERAPIST: What would you like to say to your mother?

PATIENT: (Long pause) You know, Mom, this is really weird. You feel like a mother and a girlfriend at the same time.

THERAPIST: And what does your mother say?

PATIENT: (Crying) Oh, it is hard to think of her without getting upset. I am not thinking of her as the dream character. I am thinking about her as the real person that I saw . . . recently before she died. (Sobs.)

His mother's death is the ingredient awareness that transformed his sexual guilt and confusion into actual sadness, an experience that calls for its own resolution. It is as real a theme as the original, and he elaborates the ingredients further in the following exchanges:

THERAPIST: Well, she was very sick then. But in the dream she was not real sick. The dream is almost like a resurrection.

PATIENT: She would say different things. In the character in the dream she'd say one thing and the character of her real self she'd say something much different.

THERAPIST: Well, let's hear both.

PATIENT: In the dream she would say something like, "Okay, that's all right. This is fun. Just stay here." The real one would say something like, "I did not realize you felt that way. It must be very difficult for you." She would be very helpful and concerned and supporting and all those . . . (wavering, tearful) nice things that I miss a lot. (Breaks into sobs.) She was so kind. I don't think I've known anyone as kind as her.

THERAPIST: Tell her how you feel about that.

PATIENT: (Catches breath) Oh, Mom, you're so kind, so gentle. You make everything seem so safe and so warm, so easy. If anything, anything at all upset me, I could always come home and be around you and it just would not be that bad. Even when I was angry at you and wanting to be separate from you and not wanting a mother and wanting to feel like a man, I'd sit there on the couch with my arms crossed and you could be across the room and it did not matter, it'd still be this, everything would be okay.

THERAPIST: She'd just accept you.

PATIENT: Yeah, no matter what. (Sniffling) I think nothing mattered more to her than accepting me. She made me feel accepted. I felt so bad about the times when I was real angry with her. I really tried to get her. Just kinda by withholding from her and smoldering around her I felt like I was defiling that perfect kindness.

THERAPIST: It is hard to accept a mother the way a mother accepts a son.

PATIENT: (Laughs softly; motions toward tissue, which I hand to him.) It is, isn't it. I felt like such a schmuck 'cause I couldn't do it. I felt kind of inferior.

THERAPIST: It's very common, though, isn't it?

PATIENT: To feel inferior to your mother?

THERAPIST: No. To feel that a son does not accept a mother like a mother accepts a son.

That was a tricky misunderstanding, bringing in inferiority rather than his views about taking care of his mother as she did of him. It complicated my therapeutic choices. Should I deal with his new awareness of inferiority or get back to the theme of mother's protectiveness? I chose the latter as a more immediate promise for accentuating his own independence, particularly as the session had run over and we had to end it.

What has to be evident is that he need not be a carbon copy of maternal indulgence in order to feel like a loving son. The sexual theme is no longer central, though still an undercurrent to the guilt, but I did not accent the sexually permissive side of his mother, from which he moved to her protective quality. The different emphasis was an important one, but not the one promised originally in the dream.

The basic requirement to follow the hints the patient provides is complicated when they contradict each other, as between mother's protectiveness and mother's sexuality. Which way the patient is leading is discerned by the therapist, whose work lives or dies by these discernments, each with its own directional integrity. This process of following the patient's arrows was described at length in Chapter Five.

We never got pointedly back to fleshing out the dream's sexual elements. What became focal instead was a more generalized guilt, a new composite awareness calling for new detailing. This new theme overshadowed the sexual, though it was not unrelated, since the sexual evoked it. But the new theme was connected not to sexuality but rather to his responsibilities to his mother and his sadness about not doing enough for her as she was dying. His sexual fears remained underground and a nonsexual reconciliation won out.

One could say that he was not ready to further engage his sexual awarenesses or one could say I was not sufficiently skilled to help him unlock them or one could say that the sexual element is not what mattered most to him and was only an entree into his interpersonal guilt. In any case, we settled for awareness of his nonsexual relationship with his mother. It was important, but it was once removed from the dream material itself—a happy ending, with reservations. Must we get to the generic bottom? I don't think so. The unconscious is after all unlimited and our aspirations measured.

The therapist must contend with the fact that when one theme is gained, the other (in this instance the direct experience of the sensual) may be lost. Though artists offer a guiding inspiration in their powers to achieve clarity, depth, color, and range, those are, alas, more often a therapeutic goal than a therapeutic achievement.

This dream evoked high-intensity reverberations between ingredient and composite experiences but much of therapy addresses more ordinary engagement issues. For example, in conversational ease, when I see a quizzical expression, for me to simply say to my patient that he looks puzzled may evoke new ingredient aware-nesses. The patient himself may have slid over this puzzlement even though it registered in his face. Without the sense of puzzlement, he might proceed in only dimly experienced conversation. To enhance the conversation is a therapeutic mandate because it releases the excitement underneath, impelling the person into new emotion and behavior.

Some sluggishness will usually exist, however, because there is often an uncertainty in the mind of either patient or therapist as to the best emotional or behavioral path that could evolve from the excitement. In moments of great anxiety, the patient may have lit-tle idea what the undercurrent excitement is heading him toward. This uncertainty and threat of the actual path of the excitement might be the very force that generates anxiety. The fear of imme-diate and dangerous behavioral or emotional consequences of excitement must be allayed, especially when that path is indeed dangerous. Therapists are commissioned to know the dangers of awareness, as for example when a patient's excitement has poten-tial consequences of divorce or panic attacks or losing a job for telling the boss off.

Two key safety supports are the understanding of awareness as an everyday experience freed from premature implications and con-necting new awareness to already existing awarenesses. First, the ingredient experiences foster wholeness because omitted undercur-rents are brought into active participation in the composite expe-rience. For example, for the patient discussed earlier in this chapter who was disturbed by a dream of incestuous sex, an undercurrent of assertiveness—brought into awareness—helped change his frag-mented expressiveness, giving it greater unity and strength. Second, though the experience of heightened excitement inspires new ideas and directions, it does so at the patient's pace. Close attention to the natural sequence of awareness, leaving large leaps of awareness to selected situations, diminishes the risks because each new awareness fits into what the person is already aware of. When the patient's sexual dream turned into a concern with his mother's sickness, it occurred through a succession of awarenesses. My having told my patient that he was only avoiding his sexual fear rather than honoring his concern with his mother's literal sickness may have preempted his own sequential priorities and escalated the risk.

The patient's sense of self may encompass these gradual realizations at all levels of experience: sensation, emotion, values, assessments, philosophy, and so on. Therapy expands the hospitality of the person to encompass as many common experiences as possible, ranging from how patients hold their glasses to the ambitions they live by. With such inclusion of the common awarenesses, we serve both the technical needs of psychotherapy for the relevant expansion or restoration of each person's range of selves, and people's needs for an understandable and communication-friendly sense of the foundations of psychotherapy.

Action: The Engine of Self

The last and least understood of the therapeutic pathways for forming and reforming the self is *action*, long obscured by the introspective bias of the early psychotherapists. They did therapy as though the self could be reconstituted by looking inward. Yet action moves the person out into the world. It is as integral a contributor to the sense of self as awareness and contact, its major partners. The actions we take, ranging from talking to building a house, define who we are—so much so that it would not be less accurate than the Cartesian "I think therefore I am" to say "I am what I do."

Nevertheless, the wariness about action in therapy got so bad at one historical point that some psychoanalysts were forbidding any life-changing acts during the course of therapy. Actions were often pejoratively considered signs of "acting out." Yet, if we were ever to try hard to devise a way of interrupting growth, we couldn't do much better than to stifle action.

The wariness against action unfortunately also had some merit. It evolved because actions may indeed be antitherapeutic when they are impulsively taken or when they arise from misunderstood implications of the therapy experience. Jumping to conclusions, a patient might impulsively want to end a marriage, change careers, leave the city, commit suicide. With such precipitous action as an example, it is understandable that therapists would want to cut off misguided actions. But these actions, rightly timed, may also be at least as beneficial as any aspect of psychotherapy. The therapist must be on the alert for precipitous action but must also recognize its therapeutic potential. I, for one, have often cautioned patients, especially when they are impulsive, to understand that what is desirable to talk about in therapy may cause them trouble outside therapy—until they are ready to do it well.

Action and the Experiment

Most actions the patient takes are not dangerous at all, but where they *are* dangerous, therapy offers a solution. We can reduce the dangers of the real world by replicating aspects of it in the therapy office. Gestalt therapy developed an entire range of therapeutic options called the *experiment,* which provides for safe action as a major contribution to the accentuation of therapeutic engagement (Polster and Polster, 1973; Zinker, 1978).

The experiment is a designed opportunity for action tryouts. These scenarios are introduced when particular actions do not spontaneously appear. Within these scenarios, the patient is faced with specific therapeutically relevant people, places, memories, and images. Rather than only talking about the patient's life, the therapist invents circumstances and instructions for immediate action. The range of these experiments is very large, and it greatly expands the repertoire of therapeutic procedures, including procedures created outside gestalt therapy.

Ferenczi's Active Therapy

Sandor Ferenczi, one of Freud's early lieutenants, started this expansion of procedure with his "active" therapy. In one example he writes of a woman musician suffering from manifold obsessions and phobias (Ferenczi, 1952, pp. 203–204). Her tyrannical sister used to sing a particular song, and Ferenczi asked his patient to sing the song. It took her two hours to be able to do it with all the color and coquetry that her sister had displayed. Then, memories released, the patient recalled a time when she was "the darling of all her family and friends." Through the activity of singing the song, she was able to restore what I would have called her darling self, a part of her self process that she had dismissed. She got renewed perspective and stimulation about her fixated admonitions against performing and against being the darling in her family. The action options gave a new zest and new meeting with reality, in contrast to the esoteric introspective isolation of the patient, so common in those days.

Moreno's Psychodrama

Activity such as singing the song is the forerunner of what gestalt therapy has called the experiment, but before we describe the experiment further, we must take account of Jacob Moreno, another milestone influence in shaping the relationship between activity and awareness. Moreno was far more sophisticated in methodology than Ferenczi, who made his contradictingly brave and apologetic attempts only to stretch Freudian procedure. Moreno carried no such baggage, owing no homage to Freudianism despite living in the Viennese atmosphere and being well aware of the Freudian influence. So aware was he, in fact, that his psychodrama was directly—and negatively—influenced by Freud. Moreno reacted strongly against what he described as Freudian isolation and inaction, and he was indignantly aroused to further his own communal and action-oriented procedures and to create psychodrama (Moreno, 1946, p. 8). He once told Freud, "I start where you leave off. You meet people in the artificial setting of your office; I meet them on the street and in their home, in their natural surrounding. You analyze their dreams. I try to give them the courage to dream again" (pp. 5–6).

These sentiments are key factors in the stream of modifications to which gestalt therapy has contributed. The implications of Moreno's critique and his development of psychodrama were to replicate real-life situations in which the patient would interact with other members of the psychodramatic group, each of whom would play designated roles. His improvisational methods gave fresh life to experience and challenged people to respond to novelty.

Gestalt Variations

Three modifications of Moreno's psychodrama especially characterize the gestalt experiment.

Experiment in Ordinary Therapy Setting

The first significant aspect of experiment is that it brings action into the therapy office, requiring neither preset scenery nor the presence of a group. The improvised experiments evolve from ordinary therapeutic exchanges, shifting back and forth between therapy conversation and the actions of the experiment. The experiment is specifically designed by the therapist and evolves from the theme already developing through therapeutic engagement: the patient's personal reports of needs, dreams, fantasies, body awareness, therapeutic understanding, and the like.

Thus, for example, the therapist, hearing his patient's account of a frightening experience with his father, may attentively listen to the narrative account and be moved by the patient's experience of terror, perhaps offering his own perspectives. But he may also ask the patient to imagine speaking to his father, as though contacting him on the spot.

This accessibility of the experiment to the ordinary therapeutic session contains an important complication. The flexibility in moving from the contactful engagement between therapist and patient and from the concern with awareness to the creation of experiments makes gestalt therapy a tripartite methodological system where the three perspectives of contact, awareness, and experiment are intermingled. One of the primary roles that experiment plays is to expand both contact and awareness parameters.

Shuttling among experiment, contact, and awareness, choosing the timely therapeutic vehicle is especially important. Contactful conversation with the patient, though central in therapy, gets great therapeutic enhancement from the accentuations produced by awareness and from setting up experimental opportunities. This shuttling process calls for continuing discernment of timing, content, and style as the therapist chooses among the awareness, action, and experiment modes of therapeutic work.

There are some patients with whom the therapist would rarely set up experiments, either because they are befuddled by make-believe, because they would feel overwhelmed by the directness of engagement, or because they would feel the loss of contact with the therapist, a support they need. With other patients who could roll readily into the experiment, it is an invaluable chance to make the engagements they talk about more real to them.

Timeliness is also crucial for the gracefulness of the experiment, which must be connected with what is already going on in therapy. Shuttling between the contact with the patient and identifying her awarenesses and setting up experiments is complex. Patients may easily feel disregarded or interrupted if the therapist is choppy in movement from one mode to the other. For example, when a patient is absorbed in recounting an important experience, to ask what she is aware of may be distracting. To arrange an experiment also requires resonance with what is already happening. Where the change in mode from awareness and contact to experiment may be abrupt or distracting, transitional explanations about the purpose of the experiment or guidance in how to do it may be necessary to give credibility and pertinence to the new instruction.

Patient in All Roles

The second factor differentiating the gestalt experiment from psychodrama is that it gives the patient free rein to play various roles rather than being limited to a group where other group members play them. The patient's father played by a group member would be different, probably less accurate, from the father known by the patient. Furthermore, when the patient plays the role of his own father, placing herself in her father's shoes and feeling what it is like for her father to respond to her, she often gets a new sense of what her father is like. When the patient can get into this empathic position, it is easier to know the father's own difficulties and not take them only as commentary on the patient's self.

Though the gestalt experiment expands the range of possibilities by encouraging people to take the roles of others in their lives, it is unnecessarily limiting to *exclude* others in group or couples therapy from playing the role of people to whom the patient relates. In spite of the projective inclinations of the role player and the consequent inaccuracies, the therapist may nevertheless validly see a procedural advantage in others playing the roles of people in the life of the patient. For example, if the therapist herself plays the patient's boss, that choice may provide important opportunities to the patient for expressing herself to an authority person. Though the therapist would not play the patient's boss the same way the patient would, the patient will get a valid exercise of her skills in relation to someone with authoritative qualities. People may remind us of past figures without being carbon copies.

Diversity of Techniques

Third, the gestalt experiment has expanded the variety of techniques available to the therapist. This variety ranges from the technique most widely identified with gestalt therapy—the empty chair, where the patient carries on a dialogue with another person who is not present—to the creation of homework experiments, where people carry out assigned tasks outside the therapy office.

Though the empty chair is a stereotypical representative of the gestalt experiment, there are limitless options in the use of the experiment. Gestalt therapy taps into three sources of these techniques.

1. *The therapist's on-the-spot creations.* All therapists can make their own idiomatic creations of particular experiments as they evolve from specific experiences with the patient. A heavy voiced

patient may be asked, for example, to experiment with speaking softly. A patient grieving over the home she left may be asked to imagine herself walking back into her home and to say what she sees. A patient feeling alone in the world may be asked to visualize herself on a desert island and see how the visualization unfolds (Zinker, 1978; Polster and Polster, 1973).

2. *The standard repertoire of techniques.* A large range of therapeutic inventions has flourished in the last forty years: group dynamics, psychosynthesis, behavior therapy, hypnosis, biofeedback, transactional analysis, meditation, and bioenergetics, among them. Also included are experiments in visualization, practicing new behaviors, changing posture, exploring assertiveness, doing homework assignments, and so forth (Stevens, 1971). The experiment provides opportunities to cross methodological boundaries and take advantage of the contributions of procedural diversity.

3. *The therapist's own repertoire.* Each therapist may develop a repertoire of her own experiments, techniques which she has found personally useful, and dip into this repertoire as needed. For example, if the therapist has found that asking a patient to sing her words has been useful or that spreading his arms out to feel the space she fills or slowing down her speech when it would help her to more fully experience herself speaking, these may become part of her repertoire. She may reach into this background of her own previously designed experiments for use at sensitively relevant moments.

These remarks should not be construed to mean that the development of personal style or a large procedural repertoire negates the therapist's theoretical base for what works in psychotherapy. The challenge is to coordinate the principles of the theory with the wide range of particulars that may be faithful to the theoretical orientation. The therapist is inspired and informed by the theory to expand the procedural options, which can never be wholly demarcated.

What is required of the theory is to offer orienting principles and to integrate the therapist's procedures so as to increase the chance of success.

To some patients—and also to some therapists—arranging opportunities for action through the experiment may seem contrived and will be resisted. It is the task of the therapist, as it is in all therapeutic engagement, to ferret out artifice and to get to genuinely illuminating moments. The therapist's responses to the experimental engagement are aimed, much as those of a theater director, at leading the patient to personally faithful expressions. If the patient mumbles or pretends or ignores or misunderstands, the therapist must in respectful regard deal with whatever difficulties the patient may have in permitting a more fruitful communication.

By setting up the experiment, the therapist has only begun the expressive process. The patient will need help with the limits imposed by her behavioral and emotional habits. The alertness of the therapist and her savvy about the patient's contact deficiencies and opportunities are crucial to the success of the experiment.

When the experiment is successfully used, it serves as an important measure for the management of concentration. With the heightened or expanded concentration it provides, patients will have a stronger registration of what they are doing and feeling than when they just casually talk. In one session, for example, a patient was very angry with someone and talking emptily about it. When I asked him to speak to that person as though he were seated in the room, his attention was more incisively directed to the person and the rage came out much more clearly. However, if I had asked him to speak *angrily* rather than just to speak to the person he was angry with, it might have felt gimmicky, producing sham anger, high in decibels but low in heat.

Therefore, in directing attention, open-ended options are often better than inescapable instruction. Anger, among other emotions and behavior, may be wrongfully induced by the therapist's own belief in strong expression, by failure to notice the patient's objections or reluctance, or by giving prejudicial instructions for the experiment. The person's fluency of response, interest, and zest, on the one hand, and hesitation and confusion on the other are the data to take account of in assessing readiness of the patient to do the experiment. Therapists must walk a sensitive line between facilitating the patient's expanded communication while at the same time honoring indications to the contrary.

Safe Emergency

The safety factor in setting up the experiment is so important that it is worth elaborating some of the considerations that must be taken into account. The safety factor is complicated by the fact that therapy cannot be merely safe. When stretching personal boundaries it is unavoidable that one reaches the edge of the familiar; this always contains a measure of risk. Therefore, in gestalt therapy, the concept of the *safe emergency* has played an important role (Perls, Hefferline, and Goodman, 1951).

While danger in everyday life is often prohibitive, in therapy there are sufficient support, skill, and guidance by the therapist that the emergency is made acceptably safe. The therapeutic purpose is to stretch the patient at her own pace to reassess the false safety of stuckness, to loosen the rigid self structure and rediscover the varieties of selves within. These selves are sometimes waiting inside for a new hospitality from the patient, and sometimes they lurk as devouring forces.

To call the move to experience new selves "an emergency" may make it seem more formidable than it need be. The experiment, which is designed to face new prospects, is made safe through two primary factors.

1. *Support.* The support of the therapist or of the group helps a patient try out behavior that seems risky. The fact that the patient is not dealing with people who are going to fire him, divorce him,

ostracize him, mutilate him, or exploit him is a step toward safety
in doing what has previously been too dangerous.

2. *Pace.* The therapist always has the option to adjust the level
of difficulty or arousal. Using the empty-chair experiment as an
example, let us suppose a patient begins to talk about being terrorized
at six by an older boy in the neighborhood. For years, he couldn't feel
safe walking out of his house. To reestablish the engagement with
the bully might arouse feelings or behaviors that would feel too dangerous to handle.

A wise therapist would take the cue from the patient. If he *said*
he was angry, she might ask him to tell the bully about his anger;
that would be timely. But if he had said he felt *intimidated,* to ask
him to express his anger might be skipping some steps and make the
experience more risky. Instead, leaving the pace to the patient, the
therapist might say, "Imagine the bully sitting in that chair. What
does he look like? Is it okay for you to imagine him there? Is there
anything you want to say to him now?"

These and other probings will be guides to the level at which
the experiment should proceed. The pace taken by the therapist is
affected not only by a momentary choice of words but by all that
has previously happened, including diagnostic assessments.

There are certain patients with whom one does not have to
measure danger so much as the relevance and impact of the experiment to the unfolding themes. Other patients, particularly borderline or psychotic people, for whom the experiment might be
overwhelming, may never be given any experiment to do. At whatever level the therapist is working, the experiment's development
must be left sufficiently open so the patient continues to have
choice in how it unfolds.

Though many of the ingredients of safety may be present, there
is a strange paradox to take into account. The safer the therapy
feels, the more dangerous are the experience options that the

patient may allow. Here is why. Prior to therapy many patients have already arranged their lives for maximal safety. What they will ordinarily permit themselves to be and do is well bounded. They have constructed a world that, miserable though it may be, protects them from dangers. If in therapy that world becomes "safe," the patient might take new chances, inviting danger because it has become safer to experience danger.

If, for example, the therapist asks the patient to close her eyes and visualize an important event in her life, she might feel safe enough to visualize an auto accident in which she saw an arm amputated. "Safe enough" does not exclude risk. The new danger is that the patient in visualizing the terrible accident may quiver in psychological overload or cry more deeply than is her habit or become enraged at the driver. The sense of safety is always threatened by new risk.

On the one hand, when the new risks come from a willingness to expand, based on actual experience rather than ambition borrowed from the therapist, the choices are more reliably supported by both the patient and the therapist. On the other hand, the reliability is only illusory if the patient is induced into feeling safe by the charisma of the therapist, drawn in by the quasi-hypnotic aura of the therapy office, influenced by what people say you should do in therapy, entranced by small successes that become exaggerated, or obedient to instructions that require large leaps. But the reliability of the safety belt becomes excellent when the therapist has demonstrated her resonance with the patient over and over, in many different ways.

Above all, the primary source of safety for the experiment is to create a valid extrapolation from what the person is already saying or doing, to make sense and build on the psychological leverage already developing. If the therapist observes that the patient seems confused when listening to instructions for an experiment, it is more important to explore the confusion than to do the experiment. In this exploratory process, patient and therapist, together, may come up with a new way to do the experiment, one that will make greater sense to the patient and be more doable.

Forging a Relationship Between Action and Awareness

When the interwoven relationship between awareness and action is disrupted, the individual's function is diminished. When people act without awareness, their behavior will often be mechanical, empty, purposeless, and unrewarding. On the other hand, those who are aware without action also have troublesome consequences: dreaminess, for example, or a tightened body when the energy becomes strongly compacted.

The reciprocal relationship between awareness and action is most evident in certain simple functions. In playing a violin, for example, the violinist's movement produces a sound, and she becomes immediately aware of it. Where actions are less closely connected with internal awareness, as in putting a car together on an assembly line or in typing a letter, personal awareness may be almost irrelevant.

In therapy when a patient cries or expresses herself clearly, there should be a subsequent awareness. This usually happens naturally without any added focus by the therapist. When, however, the therapist believes the awareness is missing, it may be desirable to help restore it by directed concentration. Without awareness, action may register insufficiently and lose its propellant force. When, on the other side of the duality, there is plenty of awareness but no action, the patient may feel sad and never cry. This represents another form of interruption and requires that the therapist help fill in the picture that is missing tears.

It is important to tune into the right mode. When a patient is geared to the action mode, to call for awareness may be distracting. If someone is intent on hitting the head of a series of nails, asking what they feel may throw them off track. Similarly, in a therapy session where someone is raptly telling a story, a premature interest in what they are feeling may represent disrespect for simply hearing the story. The therapist must be sensitively tuned into the mode that is most immediately recognized in the urgencies of the moment, as well as in the patient's style and habits.

Awareness and action are so pervasive in living that they represent the coordinates of existence. Each is a key ingredient in the configuration of self. The role of awareness in the formation of self was addressed in Chapter Ten, but it is also evident that if a person *acts* kindly, both this act and its accompanying awareness will comprise the substance from which the person's sense of a kind self will be composed. If she reads books, travels frequently, gives to charities, hollers angrily, and accommodates her interests to those of other people, all these acts may be registered through awareness as action elements, the raw material from which selves are formed.

An example of the union of awareness and action in therapy is the following session with Sally, a woman in a therapy workshop. What will be evident are the interweavings of the awareness and action factors and the force with which this integration impelled Sally forward into a highly charged and illuminating experience.

Sally, forty, was admired and well loved in her community, but that wasn't enough for her. She was disturbed because people never seemed to approach her. She had to make all the social moves, and this made her feel isolated. What Sally was unaware of was that, though she was an attractive woman, her face did not offer easy welcome. Her face was contracted, a curious tightness that did not diminish her beauty but nevertheless expressed detachment. It seemed to me that people might well be careful not to approach her, uninvited. The facial contradictions between approach and retreat were confusing to others but were so much a part of her that she had no sense of the mixed messages she was sending out.

When I pointed out that she did not look welcoming, she became aware that she might be dissuading people from approaching her even though they might actually want to. However, rather than being reassured by the awareness that people might actually want to approach her, she became more and more distressed. In her distress and the accompanying sadness, she put her hands to her face, an action that, possibly unconsciously, addressed her facial tightness. To help her heighten her own awareness of her face, I asked her to simply feel the relationship between her hands and her face.

This awareness, itself, might have been a therapeutic step, because a strengthened awareness will often arouse action. But to facilitate that connection I proposed further action. I asked her to move her face against her hands just the way it wanted to. Her face stiffened all the more during this movement and became numb. Then, after moments of attending to these movements, feelings began to come, replacing the numbness. Her hand and face movements swept her into remembering her drunken father, who would be "all over" her when she was a child.

While she talked about these experiences she looked as though she were in a dream or in a hypnotic absorption, feeling both futility and rage. When the movement of her hands and face became reflexively more vigorous, the rage won out over the futility and her face fought against the hands as though they were her father. The hands felt to her like a suffocating invasion by her father. Finally, in revulsion, Sally released a desperate sound, sprung from her tightness, and erupted into spasms of crying. Soon after this, when she was ready again to face the group, it was with an unfamiliar open look and an unreserved connection with the people.

Plainly, the amplified awareness of her father's oppression and of her own facial sensation became more intimately connected with the action represented by her hand and face movements and the accompanying sounds. It was through this heightening of connection between awareness and action that she was impelled forward, beyond dispirited complaint into aggression and release.

Sally's experience of tightly connected awareness and action is a special phenomenon, which I have previously called the synaptic experience, a prime creation of heightened attention (Polster, 1970; Polster and Polster, 1973). The term *synapse* is derived from a Greek word meaning "conjunction" or "union." Physiologically, the synapse operates as a conduit among nerve fibers, especially in bridging the gap between sensory and motor nerves and aiding in their union. Though the functions of the synapse are more complex than I am competent to describe, it is useful as a metaphorical recognition of the sensorimotor roots of awareness and action. The union of awareness and action provides people with special feelings of vibrancy and wholeness of experience. Thus to reincorporate the relationship between awareness and action is an important function of psychotherapy and requires a transcendence of the introspective bias.

Because of this interwoven relationship of action and awareness, it was not evident to therapists that one of Freud's most important contributions to the history of psychotherapy—free association—was a consummate union of introspection and action. Instead, free association was employed primarily as a vehicle of introspection. But action is only another term for expression, and Freud's free association served as a model of spontaneous expression. It was momentously influential in opening not only psychoanalytic patients but the society at large to broader boundaries of expression.

This expansion of expression was different from the new understandings free association produced. This new expressive option reduced the barriers to action, highlighting immediate freedom of action rather than only the complexities of understanding. This union of expression and introspection induced the deepest concentration in Freud's patients, opening them to a hypnomeditative level of attention.

The understanding of Sally's unapproachability was expanded by the actions of her hand and face, which elicited and dramatized important events in her life. In the language of selves, Sally, highly desirable in her community, felt isolated not because she was unloved but because she needed to be approached by others. However, her unapproachable self, unknown to her, was a hidden force preventing others from approaching her. Through the therapeutic action, her fighter self emerged, fierce and successful in actively warding off her father, replacing the passive rigidity that she had used to keep him away.

Then she saw the people in the group and heard their loving, unsolicited comments. What emerged then was her beloved self, always there, just below the surface of admiration she characteristically received in her community. By fighting off her father, she was freed of unwanted sexual implications. Replacing the wariness, her open face invited warmth from the group, and their reaction brought her beloved self into awareness. Though we did not verbalize the existence of her various selves, the actions and the awarenesses bespoke the deep quality of her experiences, meriting the designation of selves.

A patient's readiness and skill in concentrating on the reverberations between awareness and action are important assets in the sweep of sequential options. The magnetism of Sally's sequential imperative may have been a riskier prospect if she were not so psychologically sound.

Such a sweep of experience may not be expected or even encouraged in people with poor self-regulatory systems (as in borderline and psychotic patients). But where the self-regulatory system is intact and where the therapist is alert to signs of unwillingness and respects them, where the steps are small and the opportunity for adjusting to the patient's immediate experience remains present, the union of the awareness and action will have large revelatory effects.

The Range of Action

Powerful though the therapy experiment may be, it is important to realize two things: Therapeutic action is not limited to the experiment, and the proof of the therapy is what happens in actions taken in the patient's community, not in the therapy office.

Beyond the Experiment

Though the experiment is valuable, we must not assume that the experiment is always better than letting patients tell their stories in their own way. On the contrary, much of the time it is better to let them tell about events or feelings directly to the therapist than redirect attention to the experimental options. Though the fundamental engagement between therapist and patient has the greatest priority, in my estimation this engagement frequently lacks the necessary pointedness or potency that the experiment may add. Therapy is always dealing with the direction of attention, heightening concentration on the one hand and expanding the range of attention on the other.

Luckily and obviously, action is always going on, not limited to narrow definitions. Anton Kris (1982) is one of the few analysts to address free association as an expressive act in its own right. He observed that the act of free association itself created excitement, satisfaction, and continuity, irrespective of the understanding that may evolve. In light of the common snags in coordinating point/counterpoint factors, it is to be expected that Freud would have had difficulty giving equal weight to both understanding and action. Nevertheless, in counterpoint to the role of understanding, two key contributions of free association were its restoration of expressive freedom and its role as a starting point for the inventions of techniques in contemporary psychotherapy, most of which have been action-oriented.

Just like free association, conversation itself is also a key therapeutic activity. Usually conversation is seen not so much as an activity on its own merits but as a mere conduit toward understanding and relationship. However, the act of conversation is as much a motor event as gestures, movements, crying, laughing, and all the other actions and events that happen commonly in therapy. It is a major force in self formation, because it induces reactions and provides data for who one is. For example, a depressed person who becomes animated in speaking to the therapist is moving a step toward getting things going again. When she speaks of new experiences, the depressed person's fixed self—worthless or stupid or weak—is joined by other selves, reflected in these new experiences.

It is sometimes difficult to tap into the action component of conversation because patients may have learned to disregard the vibrancy of speech and to treat it almost as though thinking out loud. The restoration of a sense of conversational action is aided by animating the conversation through the familiar therapeutic techniques of accentuating what the patient has said and through the contactful engagement that enhances the palpability of the conversation. Once the action potential is tapped, the natural fluidity of action helps the patient to emerge from the abstractions she is stuck with.

An example of this animating process is the fresh statement of a depressed patient of mine, who in the early days of therapy saw little in his life to be pleased with. In response to the sense of hopelessness and dismissal he was getting across, I asked him why he came for therapy. He answered, "Because you like me." Then he smiled, bringing action to a previously rigid face. That touchingly honest statement injected animation into our conversational action and also showed that he cared about a likable self within. The animation serves not only to make expression feel real but it also sparks reactions from others, and this feeds new data into the process of forming selves. My patient told me how important it was to him that I liked him, and that telling was just as much an action as grabbing me by the throat. Through his action, I became all the more alerted to his likable qualities.

To see conversation as action takes action beyond certain common stereotypes. When people call certain films "action movies" or when a young man says he's going out to "find a little action" or when we say that someone finally "took some action," we limit its parameters. People who say, "Let's not just talk about it, let's do something" are more accurately saying, "Let's do something else besides talking." Talking may simply be the wrong action under many circumstances.

Beyond the Therapist's Office

My primary focus so far has been on action within the therapist's office, with only occasional attention given to the most important actions of all: those that happen in the patient's real world. Miriam Polster (1987) has addressed a facet of this therapeutic requirement in describing an integration sequence in therapy. What is pertinent here about this sequence is the accommodation phase of therapy— the management of therapeutic discoveries in the less hospitable circumstances of the world outside the therapy office.

The ultimate test of therapy lies in the actions taken in the outside world, where the patient must accommodate to objections, threats, modifications, and barriers. For example, if the patient were to discover she wants to be an architect, the effect of that discovery will vanish without the acts the discovery calls for. This patient may still have to get into a school of architecture, she will have to work hard in school, she will have to engage the cooperation of her family, she may spend a summer as an architectural aide, and so forth.

This process of accommodation can be partly supported during the therapy sessions; but most therapy happens through the actions that come in intervals between sessions or even after therapy is completed. During this process, new selves will also appear. The architect self that drove this patient to her new career may become overshadowed by a disillusioned self or a confused self or a rebellious self. The appearance of all these selves will be driven by the wide range of actions taken. Integrating them will then be the new therapeutic task.

My patient Giaccomo (introduced in Chapter Four) is driven by nihilism but has created seepage into his nihilistic self by discovering there are some worldly things he wants. Some of them, like having a family and making more money, are complicated and can be tested only through a long interval of time. But one thing he wants is simpler but still a major confrontation with life outside the therapy office. He doesn't like his body and he wants to improve it by working out in a gym. The problem is that he is embarrassed to be seen. All the personal workthroughs in the therapy office can only serve to prepare him for the ultimate requirement to do it in the real world. Even Freud (1957) recognized that agoraphobic patients should be induced to "go it alone" and deal with the consequent anxiety and that with obsessive patients "a great deal will come to light without its effecting any change in them" (vol. 2, p. 400).

Another patient whose therapy work hinged on the actions he took outside the therapy session is Jason (first mentioned in Chapter Three). Populated by his antiestablishment, ambitious, and corporation selves, Jason made a major breakthrough by making a film on the use of company day-care centers. This action option had many obstacles, and he often talked about them in therapy, getting stimulation for doing these things and also testing out some of his ideas. Through Jason's actions, free from his stereotypes of what actions corporations will permit, he was able to transform a dream into a workable creation.

The actions people take in daily life as a result of a therapeutic session—whether it be building an airplane with their son, interviewing for a new job, writing a letter to an old friend, telling a funny story to their spouse—all count as the action component of psychotherapy. Without such actions there would be no therapy, only circular wanderings of awareness.

Therapy, with its early roots in the introspective process and self-understanding, has more and more recognized its action potentials, inventing action options and recognizing action in the simplest of engagements. With inclusion of action, the interrelationship of awareness, action, and experiment makes a complete circle, accentuating the wholeness of the person.

References

Adler, A. *The Neurotic Constitution*. New York: Arno Press, 1972. (Originally published 1926.)

Agee, J., and Evans, W. *Let Us Now Praise Famous Men*. Boston: Houghton Mifflin, 1941.

Barron, J. "In Just a Word, Who Are You?" *New York Times*, Nov. 14, 1994, pp. B1, B4.

Beisser, A. "The Paradoxical Theory of Change." In J. Fagan and I. Shepherd (eds.), *Gestalt Therapy Now*. Palo Alto, Calif.: Science and Behavior Books, 1970.

Bowlby, J. *Child Care and the Growth of Love*. London: Penguin, 1953.

Bruner, J. "Uses of Narrative." Address at the American Psychological Association Convention, New York, 1987.

Bry, A. *est*. New York: HarperCollins, 1976.

Bullivant, A. *New Oxford Companion to Music*. (D. Arnold, gen. ed.). New York: Oxford University Press, 1983.

Cary, J. *Art and Reality: Ways of the Creative Process*. New York: Doubleday, 1961.

Davanloo, H. "Trial Therapy." In H. Davanloo (ed.), *Short-Term Dynamic Psychotherapy*. Northvale, N.J.: Aronson, 1980.

Eliot, T. S. *Four Quartets*. San Diego: Harcourt Brace, 1943.

Erickson, M., and Rossi, E. *Hypnotherapy: An Exploratory Casebook*. New York: Irvington, 1979.

Ferenczi, S. *Selected Papers of Sandor Ferenczi*. New York: Basic Books, 1952.

Freud, S. *An Outline of Psychoanalysis*. New York: W. W. Norton, 1949.

Freud, S. *Collected Papers*. London: Hogarth Press, 1957.

Freud, S. *Three Case Histories*. New York: Collier, 1963.

Higgins, R. "Forgoing Church, Many Find Help Is Twelve Steps Away." *Boston Globe*, Apr. 29, 1990, p. 1.

Hillman, J. *Healing Fiction*. Barrytown, N.Y.: Station Hill Press, 1983.

Horney, K. *Self Analysis*. New York: W. W. Norton, 1942.

Jung, C. *Man and His Symbols*. New York: Doubleday, 1964.

Katz, A. H. *Self Help in America: A Social Movement Perspective*. New York: Twayne, 1993.

Kingsolver, B. *The Bean Trees*. New York: HarperCollins, 1988.

Kirkpatrick, J. (ed.). *Charles E. Ives: Memos*. New York: W. W. Norton, 1972.

Kohut, H. *Restoration of the Self*. Madison, Conn.: International Universities Press, 1977.

Kohut, H. *Self Psychology and the Humanities*. New York: W. W. Norton, 1985.

Kramer, P. *Listening to Prozac*. New York: Viking Penguin, 1993.

Kris, A. *Free Association*. New Haven, Conn.: Yale University Press, 1982.

Machado de Assis, J. M. *Epitaph of a Small Winner*. New York: Noonday Press, 1990.

Mahoney, M. J. *Human Change Processes*. New York: Basic Books, 1991.

Markus, H., and Nurius, P. "Possible Selves." *American Psychologist*, 1986, *41*, 954–969.

Masterson, J. *The Real Self*. New York: Brunner/Mazel, 1985.

May, R., Angel, E., and Ellenberger, H. *Existence: A New Dimension in Psychiatry and Psychology*. New York: Basic Books, 1958.

Miller, A. *Thou Shalt Not Be Aware*. New York: Meridian, 1986.

Miller, M. "Curiosity and Its Vicissitudes." *Gestalt Journal*, 1987, *10*(1), 18–32.

Moerman, M. "Ariadne's Thread and Indra's Net: Reflections on Ethnography, Ethnicity, Identity, Culture, and Interaction." *Research on Language and Social Interaction*, 1993, *26*(1), 96.

Moore, T. *Care of the Soul*. New York: HarperCollins, 1992.

Moreno, J. *Psychodrama*. Boston: Beacon Press, 1946.

O'Connor, F. "The Nature and Aim of Fiction." In J. Hersey (ed.), *The Writer's Craft*. New York: Knopf, 1974.

Ogden, T. *The Matrix of the Mind*. Northvale, N.J.: Aronson, 1986.

Ornstein, P. H. (ed.). *The Search for the Self: Selected Writings of Heinz Kohut, 1950–1978*. Madison, Conn.: International Universities Press, 1978.

Perls, F. *Ego, Hunger and Aggression*. London: Allen & Unwin, 1947.

Perls, F., Hefferline, R., and Goodman, P. *Gestalt Therapy*. New York: Julian Press, 1951.

Polster, E. "A Contemporary Psychotherapy." *Psychotherapy: Theory, Research and Practice*, 1966, *3*(1), 1–5.

Polster, E. "Encounter in Community." In A. Burton (ed.), *Encounter*. San Francisco: Jossey-Bass, 1969.

Polster, E. "Sensory Functioning in Psychotherapy." In J. Fagan and I. Shepherd (eds.), *Gestalt Therapy Now*. Palo Alto, Calif.: Science and Behavior Books, 1970.

Polster, E. *Every Person's Life Is Worth a Novel*. New York: W. W. Norton, 1987.

Polster, E. "Introduction." In J. Simkin, *Gestalt Therapy Minilectures*. Highland, N.Y.: Gestalt Journal Press, 1990.

Polster, E., and Polster, M. *Gestalt Therapy Integrated*. New York: Brunner/Mazel, 1973.

Polster, E., and Polster, M. "Therapy Without Resistance." In A. Burton (ed.), *What Makes for Behavioral Change*. New York: Brunner/Mazel, 1976.

Polster, M. "Gestalt Therapy: Evolution and Application." In J. Zeig (ed.), *The Evolution of Psychotherapy*. New York: Brunner/Mazel, 1987.

Reich, W. *Character Analysis*. New York: Orgone Institute Press, 1949.

Rogers, C. *On Becoming a Person*. Boston: Houghton Mifflin, 1961.

Rowan, J. *Subpersonalities*. London: Routledge & Kegan Paul, 1990.

Sarton, M. "Death of a Psychiatrist (for Volta Hall)." In *A Private Mythology*. New York: W. W. Norton, 1966.

Sartre, J. P. *Existentialism and Humanism*. London: Methuen, 1948.

Spence, D. *Narrative and Historical Truth*. New York: W. W. Norton, 1982.

Spitz, R. A. "Hospitalism." In A. Freud (ed.), *Psychoanalytic Study of the Child*. Madison, Conn.: International Universities Press, 1945.

Stevens, J. *Awareness: Exploring, Experimenting, Experiencing*. Moab, Utah: Real People Press, 1971.

Towbin, A. "The Confiding Relationship." *Psychotherapy: Research, Theory and Practice*, 1978, *15*(4), 339.

Von Foerster, H. "On Constructing a Reality." In P. Watzlawick (ed.), *The Invented Reality*. New York: W. W. Norton, 1984.

Watzlawick, P. *The Invented Reality*. New York: W. W. Norton, 1984.

Winnicott, D. W. *Holding and Interpretation*. New York: Grove Press, 1972.

Yalom, I. *Love's Executioner*. New York: Basic Books, 1989.

Yontef, G. *Awareness, Dialogue and Process*. Highland, N.Y.: Gestalt Journal Press, 1993.

Zinker, J. *Creative Process in Gestalt Therapy*. New York: Vintage Books, 1978.

Index

DATE DUE
